Praise for *Confessions of a Street Addict*

"Bellicose, self-justifying, coarse, infantile, lovable, and even, at times, saintly, Cramer resembles Dostoevsky's hero in *The Gambler,* who hurls himself at the flames because life without risk would be unbearable. . . . Cramer's skill at exposition and at communicating these emotions is finally more notable than his considerable skill at trading. He is the greatest public generator of excitement and knowledge about the market today."

—David Denby, *The New Yorker*

"Unflinching, rat-a-tat-tat style . . . [Cramer's] hair-raising descriptions of Wall Street in the waning days of the bull market are worth the price of admission . . . a cautionary tale for any small investor tempted by stock market hype and mania."

—Nancy Blair, *USA Today*

"Cramer's book works unusually well because it's ultimately an addiction memoir, one that just happens to take place on Wall Street."

—Daniel McGunn, *Newsweek*

"Mr. Cramer's *Confessions of a Street Addict* is the first well-written account of the '90s bull market—an insider's tale, and also a remarkably vivid self-drawn cartoon . . . a great, pummeling read, every bit as barbed, intense, and unrelenting as its author."

—Stephen Metcalf, *New York Observer*

"In *Confessions of a Street Addict*, [Cramer] explains how it all happened and includes the insights and revelations he experienced along the way that made him not only a much feared, often hated, never boring figure on the Street but one of the most high-octane financial journalists working today."

—Dan Santow, *Chicago Tribune*

P9-DCP-449

"Cramer's message is clear: Middle-class, unsophisticated individual investors do not stand a chance against the amoral or immoral professional trader. *Confessions of a Street Addict* is a primer on how no traditional investment—especially the ever-popular mutual fund—makes sense when the little person's life savings are at stake."

—Steve Weinberg, *The Plain Dealer* (Cleveland)

"Wall Street's most notorious bull bares all. . . . Cramer's unique blend of shrewd analysis, namedropping, and unremitting egotism puts him in the great tradition of American showmen: a P. T. Barnum for the age of the day trader. A must for market mavens."

—*Kirkus Reviews*

"A lively, informative portrait of the highest levels of finance and media in the last decade."

—*Publishers Weekly*

SIMON & SCHUSTER PAPERBACKS

New York London Toronto Sydney

CONFESSIONS OF A STREET ADDICT

JAMES J. CRAMER

To Karen, my father, and Nan.

SIMON & SCHUSTER PAPERBACKS
Rockefeller Center
1230 Avenue of the Americas
New York, NY 10020

Copyright © 2002 by J. J. Cramer & Co.
All rights reserved, including the right of reproduction
in whole or in part in any form.

First Simon & Schuster paperback edition 2003

SIMON & SCHUSTER PAPERBACKS and colophon are registered trademarks
of Simon & Schuster, Inc.

For information about special discounts for bulk purchases,
please contact Simon & Schuster Special Sales:
1-800-456-6798 or business@simonandschuster.com.

Designed by Jeanette Olender
Manufactured in the United States of America

13 15 17 19 20 18 16 14 12

The Library of Congress has cataloged the hardcover edition as follows:
Cramer, Jim.
Confessions of a street addict / James J. Cramer.
p. cm.
Includes index.
1. Wall Street. 2. Hedging (Finance) 3. Stockbrokers. 4. Securities industry.
5. Journalism, Commercial. I. Title.
HG4572 .C78 2002
332.6'092—dc21   2002022902
ISBN-13: 978-0-7432-2487-1
ISBN-10:   0-7432-2487-6
ISBN-13: 978-0-7432-2488-8 (Pbk.)
ISBN-10:   0-7432-2488-4 (Pbk.)

ACKNOWLEDGMENTS

When *TheStreet.com* came public three years ago, we all knew it was going to be a red-hot deal. That meant we were given friends and family stock to dole out, knowing that we would be putting literally hundreds of thousands of dollars into the pockets of whomever we gave it to—provided they "sold the opening," or dumped the stock fast. That caused me to sit down and figure out, Wall Street style, how much I could make for all my friends and family. I sat down and thought for days about how to distribute the stock and then said the hell with it, I'd be nothing without my Dad, my sister, and my wife, so I gave it almost entirely to them.

Now, as I sit back to dedicate this book, giving thanks, not money, I reach the exact same conclusion. My father has worked his entire life to make me and my sister happy, first with sustenance, and then with kindness, love, and always with inspiration. He and my late mother always encouraged me to achieve; I took it to an extreme that neither cared for and both urged me to abandon, my mother before I started my career on Wall Street, and my father when I ended it. My dad has led his life in a way that inspired me to work hard and always tell the truth. He has been and will always be the greatest inspiration for any successes and accomplishments I may have in my life. He is also my best friend, which is something that few sons can say about their fathers, and I am so lucky for it. My sister bailed me out of unfathomable difficulties and setbacks, getting me out of my makeshift bed in the back of my Ford Fairmont and onto her living room floor in Greenwich Village, and encouraging me to come to Wall Street to realize my dreams. She, who has had to put up with me longer than anyone in the world. My wife? What can I say; read the rest of the book, and find out. I don't need to spend much time here detailing her role.

I would also like to thank Bob Bender and David Rosenthal at Simon &

Schuster, both for believing I could do this, and for backing me. They are the best, and I hope to work with them for a very long time. And thanks to my agent, Suzanne Gluck, who also believed in me all the way.

Along the way there have been so many helpful people who have encouraged me, pushed me, stuck with me, even as I have, at times, abandoned them, most importantly Marty Peretz, my best man, who I let down miserably with my own petulance. He graciously accepted my apologies and extended his for a period when greed filled virtually every pore in my body. Jeff Berkowitz, my former partner at Cramer Berkowitz, who saved my life; how the hell else would I have gotten out of that hedge fund cauldron alive if he hadn't been there to take the darned money machine over? Jeannie Cullen, my assistant, who no longer needs workers' compensation for all of the broken phone, smashed computer, and cracked coffee cup shards that flew her way as she did her best to protect me from my maniacal self when I was in pursuit of the perfect trading day. Jim Stewart, who always insisted that I keep writing even after I went to Wall Street, something that I probably would have let go by the wayside without his constant encouragement.

These days, I have a great time at *TheStreet.com,* in part because of Tom Clarke, the fantastic CEO, and in part because of David Morrow, our excellent editor-in-chief, who, at last, has turned the newsroom at *TheStreet.com* into one solid, terrific institution.

I also wish to thank Eric Seiler, my personal lawyer, who figured out how to keep me out of trouble I otherwise would make for myself. He's amazing, someone who keeps me from hurting myself. Wish I'd met him twenty years ago.

And, of course, I want to thank my mother who figured everything out in her short life and managed to get me to become a writer after all.

And, most of all, I want to thank my beautiful children, Cece and Emma, for not giving up on me when I was too stupid to see what I had become and what I was going to be if I didn't become a husband and a dad in time to matter.

CONTENTS

Confessions of a Street Addict

Early Years

When other nine-year-old kids bothered to look at a newspaper back in 1964, they turned to the comic strips, or maybe the ball scores. But when my dad brought home that three-star *Philadelphia Evening Bulletin,* I chucked *Peanuts, Archie,* and the standings and went right for the only section that has ever mattered to me: the business section, or more accurately, the stock tables. You see, I didn't care about layoffs or hirings or economic policy. I cared about the companies and the dollar signs next to them that gauged their value every day. I cared about that wonderful printed wall of abbreviations, Gen'lMot, So'CalEd, PhilMo, followed by a high figure, a low figure, another number, and a minus or a plus sign. I devoured those the way any normal Philadelphia boy might have devoured the batting averages of his beloved Phillies or Eagles or Warriors. I knew I could figure out where those numbers were going. I could figure out the patterns that drove those prices, and I could make money doing so, if only in my own well-played stock market game.

By fourth grade, I thought I understood the sequence of those numbers that came after those truncated names. I scrounged a used ledger book from my dad's jobbing business, National Gift Wrap & Packaging Company, erased his all block capital letter tallies of boxes sold—men's 9 by 12 locktops and 3 by 4 inch ladies' jewelry—and replaced the columns with stock names and predictions of where they would close that afternoon. I never missed a day and couldn't figure out why we had no pricings on Good Friday, Memorial Day, or election day. Didn't those companies keep ticking despite the holidays? I couldn't get enough, even when the rest of America clearly could. I wanted daily action.

By fifth grade, unlike every other son in America, I had to beg my father to stay later at work. The paper he ordinarily brought home, the *Bulletin*'s three star, stopped quoting prices at 12:30 P.M. What good was that? I made him work an additional hour and a half so he could snare the purple five star final sold right to your car window at 16th and Market on the way home to the suburbs. How else could I measure how right I was about my predictions of where Ling-Temco-Vought (LTV) and DougAir had finished if Dad came home with that miserable early edition with its midday prices? Each day, while others wasted time after school playing board games or combat or touch football, I'd be gaming the close. Each night, I'd rip the paper out of my dad's hands, spread out the New York Stock Exchange tables on the living room floor, and see how much money my picks would have made.

I wasn't content with my own prowess. Nah, I had to teach others, tried to get Mrs. Mixer's whole fifth-grade class to play the stock market game with me. Even showed them how to read the tables. But I had no takers. They just didn't get the process.

Didn't matter. By my count, I would have made a couple of million dollars following my own picks before I had matriculated to sixth grade. That's when $2 million meant something. My methods were simple, try to make small gains from the most active stocks, the ones that were involved in defense, because there was a war on, and defense seemed to be coining money. Seemed, and was—and will always be—simple enough.

If only fantasy equaled reality at 1401 Cromwell Road in Wyndmoor in 1965. While I beat the averages with my picks, my dad, like many of his generation, had gotten a tip from a local broker: National Video. He plowed the returns of his paper jobbing business into the prospects for National Video. I still shudder when I hear those two words. For a period of about a year, every penny my dad made at National Gift Wrap, selling paper bags and boxes to retailers, he lost to that generation's e-commerce dotcom play. Every night at dinner I would hear how National Video had done. It never seemed to go up. Although a chart I saw of the stock shows a couple of gentle rises on the way to oblivion, I can't recall a single conversation during that period that wasn't punctuated with "that goddamned National Video." It got so I dreaded hearing the most actives on the radio, a report that I used to tune in at 4:00 P.M. every day before my dad got home to get an early line on how I did, because National's decline always got prominent featuring. Eventually, the pain of National Video overwhelmed the pleasure of my own game, and discussions of the stock market, fantasy or otherwise, were banned from the dinner table as just too upsetting.

My dad has pretty much forgotten about National Video and the fellow who put him in it. But I remember Jack P., the Philadelphia broker who turned a generation against the stock market, and I hate that charlatan as if it were yesterday. He and National Video ruined just about everything a kid could want at that age.

The stock, and with it, my father's portfolio, like so many of his generation, never recovered. By sixth grade I thought it more prudent to downplay my stock prowess for my hitting and fielding abilities.

And so it stayed, suppressed, with little more than a gentle skim of the closing prices through high school and college. What was the point for this indebted scholarship kid who didn't have enough money to buy a share of a penny stock to keep up with the closing prices? If it hadn't been for the night jobs of proofreading and delivering the college paper after it came off the presses, I wouldn't have been able to maintain my day job as president of *The Harvard Crimson,* let alone complete the curriculum. Trading stocks would have to wait until I had some money.

I was a competitive person at Harvard, at least that was my reputation. Unrelentingly competitive. Mindlessly competitive. For me Harvard College was a sideshow to the *Crimson,* Harvard's newspaper. I ran for president, or editor in chief, of the paper against Eric Breindel. The presidential race at the *Crimson* is written about more than it should be, probably because every one of the top officers of the paper goes into journalism. At least a half-dozen magazine articles have chronicled this particular episode in my life, always in the same inaccurate way. Some unsophisticated hick from a trailer park in Pennsylvania runs against the most well-educated, awesomely intelligent preppy kid ever to come out of New York City by way of Exeter. Yes, I was a scholarship kid, but so was most everybody in my class. And yes, I was less sophisticated than Breindel, but I knew enough to recognize that the previous president, Nick Lemann, believed in meritocracy, and I was willing to work twice as hard as the next guy, if only because I could go twenty-four hours without sleep. I also knew that Breindel's backers had arranged a "slate" that filled all the top positions without me. When I told Lemann this, he thought I was being paranoid until he heard it from Breindel's supporters the night of the Turkey Shoot, when would-be executives declared their candidacy for the top positions at the paper. The vote was very close, 12–11 for me, and when Breindel lost, most of his slate stalked off, but not before throwing a few punches at some of the outgoing execs who had voted for me. Didn't bother me—three fantastic freshmen agreed to work with me: Mark Whitaker, who would later become editor of *Newsweek;* Jon Alter, who would become Whitaker's star columnist; and Joe Dalton, a talented writer who would pass away without ever realizing his potential. We put out a great paper. (Eventually Breindel brought his supporters back to work with me.)

Two years as a journeyman general assignment reporter, first in Florida, for the *Tallahassee Democrat,* and then in California, for the now defunct *Los Angeles Herald Examiner,* did little for my market fixation either. Not that I didn't have the desire. Never a wealthy kid, but not poor by any means, during those two years I was subjected to a series of reversals that would have provided anyone with several lifetimes' worth of catalysts to get wealthy.

Oh, I was a guy with a knack for being in the right place when it came to the news game. Only a few months after my arrival in Tallahassee, a crazed murderer broke into the sorority house down the block from my apartment. I got there early enough to leapfrog every other crime reporter in the country in the unfolding Ted Bundy national serial-killing spree. My reporting on that double murder received so much coverage around the country that editors who wanted hard-boiled crime reportage clamored to offer me jobs. In just a few months I found myself covering for the *Los Angeles Herald Examiner* everyone who died violently in California.

While my criminal reporting career was taking off, however, my personal and financial well-being deteriorated rapidly. A few weeks after moving into a bungalow on Orange Grove in the only neighborhood in L.A. that remotely seemed like home, the Fairfax district, I returned from work to find that someone had made a tuna sandwich in my kitchen while I was away—a discarded can lay in the middle of the kitchen floor, and the bread bag had been mysteriously opened. I called the police, who did a cursory check of my security against intruders and told me to change the locks. I did.

The next day, after work, I discovered that someone had broiled a chicken in my oven and eaten a couple of pouches of Birds Eye vegetables. The trespasser had left me with the carcass and some gizzards and a badly burnt broiling pan.

A call to the police again brought in a suggestion that I change the locks again. Having just done it, I said I would do so again, but I wasn't made of money.

The next morning I thought I detected someone outside my little home smoking cigarettes. I called the police immediately, but by the time they got there, the man had disappeared. However, there was a pile of Winston butts right outside my bedroom window where the person had apparently been waiting for me to get up and go to work so he could start the day living in my apartment.

I told the cops where he had been standing outside my house, and asked if they would take some fingerprints off the butts or around the windowsill.

It was then I realized how overmatched I was. One patrolman looked at the other and said, "This kid thinks we're Kojak or something." His advice was more pointed. "Look, get a gun, hire a private detective, protect yourself."

Thanks, officer!

That day I borrowed a .22 caliber pistol from a reporter friend of mine and brought out my Boy Scout hatchet that I had used in camping trips as a little boy. When I got home that night I learned that the stalker had made a nice salad, opened up a can of fruit cocktail, and taken a shower and a shave in my bathroom. He neglected to flush. He had also taken my extensive collection of John Coltrane albums and the change that I kept hidden away in a little Tupperware container in the hall. I didn't bother to call the police this time.

Throughout this period I had confided in my editor at the time, Frank Lalli, later of the New York *Daily News* and before that of *George* and

Money magazine, that the stalker was getting the best of me. I told him I had no place to turn and needed his help. He just nodded each time and gave me another assignment. He dispatched me to San Diego to cover a standoff between a sixteen-year-old sniper, Brenda Spencer, and the San Diego police. Spencer, one of the original school shooters, would later tell people that she killed because rainy days and Mondays made her blue.

When I got to the unfolding crime scene I called Lalli and told him that this was a well-covered affair with lots of press. He urged me to get something different. He suggested that I go past the police line and run toward the school to get a sense for what it would be like to be under fire. While I knew that Lalli was no fan of mine, for $179 a week I wasn't going to become a live target of some crazed teen. I told Lalli that and said I wanted to get back to my bungalow because I feared what would happen if my stalker had the run of the place overnight.

He instead told me to stay in San Diego to see if I could get some good second-day angle on the shooting.

When I got back home the next day, everything was gone. It was as if a moving van had come and taken every last scrap of my belongings. Nothing was left. No clothes, no sheets, no furniture, no books, no toiletries, no food, not even any toilet paper or toothpaste. Broom-clean save for a box spring and the heaviest of the appliances.

All I had left to my name was what was in my car, a sport jacket, my .22, and the old Boy Scout hatchet. Of course my checks were gone. He'd cashed me out of my checking account the day before. No more money for the rent, not that I wanted to stay there another night. The cops came yet one more time, said they would be happy to write up a stolen property form for insurance purposes—like I had any—and told me that I would be an idiot to stay in that apartment any longer unless I wanted to be killed by the stalker.

Good advice.

Bereft with no way to pay my rent, with literally only the shirt on my back and not more than a couple of dollars in my pocket, I descended rapidly into the world of the working homeless.

I slept in the back seat of my Ford Fairmont for the next nine months, with intermittent stays at friends' apartments, as they took pity on my plight. My favorite resting place: I-5 truckstops, huddled beneath my corduroy jacket, clutching the hatchet with one hand and the .22 with the other. For a month Don Forst, now the editor of the *Village Voice,* then the managing editor at the *Herald Examiner,* let me crash in his apartment when he could no longer stand the smell of my corduroy jacket and Gap pants that I wore every day. He asked me how come I never changed clothes. He gave me a chance to get back on my feet, but no sooner did it look like I had a place to stay for good than Forst got the job as editor of the *Boston Herald,* and I was right back out on the street, in the Fairmont, with the .22, the hatchet, and a new addition, Jack Daniel's, to keep me warm. I defined pathetic and poor. Man, and did I ever smell bad.

My city editor, Lalli, seemed to think that all of these travails were hysterically funny. He delighted in sending me to ridiculous overnight assignments where I wouldn't need to go "home" anyway. Repeatedly, whenever it was foggy, he made me stake out LAX waiting for plane crashes. He made me cover every L.A. night fire short of a barbecue or school bonfire. Of course, he made me visit the families of every murder victim and if I came up empty-handed for the first edition he would have me hound the bereaved for the second, third, and fourth editions. He had me hole up below a dangerous boulder that jutted from the Palisades over-looking the Pacific. He had hoped that it would roll down on my watch, hit a few cars on the Pacific Coast Highway, and then plunge across the street into the den of the director who made *Sounder.* When the state finally dy-namited the boulder to get it loose, he urged me to write the story from be-neath the boulder's trajectory to get the real scoop. He wanted to use a headline that said I played rock around the clock and the rock won. He cackled daily to other staffers about my poverty and seemed to relish how dirty he could make me, knowing that I had no ability to grab a shower or get fresh clothes without the help of others. Without the protection of Donny Forst, I was at the mercy of this taunting maniac.

Desperate, I pleaded to higher-ups to let me go on the road where I could have some expense money so I could rebuild my wardrobe, even if it meant staying in my car at Interstate 80's Northern California truck stops. Jim Bellows, the editor in chief, answered my prayers by making me capital bureau chief in Sacramento, and instructed Lalli to tell the cur-rent bureau chief to move on. But Lalli didn't let anyone know and when I got to the capital city the bureau chief knew nothing about the switch. I ended up camping on the side of his desk by day and on the side of I-80 by night.

I parlayed the first expense dollars into enough money to rent an apartment by taking up betting on the horses. I had taken a handicapping tutorial in college taught by a fellow who had studied with Andy Beyer, the *Washington Post* racing columnist, who had dropped out of Harvard a week before he graduated because he was making too much money at the track. I would spend weekends in my car outside the track near the Bay Meadows park outside San Francisco or drive to Los Angeles and camp out near Santa Anita. It was my only way to make enough money to stay dressed and warm.

As luck would have it, Governor Jerry Brown was anxious to promote an area of the state that was starting to boom and he arranged a multiday tour of the factories of Silicon Valley for anybody who was inclined to go. I was the only one who volunteered.

The trip was just enough outside Sacramento that the real bureau chief didn't mind my taking it, and I had my first personal brush with high-tech companies. Of course, I didn't have two nickels to buy a stock, but I got the sense in the spring of 1978 when touring National Semiconductor and Signal, two forerunners of the coming tech boom, that this was where the big money was going to be made if I ever got any to invest.

Not long after I arrived in Sacramento, Lalli, on a whim, asked me to fly with Governor Brown and his girlfriend Linda Ronstadt to Africa. I only had a day's notice, and to go I needed inoculations against a host of diseases, a series that was meant to be given over a period of weeks. The next day I came down with something that resembled cholera and devolved quickly into a deeply jaundiced liver.

Unfortunately, I had no health care coverage, because the paper's HMO only had offices in Los Angeles. I dragged myself to a farmworkers' clinic in Yuba City, where doctors told me that someone would have to take care of me if I were to get better.

Scrambling, I tapped into my old *Harvard Crimson* network to find someone who was hiring journalists in New York, where I knew my sister, Nan, would be able to nurse me back to health. A buddy of mine, Scott Kaufer, a couple of years ahead of me at college, mentioned to me that Steve Brill, a hard-charging reporter turned editor, was putting together a trade magazine about lawyers that would allow young reporters to practice investigative journalism. I was so down and out I didn't mind the notion that I would be helping start some sort of trade magazine for lawyers, and I told Kaufer that I would love to get a shot at being in New York. As I was making little with no health benefits, I figured, How could it be any worse?

Not long after, Steve Brill called. I had never met a character like Brill—never will again, either. Brill was mean, not behind your back, but right to your face. Gratuitously mean and tremendously funny. The contrast between us couldn't have been more black and white; me, five foot nine, slight, with a wild but receding head of Afro'd hair, a beat-up jacket and bell bottoms that I had turned into straight pants with a little cutting and pasting, and the big brutish Brill, with the perfectly cut blue American suit, and those split collar shirts, and Yale ties and gold collar bars. When I was ushered into his office, the first thing out of his mouth was that he would love to hire me, but he couldn't, not until he fired Mike Vermeulen, a long-since-departed-from-this-earth reporter. He needed Vermeulen's desk first. He looked at me, up and down, eyes lingering on the corduroy jacket's grime-blackened lapels, and said that I looked like I could use some extra money. He offered me a thousand bucks if I would personally fire Vermeulen right then and there. He had no idea how desperate I was for money—I owed everyone in California a couple of hundred dollars—and I jumped at the chance. When I said I would do it unhesitatingly he hired me on the spot at $20,000, an immense amount for 1979, almost doubling my pathetic *Los Angeles Herald Examiner* salary. He kept me from doing the firing—and believe me I would have—and gave me a couple of hundred bucks and told me to go buy some clean shirts and a jacket and report to work in two weeks.

Job in hand, I flew back to California and immediately called down to editor in chief Bellows and told him I was quitting because I could no longer take the torture of Lalli's brand of journalism. Of course it had no impact whatsoever, as those things never do, but at least I felt like I explained to Bellows what a sadistic son of a bitch Lalli was. Only now, after I have made millions in the stock market to get away from that poverty, do I perversely—in a way that Lalli would certainly understand—credit that strange bully with the inspiration to get rich as quickly as possible.

I vowed that I would never again allow myself to be as poor and lacking in material wealth as I had become. My older and only sister, Nan, an associate at a downtown law firm, allowed me to sleep on the floor of her studio apartment in Greenwich Village so I could begin to save a little money to buy some clothes and get my health back. Once at *American Lawyer*—as Brill's magazine would be called—I contacted the slew of bill collectors that had dogged me for everything from phone service to Southern California Edison to Mobil to Allstate and agreed to pay the money I owed over a four-year period.

With what was left with my paycheck, I decided that the time had come to try my hand again at the game I had given up years before: stocks. I bought shares in some of the companies I had visited in Silicon Valley a few months before. I only had enough money to buy five shares at a clip, and sometimes the commissions were as expensive as the stocks! But that didn't deter me. I remember those first trades like yesterday. I piled into seven shares of Bobbie Brooks, the dressmaker, after *Forbes* gave it a nice write-up. I snared ten shares of American Agronomics, the orange juice company, also a *Forbes* write-up. Then I bought twenty shares of Bob Evans Farms, a Midwestern restaurateur. Magazines, such as *Forbes,* then as now, are chock-full of good ideas that you can turn into profits. I got the old ledger out from the 1960s and put in new names, with real hard dollars, not play money. I matched ideas from *Business Week* and *Forbes* with the miserly stock research then available publicly through the New York Public Library. Even though we were still in the tail end of the 1970s bear market, my selections worked. It was just like the old days back in the Philadelphia suburbs. Nothing had changed my ability to splice the headlines of the day with stock prices to derive some serious winners. With the winnings, always taken off the table, I plowed into SPS Technologies, an airplane fastener company, catching an aerospace cycle move for a quick doubling of my money.

Within a few months' time, I could barely do my reporting work, I was so busy running to the Midtown Business Library in Manhattan investigating tips and ideas for my next score in the market. I had even engaged the boss, Brill, to tag along with me, after he asked me what the heck I was doing calling my broker all the time when I was supposed to be writing. I told him that I was developing a thesis that Natomas, the oil company with giant shipping interests, would soon be getting a takeover bid. When the bid materialized a few days later, he too became a believer. Soon Brill let me have time off to develop my next big idea, provided I let him in on it. We made some good money together.

I also gave up the ponies for the equity market, taking with me the disposition to plunge big when I was right and to cut back dramatically when the odds didn't favor me. Those, after all, were the true takeaways from *Picking Winners* and *My First $50,000 Season,* two excellent racing books by the *Washington Post*'s Andy Beyer. While others read them for their horse handicapping insight, I saw them for what they truly were, a rigorous, disciplined way to handle risk in any endeavor involving wagering, whether sports or stocks. I combined an ability to read the fundamentals behind the stocks with insights gleaned from Beyer to generate an investment philosophy that allowed me to let my gains run but cut my losses immediately. He preached discipline in the face of fallibility. He backed a philosophy of betting large on out-of-the-way races and tracks that weren't on the radar screen of the big-time gamblers, perfect traits for the mastering of any stock market.

There are tons of investment texts out there, most of which preach buy and hold and many of which emphasize how to analyze value and growth stocks. However, few if any tell you about a disciplined style that melds conviction with the changing course of business fundamentals and emphasizes putting the big bet down when you think you have something really special, as Beyer insists. None of these investing books talks about flexibility and the need to reevaluate and change your portfolio on a regular and rigorous basis, as Beyer does his horse wagering. It was Beyer's insights that put me on the path of massive profitability. Many years later, when I was making millions of dollars a week buying and selling stocks, I would often marvel at how wasted Beyer's talents were on the small money of the ponies. The man had it in him to write the greatest investing book in history if only he knew how much horses and stocks were alike. But it was either lost on him, or he just liked the horses more than stocks.

I could have stayed with Brill forever. His mean spirit extended only to those who didn't hustle. He ultimately was the most gracious boss I ever had, even as he would scribble the endless "You should be fired for this crock of shit" in red on the top of pieces that you rushed or didn't think through fully. When I had a difficult operation that kept me in bed for a month, he bombarded me with gifts and books and insisted that I listen in to every rant against every writer he knew I didn't like in the office. He introduced me to Jim Stewart, a senior staff writer who would win a Pulitzer for his reporting at the *Wall Street Journal* on Ivan Boesky and Michael Milken. He's the best pure writer and reporter on the planet; we became friends for life. Brill taught me I could write whatever I wanted, as long as it was true, and he backed me up against a slew of people who tried to get me to write more positive articles than I would have otherwise. He was truly owned by no one and encouraged me to be the same. He was rarely wrong about a lead, had an impeccable nose for a great story, and would spend a fortune to allow me to track down whatever investigative story I wanted to do. No questions asked. If you ever wrote a tough piece, when the inevitable call from someone big and important came to suggest you should be fired, Brill would get on the phone and scream bloody murder at the powerful person, because he was backing his reporter. That made you love him. I am always amazed how few bosses in journalism react with such loyalty toward their own.

Brill loved to pit talent against each other. Brill had just hired Stewart and Connie Bruck, both now of *The New Yorker,* right before he had hired me, and we would all compete to be on the cover of this little trade magazine with seventeen thousand circulation. He always promised the cover to all three of us and we would actually be severely disappointed if we ultimately didn't make it. Amazingly, he made us actually care!

He never did know when to quit, though, and could not bear to lose at anything. At the firm's summer outing at Brill's Westchester mansion, he divided us into teams, placed us in his pool, and insisted we play a vicious game of water polo where dunking was encouraged and expected. He relished the contact, being a head taller than just about anyone else on the opposing squad, including me. Just as I was about to score what would have been the tying goal for my team, Brill sank his teeth into my throwing arm, spouting blood into the clear water in a steady stream. As everyone looked on in horror, I could only laugh. That was Steve all over. He stopped my attempt, won the game, and gave new meaning to unsportsmanlike conduct, all with one bite.

It wasn't until I sickened of writing about wealthy lawyers for *American Lawyer,* and decided to go be one, that I was able to spend the amount of time I needed to pick stocks not just as a hobby but as a profession. When I applied to law school I thought I wanted to be a prosecutor; I figured it was like being a reporter, but with subpoena power. However, after getting into Harvard Law in 1980, and then deferring to 1981, I had set my sights more toward business; I was making too much money in the stock market by the spring of the year that I hated to give it up for full-time legal study. Although the brochures—and your parents—don't tell you this, law school is an ideal place to take off three solid years to figure out what you really want to be in life. One thing was obvious from the get-go, you needed a lot of hard work and good grades to get one of those poorly paying prosecutor jobs. In the counterintuitive world that is law, the most sought-after jobs required the best grades and paid the lowest wages.

In my first year of law school at Harvard, something happened that put an end to any possibility that I would ever work hard or get good grades. The Financial News Network had just started, and a UHF channel in Boston had picked up the feed. Along with constant commentary about stocks, FNN gave you a ticker, an actual tape of the action, delayed by fifteen minutes, of what was happening on the floor of the New York Stock Exchange. I was mesmerized. After months of having to sneak into the Merrill Lynch booth at Grand Central Terminal to get quotes, suddenly I had the whole market in front of me on my nine-inch black and white Sony. I couldn't believe how easy it would be to trade while watching TV from my dorm, and make money under the guise of getting a degree. Once I was sure that FNN was there to stay, something that wasn't easily foreseen given how horrible the market had been for so many years, I juggled my schedule to take early morning and late afternoon classes so that I wouldn't miss the trading action. I made up my mind that I could put myself through law school trading off the FNN ticker.

Sure, there were nagging classes that had to be attended to, but as long as you sat in the back with the *Journal* and some Wall Street research cribbed from the library, nobody cared. I figured I could make a killing and get the degree at the same time. Turns out that no professor cared as long as you didn't crinkle the paper too loudly. By the end of the first year,

I was reviewing the portfolios of most of my professors anyway. I got my labor law professor, Charles Fried, later the solicitor general of the United States, out of some nasty gold stocks and rescued evidence professor Charles Nesson from small cap oblivion.

Soon after, I hooked up with Alan Dershowitz, who was running a law office out of Harvard Law. In return for his being on television all he wanted, a bunch of us made him look good by doing research and writing briefs for his celebrity clients. The pay was excellent, the hours didn't interfere with the market, and by the beginning of my second year of law school I had made enough money in the market to pay for the whole three years and then some.

By the fall of 1981, the market hadn't yet begun to welcome the bulls. In fact, the stock market held very little interest for most people. It's hard to imagine now how impenetrable it all was. Only the super-rich were in; it was considered reckless to "play" the market, because so much money had been lost in a previous generation. In fact, the averages were basically in the same place they had been for fifteen years. But the oil stocks were still benefiting from the shock that came after the toppling of Iran's friendly government, and takeover activity still abounded, both in finance and in oil and gas, even as stocks, even growth stocks, foundered. I had a special talent for picking potential takeovers then.

Sometimes I couldn't resist crowing about the ideas I found. While people talked about who they married and how many years they had worked at Cravath or Morgan Stanley in their Harvard College Fifth Year Reunion book, I submitted a brief in the fall of 1981 for buying Dean Witter below $40, with the idea that it would not be independent by the time our reunion rolled around in June. It received a takeover bid not long after everyone got their class book. Name me another entry in that red-bound volume that made anyone any money. I guess you could say I couldn't help myself. I just couldn't get the market out of my head.

That summer of 1982 I labored as an associate at Fried Frank, a large New York law firm dedicated to the proposition, like the rest of them, that lawyers were smarter than the businesspeople behind the deals but had to keep their mouths shut and work longer hours for less money. I found the work stultifying. I tried to keep my head down and focus on the possibilities of being a corporate lawyer, but it wasn't for me. I had to ask the kid who delivered the mail three times a day to wake me up.

Midway through the summer, I begged off the endless Mostly Mozart, fancy dinner, Broadway play, third-row-behind-the-dugout treatment that they gave all summer associates and asked to see what it was really like to work in one of these legal factories. So, one weekend, they put me on the legal team involved with a hostile takeover of Giddings and Lewis, a sleepy Fond du Lac auto machine tool manufacturer, by some Canadian steel-maker that didn't know jack about the car business. The lunacy of paying above-market prices for such a stupid iron bender was beyond me. And, late one Saturday night, while I was proofreading documents alongside the principals, the bankers and lawyers representing the Canadian raider, I spoke up, telling everybody in the room that it had to be someone's job to tell the client that the acquisition was moronic given that the Japanese had decided to move into machine tools aggressively and would decimate the profits of the likes of Giddings and Lewis. If no one else would speak to the lunacy of the bid, at least let me see the client for ten minutes and tell him, I said, while I fixed tiny punctuation errors that I could have spotted without the benefit of a high school diploma. The business guys recoiled as if someone had farted, and the senior lawyers took me aside as soon as possible to tell me that I better keep my trap shut lest they get kicked off the deal. Nobody likes a smart-ass lawyer, they told me.

A few years later the buyer filed for bankruptcy.

After returning to law school in the fall, I decided that I couldn't go back to a law firm no matter how much they paid me. I had to make enough money in the market to show Wall Street investment firms that they should hire me. That fall, a few weeks before the great bull market began, I had an epiphany that we were due for an explosion in prices that would make anybody who was heavily invested a fortune. I could see things coming together for a major run at new highs under a Reagan presidency after a prolonged period of totally stink-o performance, hobbled by Carter's anti-stock presidency and a Federal Reserve chairman determined to destroy anything financial with astronomically high interest rates.

I took the money I made from helping Dershowitz try vainly to bail out a couple of white-collar crooks and made a massive bet on technology, then still in its infancy as an investment sector, catching fully the first big semiconductor move right in the kisser. I began purchasing call options—contracts on common stock that allowed you to profit if the stocks went up, but wiped out your investment if the stock went down—on Motorola and Texas Instruments every morning before Constitutional Law and selling them for five- and six-point profits after that two-hour yawner finished. Sometimes I would leave early rather than hear the professor drone on about *Marbury* v. *Madison,* but that often made me sell out before the trade reached full fruition. That's how heated that tech market was that first fall of the new bull market and how astoundingly boring the classes were.

I also enrolled in a class across the river at Harvard Business School to learn more about these options that I traded every day. The professor's thumbnail description in the catalogue described his course as a way to learn the intrinsic reasons behind the pricing of the instruments I was making so much money from. It wasn't long, however, before I realized that the professor, with all of his fancy calculations that showed the "true" pricing of call options, didn't have a clue about how options really worked. In fact, in almost every case that he gave, the real option world would have produced a far different answer. It would not be the first time that I found it fascinating how academics knew absolutely nothing about the way securities really trade. After about four weeks I gave up the class in disgust, muttering that the clown teaching it couldn't trade his way out of a wet paper bag. Thank God I took no notes; I might never have made a dime in the market with that "knowledge." The only place you could make any money at that school was the library, because they kept microfiched annual reports, vital for finding the next big trades.

At the same time that the bull market was erupting on Wall Street, Alan Dershowitz managed to snare the von Bülow appeal, the one that was the subject of *Reversal of Fortune.* (Dersh told me I was played by some Indian guy in the movie, but he said the same thing to the dozen others who were on the case.) I got to argue in the pleadings about some bogus Fourth Amendment search and seizure position about a black bag containing insulin that may or may not have been touched by Claus. At $18 an hour, I was making enough to increase my average position from five calls to ten, a major boost considering how much the commissions took from the trade. For what it's worth, I thought the guy was really guilty, but in our bizarre system of justice that played only a minimal role in the process.

Within a few months of the start of the bull market in 1982, I was so confident that these markets were going places that I wanted to get others in. In my first year at law school, I had been writing a newsletter called *Mr. Bullish* to my parents and a few select friends every week, containing some good stock tips, mostly on the red-hot apparel and shoe businesses and the reasoning backing up the tips. The folks got the hard copy; friends the carbons. Looking back it was an astoundingly geeky thing for a twenty-six-year-old to do, but it forced me to think about stocks in a coherent way. I was not, however, getting any traction. Not enough people were hearing about this great new bull market. Nobody should miss out on this one, I told myself. Gotta get everybody I know in. So I took the answering machine that my sister, Nan, had bought me, and decided to get into the stock business by leaving a message recommending select equities: "This is Jim Cramer, I'm not here right now, but you should take any spare cash you have this week and buy People Express up to $14." Or, "Hi, I'm not here right now, but IBM looks good for a trade up to $70." Each week on Sunday night I would change the pick, until I had built a ten-stock portfolio with a mixture of financials, airlines, and semiconductors. I caught some real scorchers on the machine, including Monolithic Memories, National Semiconductor, Northern Telecom, and a couple of the Canadian oils that were acting jiggier than anything in our markets. On big weeks I urged callers to take profits in airlines and roll into the semiconductors, or vice versa if the plane stocks took a hit.

I would cut a lot of class, trade all day off Financial News Network, then go to work researching the law for Dershowitz. It was at that moment that I got my biggest break of my business life, and it was when I least expected it to happen. For a couple of weeks straight, a guy named Marty Peretz kept calling and leaving messages. Everyone knew Marty at Harvard. He was loved by those who took his courses and had always discovered terrific young talent from his social studies lectures and from his freshman seminar. I knew him slightly, having been introduced a few years back by then-*New Republic* editor Michael Kinsley, whom I had met through *Crimson* connections. I had spent a summer just out of college in

1977 working on a piece for *The New Republic* about meritocracy and the Philadelphia Eagles under Dick Vermeil, but I only got $179 for my troubles.

Peretz called because he wanted me to write a "fix is in" book review about *The Partners,* a new book about the legal profession by my friend Jim Stewart from *American Lawyer.* Peretz and Stewart were buddies and Marty wanted to help Jim, so he reached out to me. I didn't know at the time that reviews could even be assigned to friends! Wow, was I painfully naive about the ways of journalism even after spending a few years with Brill. Perhaps I was too steeped in the *Crimson* ethic of bashing friends rather than helping them. That's not the way Marty—or the world— worked, I later discovered. I really had no interest in writing the review anyway, but Peretz was insistent, leaving me messages every Monday. I didn't bother to return the repeated calls. By the fourth week, though, Peretz, whom I knew as someone with riches beyond anything I had ever dreamed of, left a message saying that he no longer cared about the review anymore. He just needed to meet me, he said, because he had made more money off my answering machine than in twenty years of investing by so-called professionals. He liked me for my stocks, for my pick of the week that I put on my machine every Sunday night. Peretz wanted to meet me and talk about running some of his money. "Meet me at the Coffee Connection tomorrow morning at 8:30. Bring your best stock tips," said the message. Oh man, did I ever not know what I was getting into.

I schlepped across the street dutifully at 8:30, and Peretz, after shaking my hand and ordering a couple of coffees, whipped out a check for $500,000 and told me to take it. I said I couldn't. What the heck did I know about running other people's money? I wondered to the bearded professor. "Everything," he assured me. Marty had married a terrific, wealthy woman, Anne, and had spent much of his time augmenting that wealth with some great investments of his own, mostly in private companies. Now, he said, he had found someone whom he could work with to hone those hunches and make the most money out of them, and he wasn't going to let me return to school until I took the money.

Marty then had me review his family's portfolio right on the spot. He was way overweighted in the oils and the rails, definitely making the wrong bet now that oil had peaked. One of the goofy things about me is that I have an unbelievable ability to retain stocks and prices, even as I may not know names and faces very well. As I had studied the stock pages before going to the Connection, I knew where all of the stocks were in his massive portfolio, and their ranges for the last year. I gave him my high-tech epiphany and asked him where his tech stocks were. Sadly, he said, his managers had picked none. His stocks, I told him, had limited poten-tial. The oils had had their day, I said, and were unlikely to beat the aver-ages. The rails were incredibly boring places to be. (Still are.) He insisted again that I take his money. He begged me. Five hundred thousand dollars. The man was going to give me $500,000 because of my stock pick of the week, $500,000 to a person who didn't have $5,000 to his name, and I am giving him a fight on it? Why am I arguing with him? I thought to myself. The guy is trying to let me do what I think I can do best, what I think I have been put on earth to do, and I am telling him no? I could beat the returns of those family partnerships of his even while attending class. I could beat them even if I never left the classroom! Did I expect another person to turn up in the next hundred years with a check for $500,000 begging me to manage his money for him? What was I fretting about? What was I wait-ing for? So I grabbed it and shook his hand, even though I was frightened beyond belief that I would lose the money and that Marty had just, expen-sively for him, called my stock bluff. It was the beginning of an incredible partnership that made us both tons of money, for which I will forever be indebted to Marty.

I remember getting on the subway at Harvard Square a block from the Connection, with a folded-up check for half a million dollars in my chi-nos, and a couple of law books under my arm. Twenty minutes later I was at the window in some downtown office of Fidelity in Boston. As I've said, there wasn't too much interest in the market way back then and no-body was on their quote machine. While I had a full day of classes ahead, I just sat there for hours, hitting up symbols. After a long afternoon of quote hitting, I handed over the check to the discount house and began my professional trading career. They looked at me, looked at the check and a letter I had from Marty saying that I could do what I wanted with the money, and seemed completely perplexed. With my sneaks and my torn blue Sierra Designs jacket and a ratty black cotton T-shirt, I didn't look like a guy with a friend, let alone a half million bucks. But after a couple of calls they let me set up the account and gave me trading authority over the money.

The next day, I skipped class to get the half million into the market. I didn't want to waste any time. I was brimming with good ideas. Or so I thought. I put up chart after chart of important stocks that I wanted to buy. Nailed them to the walls and covered the floor with them. With some degree of trepidation, I picked up the phone, punched in seven numbers, and reached a Fidelity representative. Within two minutes I had put the $500,000 to work.

Wouldn't you know it, I dropped $14,000 the first day, getting impaled on some data switching company I had picked out of the Value Line Special Situation Survey report. I then proceeded to drop another $64,000 on Pulte Homes, Time Life, and a couple of chip stocks that had been oh-so-good to me for so long. Seventy-eight thousand dollars just up and vanished. Gone. Vaporized. I couldn't believe that, after two years of making good money pretty much every week for myself, I could turn $500,000 into $422,000 in only days. What an idiot! The losses were staggering. I had the first of what amounted to two decades of consecutive sleepless nights as I woke up at 3:00 A.M. trying to figure out how I could ever make the money back for this man I had met just one time for a cup of coffee. At $200 a pop, that's an awful lot of *New Republic* articles I would have to write to make good on Peretz's trade. I couldn't imagine how I could ever come back from that loss. Sweat would pour down my back as I waited for the market to open. I would gasp every time one of my ticker symbols came up with a minus sign next to it. By day four, I couldn't bear to look at FNN. I dreaded the stock tables for the first time in my life. I was a fraud, a huge fraud, and had just been incredibly lucky. I would cash out the remainder before I lost it all and begin working as a servant for Marty until I could make it all back, cleaning his house, maybe raking a hundred years' worth of leaves from his yard in tony north Cambridge.

The next week Marty left word on my now recommendation-less answering machine that he wanted to review how we had done. I was horrified that I could lose so much *real* money after playing so well first with paper money and then with small amounts of cash, my cash, not someone else's. After an entirely sleepless night I could barely think straight as I crossed Dunster Street to go back to the same table at the Coffee Connection where, a week before, $500,000 had been handed to me, $500,000 I had now turned into $422,000.

As soon as I saw Marty I dropped the bomb of the "lost" $78,000. I promised to give him the rest of the money back and work at any job he wanted until I did. It was then that Marty shocked me by laughing at the losses and telling me that I should just make it back in the market, that his faith in me was undiminished, and that if anything I was handling the market's downturn—it had started its first serious sell-off since the Federal Reserve had started cutting rates in 1982—perfectly, much better than his other managers. I remember choking back tears. "You mean you don't want me to repay the money right now? You don't want me to just owe you what I lost?" No, he said. In fact, he wanted to give me more money. He was ready to give me several hundred thousand dollars more right then, just to show that he had confidence in me and believed that I would make even bigger money for him down the road, when I got a better feel for the tape.

"Go make it back," he said.

And so I did.

I immediately broomed the whole goddamned portfolio that I had intended to buy and hold, and set out to trade my way back to the black, rather than owning stocks and hoping for the best. I started placing $2,000 and $3,000 bets on call options on computers and semiconductors until I made back about half the losses. (Calls are super-juiced investments that allow you to control a lot of stock with much less money than you'd need to buy the stock itself. Until you have to take delivery you can trade the value of the option, which goes up if the underlying stock goes up. There comes a time when options have to be exercised, though, and if the stock doesn't go up in the interim you lose everything. You don't buy calls to hold them. Owing to their volatility, you have to trade them, and trade them constantly. They are addictive and when you are right they can make you money with greater velocity than any other bet on earth.)

Then I switched aggressively to the short side, betting against Motorola and Texas Instruments, as well as many of the oil and rail stocks Marty had in his other portfolios, believing momentum had peaked for the moment. ("The short side" means that you make money when something goes down. It is no different from betting against a team in football. You get paid if it goes down, not up. In the money-managing world it's much more gratifying to be short than to be long or to own stocks, because you make money when others are losing money; think of it as getting paid for Schadenfreude.) Soon, almost every bet was a bet against the market. I traded some stocks eight or nine times a day, trying to catch little moves. I sneaked back to watch FNN every lunch. I gave up the Dershowitz gig entirely, in order to read up on more companies, get more ideas, more shorts. I had stacks of research in every corner of my dorm room and sheaves of annual reports. Anything that I thought could go down I would buy puts on, and as the market rolled over, I began to make some big money. (Puts are like insurance on something you don't own. You buy an option on a stock, for example, expecting it to go down. When it does, you get to collect the loss as a profit.) Sometimes I made as much as $2,000 to $2,500 a day, trying to get back to even.

Marty didn't even care that, a few weeks later, without any dish cleaning or lawn mowing or, most fortunately given the paltry sums paid out by *The New Republic,* article writing, I had made the money back. When I again offered him the original $500,000 with an opportunity for us to go our separate ways, he wouldn't hear of it. He again implored me to take more money. He wanted to know whether I had gotten my hot hand back, the one that made the answering machine tips so spot-on, and if so he insisted that I take more money. He had found his stock picker and he wasn't going to give up on him.

CHAPTER 2

Goldman

That winter of 1982–1983, after trading Marty's money for five months, I couldn't bear to think about having to go back to a law firm for the summer. I knew I hated the law. I hated litigation. I hated corporate work. I hated proofreading documents. I hated being a toady to others. I hated working for miserable mean partners. I knew I would never last. I knew I liked business and wanted to be in business, not law. So, I decided to blow off the crucial second summer at a law firm, and apply to every major investment banking house in town and see if I could catch on. I went back to the Harvard Business School Library and looked up the biggest and toughest investment banks and applied to every one of them. Within a week every firm rejected me, except the best one, Goldman Sachs, which seemed genuinely interested. I got a letter from Goldman saying that it would consider me for its summer associate program but that I would have to battle hundreds of others. In retrospect I think it was a rejection letter that I treated as an acceptance letter.

There were flyers on the corkboards of the Harvard Business School Library inviting students to attend a cocktail party at the Ritz-Carlton in Boston for potential Goldman hires. I talked my way past the receptionist by showing her my "acceptance" letter, and next thing I knew I was face-to-face with the people who did the hiring. I figured that my law degree coupled with my love for stocks could put me in line for one of those fancy corporate finance jobs that were and are all the rage at business school campuses. I wanted to play the role of the erudite bankers who had bossed around the lawyers on the deals I had witnessed at Fried Frank. I wanted a chance to be a well-paid, arrogant, corporate finance or merger and acquisitions associate. That would be the perfect fit for someone with my skill set I figured. And now I was in the room with the people who make the decisions about who gets those jobs. Within a few minutes of my arriving, I found myself talking to a towering man who seemed to be the reigning Goldman honcho. Indeed he was; I had stumbled on to Richard Menschel, head of all Securities, Sales, and Trading and one of the most influential partners ever to work at Goldman. I was all set to tell him about how I thought corporate finance should be my next home. After a minute of banter he said he had a most important question to ask me. He wanted to know why a Harvard Law School student would want to take a job selling stocks at Goldman Sachs. I thought for a second. Huh, sales, sales, I mean like, sales—what is this guy talking about? Sales? I'm here for corporate finance. Wasn't this the corporate finance reception? Were there salespeople at places like Goldman, people like the broker who sold my dad National Video? Did they have brokers there, at the esteemed and august Goldman Sachs?

But right before I could utter, "Beats the heck out of me, pal," I came to my senses and simply said, "Because I think I was put on earth to sell stocks." He asked me what distinguished me from the pack that would be seeking these jobs. I thought for a second and I said I represented the most massively undervalued security in the whole room and if he would give me a chance, I would prove it worth his while. I told him I was like Exxon, overlooked and undervalued. He laughed and told me I might get a shot. I thought I was in, but I had no idea what awaited me. If the gauntlet for a Goldman job from even the top of Harvard Business School was a tough one, it would be nearly insurmountable for someone from Harvard Law.

Not that long after, while visiting New York for one of those torturous law firm interviews, which I was using as a backup if the Goldman gambit failed, I dropped by Goldman Sachs at the appointed hour that the head recruiter had assigned me after Menschel had checked off on my existence and didn't flat out say no. The receptionist put me in a little interview room the size of two phone booths at around 11:00 A.M. I waited, patiently, reading some annual reports, for what seemed like hours. And it was hours.

Nobody came to see me. At a little after 5:00 P.M. a cleaning person told me that everyone had left and that I better be heading home myself lest I get locked in overnight. I debated that possibility momentarily and then exited.

I took the six hours in the phone booth as a sign that while it would be a little bit harder to get the Goldman summer gig than I had thought, I shouldn't be discouraged. Once back in Cambridge I wrote again, asking for an interview. The person in charge of the summer program, I recall, was concerned that I might not have gotten the message that my full-day wait had implied. I said I had, that Goldman was a tough place and only those who waited all day in a windowless holding pen would make the cut to the next round. I told the recruiter that while the test had been debilitating so far, I was more interested in selling stocks than ever before.

A week later, I was back in the booth. This time, though, a dozen young associates took turns whacking the law school piñata. Each one tried to rattle me by asking me for a half-dozen stocks I liked, where their closing prices were and what their price-to-earnings multiples and book value— yes it was a long time ago—were. I thought I had died and gone to heaven. I had been born to answer these questions, after I had finished naming the prices of every stock, their fifty-two-week lows and highs, what multiples they were selling for, and what I thought they would earn next year, I eagerly critiqued *their* favorite stocks and mentioned some I thought would be stronger performers than those on Goldman's recommended list.

I felt so good about the full-day slate of interviews that I grabbed my coat out of the fourth-floor closet in the reception area and dashed out of Goldman almost as if I were on fire. It was only when I got to the 59th Street Bridge and I realized that I had snared the wrong coat—mistakenly walking out with the raincoat of the last partner who had interviewed me—that I had a pang of worry that I wouldn't get the job. Five subway stops later and I was returning the coat to its hanger just when the partner was heading out. He looked at me and marveled that I had stuck around so long after being dismissed, and I said, I couldn't stay away from the action. He said he liked that in a person, someone who didn't know when to quit.

Shortly after, I won the coveted summer slot. I was to be the guy from

Harvard for sales and trading. Never was a guy from Harvard Law School more excited about going into sales than I was. I knew there was no way I was going back to the law after this move.

That summer I got my first taste of the basic training that was Goldman Sachs. Goldman was the polar opposite of a law firm. Bill Gruver, the tough taskmaster in charge of the program, immediately got to the front lines of action. I was thrown in, from the moment I got there, to the trading desk, where I had to field calls from arbitrageurs interested in buying Diamond Shamrock in a takeover bid. I had no idea what I was doing. People spent the whole day screaming at me about what a knucklehead I was. I wasn't sure if I was supposed to come back the next day. But I did, and sat down in the same place, and got screamed at all day again, until some other desk asked me to sit with them where *they* screamed at me all day. I was called an idiot, a moron, and a stupid dope, and all I can say is I am glad they didn't know I went to Harvard Law because then they would have had a field day with me. This trading stuff was hard. This wasn't my seven Bobbie Brooks shares, nor my ten Amoco calls. This was "trading 250,000 shares of Crown Cork and Seal on the bid side, open to buyers." It was total firing line indoctrination, and I loved it.

We in the program, as it was called, would do our best not to be tortured too often with the mindless errands we had to run for unimportant associates trying to feel important, and we held up under the nonstop ridicule all day, until after the close of the market we attended night classes that often didn't begin until hours after they were supposed to. These were truly brutal. We would always be asked a series of questions we didn't know the answer to and if we got them wrong we would have to leave the room and wait outside until we were invited back. Sometimes we weren't. Everyone in the program seemed to be made of tungsten, they were that tough. I remember, at an early meeting, giving an introduction about myself, talking about how I had lived in my car with a .22 caliber handgun and a hatchet and covered violent crime. I figured that put me in the toughness room. But the guy after me looked at me as if I were a sissy. I guess he figured I should have had a Magnum or maybe a flamethrower and grenades. I will never forget what he said he did. He explained that right before he was hired, he was a naval submarine commander and when he entered the killing profession he could fire a nuclear warhead from Diego Garcia in the Indian Ocean and hit Yankee Stadium. And when he left five years later he could fire that same missile but this time he could hit home plate. Another time I would have said, "What the heck are you firing nuclear warheads at Yankee Stadium for?" Instead, I was just in awe. I hadn't done anything that could start World War III.

Goldman was still looking to shake people out, not take them in. They were trying to find ways of limiting the number of people they hired. They knew they would make you rich if they hired you, and with that promise came a devotion to the firm that knew no bounds. Day four of my training proved to be more of a test than I had bargained for. My sister, Nan, was getting married during the first weekend of the summer school program and when I accepted the job I had asked to be able to attend her Friday night prenuptial dinner. I had assurances that it would not be a problem, as long as I attended the class after work and asked for permission then. I had again asked for permission that morning and, anxious that I not miss the event, had around lunchtime reminded my boss that I had to be in Philadelphia at 8:00 P.M. He assured me not to worry about a thing. Class would start right on schedule after the close because everyone wanted to make an early Friday break for a summer weekend.

But the instructor, who was the same soul who repeatedly assured me I would not miss the event, showed up two and a half hours after the four o'clock close of the market. Before we started class, in front of about thirty full-time trainees who had just graduated from business school as well as the elite group of five summer associates I was part of, I explained to the instructor that if I left right then I could still make the big dinner the night before my sister's marriage. I asked for permission to hightail it to the occasion. The instructor looked at me and noted that I had worked hard to get the summer slot and that now was a moment of truth. Sure I could leave, but if I did, I shouldn't bother coming back to work on Monday because Goldman would give the job to one of the thousand other people who had wanted it but had been turned down to let some kid from law school take the position. "Your call," he said, immediately starting the class.

And that's how I came to miss the prenuptial party for my sister.

I still can't explain the choice to anybody in my family. I still can't explain why I wanted Goldman Sachs so badly that I risked the wrath of my family and the anger of my conscience. I knew, however, that I loved the rigor, the intensity of the company. And, yes, I wanted the money. I wanted to be successful at the pinnacle of capitalism and there was no sense going back after you finally made it to base camp. I wanted it, in the end, too much, because, as I would later learn, I was always too willing to postpone or sacrifice the people and things in life that mattered in favor of the need to be successful.

As rigorous as the boot camp may have been for the rest of the summer, I couldn't get enough of Goldman Sachs. By midsummer I was even more certain I could never become a lawyer and yet I would have to endure another whole year of law school before I could get back to Wall Street. Every day I immersed myself on the trading floor, every night I headed to the research floor. I tried to spend eighteen hours a day chatting up anyone I could find to talk stocks. I couldn't get enough of the stock-oxygenated atmosphere of the joint. By the end of the summer the hazing stopped, and I was allowed to talk to associates without total subservience. Come August, I stayed until the day before third-year classes began. By August I had been allowed to trade, and I started increasing the size of the positions for my own account. August of 1983 proved to be a strong month for the market, and I made as much money trading as I did at the firm. Now that I understood the lingo I knew the place rocked with energy. I knew that the people were incredibly smart and fast and exacting and, above all, hungrier than you would ever believe people who were making fortunes weekly could be. It was a precision-crafted money factory. I never wanted to leave.

Once back in Cambridge for the fall I threw myself into my trading for the Peretz account, choosing to "attend" law school by using those ubiquitous outlines where you attend one class out of thirty, take copious notes, and then let twenty-nine others do the same until you had thirty great sets of class notes. This was an ideal way to play around and still have a legitimate cover for doing it. Actually, all of law school was a terrific way to have a good time and have a great alibi for doing it, provided you didn't care about where you stood in your class rankings, and, as someone who was going into sales at Goldman, I couldn't have cared less. It was also an ideal setting for trading stocks, with the need to miss only one trading session per class taken.

That fall of 1983 and the spring of 1984 saw big setbacks in tech, which I had pounded on from the short side, making a monster bet against Motorola and Cray Research as well as Data General and Digital Equipment. On the long side I had moved on to playing a high-stakes game of call buying in the oil and gas equities, as the takeover action had reached a frenzy in the patch.

As I took our account well into the black in mid-spring of 1984, I found a class, at last, with relevance to what I was trading in: anti-trust. Most of my call option positions were in oil stocks, which I thought would get takeover bids or had bids on the table. Only antitrust, the federal doctrine dating back to Teddy Roosevelt's time, stood in the way of making some huge coin. I didn't know anything about it, but I had the best professor in the business teaching the body of work, Phil Areeda, former head of antitrust for the Justice Department.

As usual, when I attended, I sat in the back, charting stocks and checking out the stock tables, as I did in the handful of classes I bothered to attend. It was then that I decided I could commit to memory all of the closing prices of all of the stocks on the New York Stock Exchange, just to relieve the in-class boredom between April and graduation.

My bets had grown from ten and twenty calls, usually about $5,000 to $10,000, to about $25,000 to $50,000 at a clip after I got back from my summer at Goldman. I loved the oils so much that I did my third-year paper on the DuPont-Conoco takeover and spent oodles of time interviewing partners at law firms for the paper, all of whom assured me, the student, that there were many more deals like Conoco in the pipeline. So I drilled for and hit call option gushers in Sinclair and Getty and then rolled the profits into Gulf Oil, which was a perennial target. Sure enough I hit a big one, a huge bid by Chevron for Gulf, the smallest of what was then the sovereign Seven Sisters of the oil world. Surprisingly, while Gulf Oil's stock took off for a half-dozen points, giving me a tidy gain, it didn't get nearly as high as it would have if the government weren't going to step in to block the deal. In other words, it traded at a huge discount to what could be a final bid if one were to be allowed. I figured there could be fifteen big ones, fifteen huge points that I could play with if only I knew whether the government was going to let the deal through. The newspapers were filled with wary arbitrageurs worried that the deal would never be allowed. Gulf began creeping back down to where it was before the deal was announced. I started giving back a huge gain. I wanted to double up on the bet, but the Justice Department's move was just too hard to call, according to the parade of talking heads I watched on the screen and read about in the *Journal*. You just couldn't know whether Justice would green-light the merger between the second- and seventh-largest oil companies.

In three years at law school I never said a thing about the law in class if I could avoid it. I would hide rather than be called on, and frequently passed, even if the professors reminded me we weren't playing bridge, a joke that I laughed at the first time, but by year three had gotten sick of hearing. I just wished they would let me alone. I sleepwalked and backbenched through the whole experience. But for once, I figured, let me get something out of this high-priced education. A few days after the Gulf-Chevron deal, with Gulf in free fall as rumor-mongers on Wall Street bet that Justice would stop it, and my calls caused me to bleed red from my eyeballs, I did the unthinkable. I approached Professor Areeda, the reigning antitrust teacher in the country and the acknowledged dean of the subject, and asked him about the Gulf deal. He slowly looked me up and down, wrinkled his nose as if I needed a shower, which I probably did, and asked if I was the guy who kept reading the *Journal* in the back of the room, paying no attention to class. I said that was me, no denying it. He said he had no desire to help someone who was obviously so uninterested in the subject, but because I was his student, he felt obliged to tell me that he was sure that the deal would go through and it would not be blocked. I looked at him again and said, "Mr. Areeda, I am a bit of a betting man. How certain are you?"

He said he knew Justice wasn't going to stop it. I told him I was going to bet that way and that it would really screw up everything if he were wrong.

He looked at me with total contempt and asked if I thought he really wasn't the expert he knew himself to be. Was I challenging his knowledge or his sources in Justice?

Oh no, I assured him, I was just pretty stupid about the subject, an opinion he readily acknowledged.

With that, I thanked him, looked at the clock and saw that there was still enough time to bolt from class and get to the phone booth outside the lecture hall. I took all the available money and borrowing power I had and put it all on the Gulf Oil April 45, 50, and 55 calls, betting that the stock in the low 40s was about to roar right back up because the government wouldn't block the deal. I would make almost ten times my money if Areeda knew what he was talking about.

I had to wait until some woman got off the phone to her mother, bragging about how she had gotten a job at one of those New York sweatshops, knowing that if she didn't shut up, I wouldn't beat the closing bell. She hung up just in time for me to punch in Fidelity's numbers and place the shootin' match bet on Gulf calls.

The next day Justice leaked that it would bless the merger. The move paid for the entire three years of law school and then some. It would be two years before I had a hit as big as that one. It also reminded me that as much as you like a diversified bet, if you have an edge, you have to be willing to bet the house on it.

For me, the journey, and the addiction, were just beginning.

I counted down the days to the end of law school. On graduation day, Marty threw a terrific party and introduced me to dozens of friends as his broker, thereby assuring me that I would have a strong client base when I got to Goldman. It was an act of generosity he would repeat over and over in the next dozen years. On the last day of exams, however, as I packed my bags for New York and a summer of studying for the bar exam, I got the phone call that would scar me for the rest of my life. The registrar claimed I had failed to drop a class and that I was fifteen minutes late to an exam of a civil procedure class that I would have to take if I were to graduate. I said I knew nothing about civil procedure and wasn't about to take an exam I had failed to prep for. Then I wasn't going to graduate, she told me.

A few days after everyone had left the campus, my case came before the administrative board. I remember telling my interlocuter that I had never even showed at the class and that must have been a sure sign that I had dropped it. But the questioner knew I had barely attended any other classes, so that couldn't be proof. After getting a couple of professors whom I had impressed as a stock picker to speak up for me, I was allowed to graduate. For the next sixteen years, until I retired from the hedge fund business, I would dream at least three times a week that I had to take an exam for a class I didn't attend.

Studying for the bar exam was pure hell, because there was only one phone booth at the corner of Sixth Avenue and 45th Street in Manhattan, where the classes were held, and they gave you no break before the opening to place orders. Pre–cell phone it was almost impossible to trade unless you were at a desk.

So, for two months, I let my call positions ride, trading only when I could get to the pay phone, and then rarely taking much off the table. I almost got killed betting that Amoco would be the next oil to get a bid. It would be more than a dozen years before that takeover would come to fruition.

Goldman Sachs had made it clear that I would not be able to manage Marty's money when I was in the three-month training period to be in sales. That meant I had to gun Marty's account to maximum size before I cashed it out. That meant making a sizable tech bet right at the time of the bar exam, with huge outsized wagers on Texas Instruments, IBM, and Motorola. I bought massive amounts of calls a week before the bar exam. As I was going to start work the day after the exam, I had no choice but to cash out all my positions during the break in the bar between the multistate and the New York State portions. I rang the register for about $3 million of call options—I had built the original money into a substantial sum over the years—from the only working pay phone three blocks from New York Law School, where the exam was given, and got back just in time for the next part of the exam.

I got out of the Goldman training program early because I had taught myself a lot of what there was to learn, and I had withdrawal when I couldn't trade. And then, once out of the training program, I could see there would be this huge obstacle to performing as well as I would like in the market: when you are a broker at a firm, even a great firm like Goldman Sachs, you only have one task in mind, and it isn't making money for your clients. It is finding new money and bringing in "elephants," as we called them at Goldman. Every day, day in and day out, I would have to make thirty cold calls to people I didn't know and who had no desire to talk to me. I would get hung up on as I tried endlessly to get through to people. Didn't matter. My job was to call and I would have to submit a log of calls each week. (This came easy for me after having to call the next of kin of dozens of homicide victims when I was a beat reporter.)

I searched endlessly for good lists to call. Those who donated money to virtually anything and were not already clients of the firm would get a call from me. I called every patron that I could find of the Metropolitan Opera, Metropolitan Museum, any ballet company. If you were in a program at Lincoln Center, I called you.

Most of the time people would have secretaries screening calls. If I could get the name of a receptionist or a secretary, I knew I was as good as in because most brokers treated these people awfully. Any dose of non-wiseguy kindness would get you far. I would give people presents if I could find out it was their birthday, or buy them flowers. They would eventually let me, that nice guy from Goldman Sachs, through to the elephant. I know, I know, it sounds familiar, sounds like Bud Fox from the movie *Wall Street*. It sure should; as part of their research for the movie I met with the filmmakers to describe how I would get through to Gordon Gekko. Bud did exactly as he should have and it worked.

Once I got my meeting, I would always make the most of it, critiquing their portfolios and urging them to buy something I loved. I would almost never leave without an order.

After the meeting I would go to the top floor of the building and work my way down, knocking on doors to see if anyone wanted to talk stocks. Any door with the words "Equity" or "Partnership" or "Securities" was fair game, in case you are trying to figure out how to discourage guys like me from coming into your office. While my hit ratio on my walk-downs wasn't high, it kept me from getting prodded into making even more cold calls if I were in the office. Eventually, I came to know all the skyscrapers in Midtown Manhattan by looking at their directories and visiting any office that even sounded remotely like a money management partnership.

Soon, I exhausted Manhattan and would rent a car to go to the libraries of rich neighborhoods and read the local paper about who the big movers and shakers were in those towns. I would jot down dozens of names and with bags of quarters make call after call until I could make an appointment. Again, the persistence paid off, and once in, I would know something in their portfolios that should stay and be bought more heavily and something else that should go.

That's all the firm wanted me to do. But I had other ideas. I missed terribly the idea generating that I used to do, and I felt so hemmed in by the firm's recommended list, even though there were something like 500 companies that could be considered to have some form of buy on them. They were all staid, solid companies, and there's no sense deviating from the list if you want to bore rich people with rich ideas.

Not me. I wanted to be out finding the next great idea. While I was out looking for clients, I hit upon the idea of visiting stores to see what was hot. It was only after a few weeks that I realized how much you could get out of store clerks if you knew what to ask. While walking up and down the Woolworth Building one day, I stopped in at a nearby Foot Locker to see what was moving.

Reebok's aerobic sneaker, the clerk told me. Can't keep them on the shelves. For the next week, any time I canvassed a building for clients, I checked a nearby shoestore. I always got the same answer: "We can't stock Reebok fast enough."

Reebok, a stock in the low teens, had just come public. Nobody knew much about it. I read up on the documents in the Goldman library and found out that the stock was barely covered by analysts, including Goldman Sachs. I knew I had a home run.

From that one piece of information, gleaned from going to more than forty stores, I called every shoe executive in the book. (Industry execs always want to buy shares of stocks in their own industry.) Some of the people I called worked outside the New York area—which amounted to poaching on some other Goldman employee's turf, but so be it—and I jammed everybody I could with Reebok. Every cold caller got the Reebok story. Every time I got in the door I mentioned Reebok. I even called up accounts that weren't mine, that were short Reebok, betting against the stock, and urged them to cover (buy back to close out a short). I called Michael Steinhardt, Wall Street's legendary bear, when I read in some newspaper that he was short Reebok and I demanded to see him. I got in and I told him he was nuts and that Reebok, which had moved up to the mid-30s, would go to 100. (I used to sell a lot of stocks like that, find ones that were in the 30s or 40s and say that 100 was the next stop.)

Steinhardt told me I had no idea what I was talking about and that Reebok was a fad, a joke.

But no one was laughing when a few months later Reebok hit $100 a share. I called everyone and told them to sell. I didn't want to wait to find out the show was not hot anymore. (The stock went a bit higher, then plummeted for years.)

During the unprecedented run by Reebok, when account after account of mine would be seen buying it, my manager called me in to ask why so many people were buying a stock that was not recommended by Goldman Sachs. I told him about my research. He told me that the firm spent millions of dollars on research and that I better stick to the recommended list. I asked him what was the point of hiring thinking people if they couldn't recommend something they had researched themselves? He told me that my freelancing days were over and that from now on no client was to buy Reebok unless the client brought it up.

It made no sense. The goal of the process was to make people money. But in a way it did make sense: the firm had to be careful; you couldn't have brokers out there recommending stocks that weren't backed up by official research.

It was a cowboy act in a firm that doesn't like cowboys. I got the impression that if my commissions hadn't been among the highest in the firm, I might have come under even tougher scrutiny. The manager also frowned on my calling on people who were not in my territory of New York. I could never figure out whether he was out to punish me or not, but the next thing I knew I was going to Rochester, Syracuse, and Elmira every other week as part of a lesson in territory. For each town I would go to the library and look up the patrons of all of the arts, but together they didn't add up to one big New York client. I know my boss thought I got the message that I had to stay in my New York territory no matter what, or I would soon discover the wonders of the Southern Tier and the Finger Lakes. These trips were real boot camp to me, because Goldman didn't want me to open an account unless the individual had $10 million to buy stocks or bonds, and, frankly, there weren't a lot of multimillionaires in Glens Falls, Horseheads, or Binghamton.

But soon after I began my weekly rounds to Chemung County, home of the Chemung County Bank among other robust institutions, I got a call from the man who served with me as my business manager when I was president of *The Harvard Crimson*. He was looking for some honest information about the market, looking for a broker his firm could trust, who was not out to rip them off or gouge them. He was in Seattle and he wanted me to come out and see him to give him some advice about what to do with his stock and his money.

We chatted, and I told him that I would love to come out sometime. I had a terrible cold and didn't want to make the trip. But the caller, Steve Ballmer, now CEO of Microsoft, said the firm was thinking of going public and that if I didn't mind he would like to see me sooner rather than later. How soon? I said. "How about tonight, for dinner?"

I was supposed to drive to Glens Falls the next day to prospect. My head was spinning, partly from my cold and partly from the knowledge that if I didn't go prospecting in Glens Falls but instead got on a plane to Seattle to meet Steve Ballmer for dinner, I was a total idiot. I paused for a second, during which he said that if I could come tonight, I could also meet Bill Gates, Sr., who was also trying to figure out what to do with his and his son's possible riches.

"Sure, Steve. In fact, I am leaving right now," I said.

Next thing I know I am on an airplane to Seattle, sick as a dog, but determined to bring in what could be the greatest herd of elephants of all time.

But as we climbed into the air, I began to feel a searing pain and a monstrous pressure in my left ear. It built throughout the trip. I told the stewardess, who suggested I chew gum, to no avail. As the pain increased, she put steaming hot paper towels in cups and asked me to hold them to my ear. Again, no cessation in the pain.

As we drew closer to Seattle-Tacoma Airport she told me that it might be excruciatingly painful for me to land but that we, of course, had no choice. As we descended, something wicked popped in my ear and then everything just went muffled. I could see people talking but it sounded as though they were underwater.

I had blown out my eardrum. My head was splitting, my hearing shot. But I had to get that account. I had to get that elephant.

I remember nothing of the dinner other than how much my head hurt. Steve did most of the talking. Whatever I said, it worked, because I flew back that next morning, minus the hearing in one ear but with an awfully big chunk of business. Before I went to the office I went to an ear specialist, who simply confirmed that I had burst my eardrum, something that can happen when you fly with a terrible head cold.

I didn't care. I was so thrilled to get that business that I couldn't contain myself. I told everyone the good news.

Within minutes I was summoned to my manager's office. What was this about going out to Seattle?

I started explaining to him what had happened. He was furious, saying that nobody was allowed to poach like that. He wanted me to give the account to the San Francisco office, whose territory it was. I refused. I told him that if I hadn't made the trip, Ballmer would have gone to another firm. No matter. My manager wouldn't pay for my airfare. There was nothing I could do. In a few years Ballmer became one of the largest clients in the firm. I was never reimbursed, though. And you would do best to sit on the right side of me if you want me to hear you.

For the most part working at Goldman Sachs meant being as creative as possible at getting people's assets handed over to your custody. That's what brokers do best and I was darned good at it. Rarely did it matter *how* you *did* for clients. In fact, that was an abstraction, left unmentioned.

Performance was out of our hands; we were graded by our asset gathering and ticket writing. Only occasionally did I feel that there was an intellectual intersection between doing well for the client and doing well for myself. What mattered was a constant stream of new clients, and everything from payday to review time revolved around how much new business you were doing, not what you were doing to keep your clients happy. In a sense, your clients were supposed to be so rich to begin with that it was your job simply not to screw up their wealth; making wealth was a total afterthought, something you did on your own time.

That meant selling bond "paper" that paid you well and paid the customer well, and trying to stay away from the marginal pieces of merchandise, the Bethlehem Steel convertibles and American SouthWest collateralized mortgages that paid you *huge* and shafted your client. But no one ever got in trouble for shafting a client, whereas you were in trouble in an instant if you shafted the franchise. I bought it; not to buy in is to court failure and dismissal.

I also struggled at Goldman to attempt to balance what was once a liberal-arts-leaning life with the automaton in me that needed to beat the numbers at all costs and make the money any way Goldman felt was fair and honest. I tried to keep my hand in writing, but it wasn't something that anyone endorsed, except for, amazingly, Bob Rubin, who had been running arbitrage for Goldman at the time and was perceived, correctly, as the partner who would ultimately run the firm. He loved that I wrote and only asked that I run everything by his desk before it appeared. I did a couple of innocuous pieces about the market, published in *The New Republic,* that he liked but said little about. Most of these were little snapshots of the market, about how I felt we were at the beginning of a major bull market and how you couldn't be scared about the sell-offs, that they were to be bought not sold. I was considered a reckless and hopeless bull internally at Goldman, but in retrospect, even I was way too conservative about the upside.

Then one day Marty Peretz asked me to do another sweetheart review for a friend, this time Ivan Boesky, who had written a book called *Merger Mania.* This was a year before the feds collared Boesky.

When I finished my draft of the review, which praised Boesky for his insight into how he made his money, it came back from Rubin trashed, with notes scrawled in the margin about how Boesky didn't make his money that way at all. The notes made it clear that Rubin didn't believe that Boesky was telling us the truth about arbitrage, Boesky-style. Rubin told me to come see him. I jogged up the stairs to his office, where he was lying on his back—he had a perpetually thrown back—on the floor. He asked if I knew anything about Boesky. I said I had met him once and had read his book. Rubin told me that if I didn't put a caveat in about how Boesky really made his money, it would come back to haunt me. I told him that the changes he wanted might embarrass Boesky. He didn't care. He simply smiled and said that the only person who would ultimately be embarrassed by taking Boesky's book seriously would be *me.* So I adjusted the review to suggest that while the book had excellent information from Boesky, we would have to wait for another work to find out the true story of the Boesky legend. Rubin loved this and *The New Republic* printed it. Later, after the feds busted Boesky, I realized that I owed Rubin big. But he never wanted an ounce of credit for anything. He had just wanted me to look good.

Money Man

At Goldman I was always looking to make people more money than the firm wanted them to make. I had a terrific client base, and a well-rounded one, in part because Marty Peretz had turned me on to his considerable network of friends, many of whom were doctors. These doctors had always been trying to find a broker who could translate their medical insights into profits. I was always looking to do the translating. It was then that I discovered my single greatest investment of all time: Merck. At the time Merck was a dowdy company without much excitement. Nobody disliked it but nobody liked it much either. In fact, it was a stock that was frowned upon at Goldman Sachs because it did not have a single blockbuster drug in the pipeline. Or so the research department thought.

I knew otherwise. Merck had an anticholesterol drug that several of Marty's friends were testing and the results were spectacular. In 1986 I took everyone out of everything and put them into Merck. It was a great call and we made tons of money riding Merck the whole year, but it was never on the recommended list at Goldman so the whole act of making millions upon millions of dollars for people, and many hundreds of thousands for myself, was viewed as one more rogue act that branded me a cowboy. But it wasn't as big a rogue act as my short-selling of Bethlehem Steel. That once great steel company had come to Goldman Sachs to do a financing, a convertible preferred. As part of the dog-and-pony show where management goes around the country and tells you why you should

buy its stock, Bessie, as it was known in the firm, came to Goldman Sachs
to talk. I was one of the only sales guys who attended the meeting. As the
Bethlehem folks could not answer questions about how they were going to
beat back exports, shrug off declining demand, or pay their considerable
health care benefits, I walked out of the meeting convinced that the $25
stock was about to go much lower. I talked Marty Peretz into buying a
massive number of puts on Bessie. When the stock plummeted to $5 not
long after, Marty made more money than we had made on any bet in favor
of a stock except for Merck. Once again, though, the firm wasn't happy
with my buying the puts. It was bad enough we had made a lot of money
with Merck, a nonrecommended stock, but to make a lot of money betting
against a recommendation that was also a client, now that was plain
heresy.

It should have been a great time for me, with my business taking off and
my Goldman clients making big money. But in early 1985 my mother, a
metal sculptor, was diagnosed with kidney cancer, the type that has been
known to strike welders. She had never been sick a day of her life but this
cancer was incurable. I wanted to spend as much time as possible with her,
knowing that time would be short. I went to the men who hired me,
Richard Menschel and Bill Gruver, and told them about my mom. Both
men, who I thought were heartless when I was being recruited, now explained to me the way the Goldman family really worked. They wanted
me to take as much time off to be with my mother as I needed. They didn't
want to see me. They urged me to stay with her and my dad in Philadelphia
and to be helpful. It was the side of Goldman you saw when you were inside, and it allowed me to be with my mom as much as possible in her remaining months.

My mother, who was working on a one-woman metal sculpture show at
the Art Alliance in Philadelphia—a show she would live to see, passing
away only days after its completion—wanted me to go back to being
someone creative again. She liked the market, liked it for fun, but she
thought that I had been devoured by it. She thought that the money business was a crude and rapacious one that would turn me into someone who
cared only about money, and not family or personal fulfillment. She urged
me to go back to being a journalist, because she knew I loved writing, as
soon as I had enough money. She was repulsed by my talk at the dinner

table about how well I was doing, and how I was respected as a good sales-person who was going to do a lot of commission. That's not something to be proud of, she would say. She had a strange and angry clarity in her final months that made her rage against what she thought I would become, and long for the boy who wanted to do good, to do something important, not something mercantile.

She was confused about my relationship with Marty Peretz. On the one hand, she thought it terrific that I had found someone who believed in me, and wanted to help me advance within the ranks of Goldman Sachs. She was so proud of the party Marty threw at graduation and she had seen our business friendship blossom into a true personal friendship. But she also thought that Marty contributed to my incessant focus on the market. She was astonished that Marty would call at all hours, that we would talk about stocks from 6:30 A.M. to 11:00 P.M. Takeover stocks. Stocks with bright earnings prospects. Stocks and more stocks. She was worried that I had become addicted to the money, even as I told her that I was sim-ply enjoying the trading. I had gotten her and my father dabbling in the market again, and she enjoyed it, but she felt that the constant trading, which did not let up even while I was at her bedside in her final months, was just nuts.

I wasn't sure myself where I was going with this obsession. I knew that my relationship with Marty had taken on an intensity that demanded total focus on the market. He felt the trading was a helpful diversion from the sadness of my mother's illness. I would come in on Fridays, sit with my mother, talk with Marty about the market by phone, check in with Gold-man, watch FNN, and place orders all day from home—literally until the day my mother died. The conversations with Marty were the only diver-sion from the incredible sadness that occurs when you watch your fifty-five-year-old mother die just when she had been so happy and so proud of her career and her family. At the time, Marty seemed right: the trading was a good place for my mind to hide, even as others thought it crass and cruel, a What Makes Sammy Run moment.

But I had no idea how far gone I was until the day my mother died, and Marty, while offering condolences and making preparations to come to the funeral, fell into the easy cadence of asking about his soon-to-be-expiring November call positions in Union Carbide and GAF, and whether we should roll them over to December. In front of my astonished father and sister I talked to him about it as if it were any other day. Could a trading obsession really be therapy, a tonic that made me sleep easier and diverted my mind from a world without my mother? I wrote in my journal that horrible night. Was it something I was doing for my own mental health? Or was I just kidding myself, and had my feeling of indebtedness to Marty for all his help just overwhelmed my better judgment? Was it Marty's financial health that had become paramount even when my mother's now empty bed was right in front of me? I knew this: taking a break from the trading seemed impossible to me. I knew I would be letting Marty down if I did, because you can't let quickly expiring calls and puts lie idle. To do so is irresponsible: they have to be traded to be effective.

That was the strange nature of the relationship I had with Marty; we talked about the market as others would talk about life and death. It was our language, our way of dealing with events, and it had become so natural to me that it became a comforting diversion from the reality of my loss. I wanted to do the right thing for my clients and do the right thing at home, so I tried to strike a balance between money and performance and everything else in life, but I really couldn't, even if I thought so then.

That would not be the first time my desire to please Marty and the desire to trade would get in the way of my real life. Far from it; it was just the first time someone I loved questioned it. I knew I answered unsatisfactorily. And I knew the issue would come up again if anyone else were ever to be close to me.

Of course, after sitting shiva for my mother, the Jewish tradition of mourning a soul with stories of love and laughter, it was back to work at Goldman, back to work with a vengeance. I made dozens of trades each morning, and dozens of cold calls each afternoon: the mind-numbing process of trying to set up an appointment, win over an account, and convert that person to be a customer of Goldman came easy to me after my mother's death. You could think of nothing else during the day, it was that all-consuming.

While I had seen the softer side of Goldman when my mom was ill, I was about to see the harder side. Soon after my mother passed away I got snookered by the *New York Times* to talk openly about how much I loved my job. Every once in a while, the press decides to have some fun with young brokers who are breaking into the business. The press knows that brokers make a lot of money. The press is eternally jealous because most of its members believe that brokers are a bunch of boastful ignoramuses.

One day a reporter called to set up an interview about how I had moved from law school to business without practicing law. The reporter, Sandra Salmons, said it might be an interesting trend worth writing about. Later, much later, I would find out that a *Times* reporter had been given my name by someone who knew that the article was meant to make young Wall Streeters look like heartless greedy folk, and that this person wanted to pay me back for a slight at *The Harvard Crimson* ten years before! Pretty typical of the hard feelings that the *Crimson* seemed to engender in people. Ah, I thought, naively, not knowing that a setup was at hand, this law school angle dovetails nicely with what I was trying to do at Goldman, recruit talented people from law schools all over the country who wanted to be in sales. I could not think of a better way to connect with so many students at one time as with an article about going from Harvard Law School to Goldman Sachs. And that's exactly what I told my bosses about the call. They agreed to let me sit for the interview.

Salmons seemed genuinely interested in why a law school graduate would end up peddling stocks. We spent several hours together and I enjoyed telling her about how I found and picked stocks and how much I loved the market just then. She asked me dozens of innocuous questions while a photographer snapped away. I answered them all and mentioned repeatedly that I wished others from law schools would seek to do the same as I had done. My antennae should have gone up when the photographer kept pushing for me to put my feet up on my desk. I am surprised he didn't whip out a stogie to seal the indictment.

At the end of the interview she said that her editors had told her she had to ask me how much money I made. I told her it was none of her business. She then asked me whether it was in the high or mid-six figures, and again, I told her it was none of her business. She asked again. I refused yet again and told her that it might be time to end the interview. I told her it was totally irrelevant to an article about why I loved the stock market more than the law. As I walked her out she badgered me again about how rich I was. I told her that I lived in a studio apartment, had a beat-up Ford Fairmont, the same one I lived in in L.A., no summer house, no art collection, no nothing, and that I saved everything I had and put it in the stock market. But, she insisted, didn't I make enough money to buy anything I wanted? I told her if I went to the supermarket, and I wanted to buy anything I saw, I could certainly, but that I had been and was a modest guy given to saving money, not to spending.

A week later I opened the *Times* to the business section on the way down to work in one of those cab shares at 72nd and York. There was a picture of me with a caption underneath that said, "James Cramer says he can buy anything he wants." All my life I have had a habit of getting flushed in the face, beet red, when I am embarrassed. I must have looked like a stopped traffic light to the three other guys in that cab. "My obituary is in the paper," I said to the other riders. Everyone laughed. I then showed them the picture and the caption. Each one mumbled that I truly was a dead man.

When I got to Goldman I went right to my boss and tried to explain what happened. He told me that if it were up to him, he would not have a problem, but that John Weinberg, the co-chairman of Goldman, wanted to see me immediately. I was a peon at Goldman. Peons didn't go to see John Weinberg. I flew downstairs to see him and after less than a minute of waiting he called me in. He told me that I had good numbers but that there really wasn't any way for me to work at the firm anymore. I told him that I loved the firm dearly but that I would, of course, resign if I caused the firm any disgrace. I did, however, want to tell him about how I had been fooled. He listened and called the *Times* immediately to find out what had happened. He then told me to go back to my office. He would tell me what I would have to do.

A few days later I found out through the grapevine that the *Times* had confirmed my story to the chairman. I had indeed been set up. They had no interest in doing the story I had requested approval for. So I was forgiven internally by my betters, but this incidence radically changed the perception of me in the firm.

In an article that appeared the following Sunday about Goldman, Weinberg acknowledged that his firm discouraged a star system and didn't like anyone mouthing off to the press. It was a direct shot at me. Life was never the same after that article. While I still had excellent numbers and continued to be among the highest commission generators in the firm, I always felt that my days at the firm were numbered. I had popped off. I had broken the code. There were no stars at Goldman, no showboats either, and my flamboyant personality marked me as someone who would never be able to stay within the organization and advance even though I had led my class in commission generation for every year running.

Toward the end of 1986, a few months after the *Times* incident, I made up my mind that I was going to leave the firm to start my own hedge fund with Larry Levy, another fellow from the company. As much as I thought that Goldman Sachs was the best company in the United States to work for, a firm that allowed me to make millions of dollars personally in a very short period of time, I wanted to be free to pick stocks for a living, and not spend the rest of my days prospecting for business. Perhaps one day the brokerage business will be based more on performance than on attracting new clients, but until then I knew I could make more money taking a percentage of what I made for people than I could in commissions from trading. Marty thought the move out of Goldman a wise one. He vowed to help me raise as much money as possible, and made good on that promise. I went to everyone I had made a lot of money for in the last few years and asked them to give me some of the profits that I had made so I could run that money for them. I promised my bosses at Goldman that I would be a great client of the firm—since I needed someone to execute my trades— and exited with much more goodwill than I had expected. (I did start the fund with Levy, but he would return to brokerage after a few months, as the money management job didn't suit him.)

After a couple of months of setting up and looking for office space, I went to see Marty's good friend Michael Steinhardt, the same man whom I had told that Reebok was a great long and not a short. Steinhardt had not covered the Reebok. He had let it run, against my advice. He told me, however, that he would have saved millions of dollars had he listened to me and that he wanted to put money with me and give me office space so I could learn how to trade. I told him I knew how to trade. He told me no, I knew how to spot good ideas, but I would have to learn how to trade from his traders. He was dead right; I had no idea really how to run money, even though I had been trading for almost a decade.

As alien as the brokerage world is to those who have never sold stocks, the world of hedge funds is more mysterious, even to those who have toiled for years in what everyone refers to as "the business." When I went out on my own from Goldman Sachs there were probably only about 600 or 700 hedge funds. There are now more than 10,000.

These days, after a rip-roaring bull market defined the 1990s, it is hard to imagine anyone having trepidation about going out on his own and making money in the market. In the last five years people quit their jobs with regularity to plug into the Web and start trading, with little or no capital. But in 1987 it was considered almost suicidal to give up a high-paying Goldman job—I was making $1 million a year in my fourth year—for a job in which you would have to match wits with the market and take a percentage of what you made. Only a handful of people believed they could make enough money in the market that they would do better than by taking commissions for buying and selling stocks. I was one of them.

I sure wish we could come up with another name for the kind of company I established, because "hedge fund" doesn't really explain much. The nomenclature comes from a fund that can hedge its bets. That's somewhat self-explanatory. Actually a hedge fund is simply the only legal method allowed by the U.S. government to pool people's money and take a percentage of the winnings. After the Depression, the federal government decided that it wanted to regulate money managers, allowing them to take a percentage of the money they managed as a fee, not a percentage of the gains. That's the mutual fund model. The government also created an exception that allowed managers to run money unregulated by the government, provided that all of the clients of that manager were wealthy. Rich people didn't need the protection of regulation, according to the intent of the legislation. They could fend for themselves. That's a hedge fund. I went with the hedge fund model because I believed that it allowed you to do the best both for the client and for yourself.

Ironically, the hedge fund model would do much better for those who are not wealthy. Right now they are at the mercy of the market and mutual fund managers who don't give a hoot if they lose their clients' money; they get paid anyway. That's not how it works in the hedge fund world. You get paid only if you make people money. Here's why: hedge funds typically take 1 percent of the assets as a management fee and 20 percent of the gains—both realized and unrealized (that is, whether you sell your holdings or not)—as payment for the fund. If you make money you do extremely well. But if you lose money, you have to get back to even before you can take a fee again. That's known as the "high-water mark" provision and almost all hedge funds, including mine, had it. It means that if you lose money in year one, you don't get paid until you get your people back to even. If you fail to make it back in year two, you still don't get paid. That's a model that really forces you to be creative and cautious about stock selection. It means that you can't just blame the market and take your fee, as mutual funds do. You have to bet against the market if you think it is going down, so you can still make money. You have to short stocks and short the market as a whole at times, to be sure you don't lose money when the market comes down. You can't just be fully invested in stocks all the time, a position I regard as extremely reck-less, yet one that is embraced by virtually every mutual fund family in the country.

Why the government continues to allow only the rich to benefit from this setup, which is so naturally more conducive to better performance than the mutual fund model, is beyond me. The hedge fund model puts you on the same page as the investors. The mutual fund model makes you a slave to gathering assets and marketing. You can underperform for years and still take in plenty of money, as we are discovering now after the awful performances of so many mutual funds. That's not how the game should be played.

As a brand-new hedge fund manager I put in another provision to safe-guard the funds of my partners (as investors in a hedge fund are called): a provision that would make my partnership open up and disband if our per-formance were to dip below minus 10 percent. I put it in because some of my partners didn't like the fact that they could not get at their money if I started off badly.

Wouldn't you know it, when I started, in the first week of April, the market got hammered and I was caught, just like when I started with Marty Peretz. Frankly, I got hammered because I didn't know how running real money worked. Until I set up the hedge fund, I simply used to talk with analysts at Goldman, look for one good idea at a time, and then sell that idea to my account base. When I started in the hedge fund business, I still totally relied upon Goldman Sachs. I had my account there and I pretty much listened to what the salespeople from Goldman told me that Goldman was doing. I felt horribly alone at Steinhardt's office, with no Goldman contacts. I didn't know that the key to hedge fund management is to *bet against* Wall Street. To do that you have to know what Wall Street is saying.

I learned this the hard way. One night in my third week on my own, after a particularly brutal beating at the hands of the market, I calculated where we were and realized that we were down almost 9 percent—a little more than 1 percent away from having to open the fund and disband it. I had been in business only a short time and I was getting crushed. As I worked at trying to figure out what I was doing wrong, John Lattanzio, a legendary trader who ran Steinhardt's trading desk, dropped by to see how things were going. He had been ribbing me as the Harvard kid who knew nothing, regularly making fun of me as being too smart to be a hedge fund manager. The last guy I wanted to talk to was Lattanzio, a scrappy but impeccably dressed silver-haired tough guy, who I knew would ride me mercilessly when he heard how I had lost so much money so fast. When he asked me how I was doing, I told him that I was doing fine. He said he had been betting with people that I would be down big by now and he was glad to hear it.

I couldn't hold back then, thinking that it would just complicate things more if I had to disband the next day after telling Lattanzio I was doing fine. Performance is something that is never cuffed in my business; you can't fool people if you are doing poorly. So I told him the truth.

He smacked me on the side of the head when he heard it. That's his style. "Listen, you piece of shit, and listen good, 'cause I'm going to save your sorry little dick," Lattanzio said, in a notation that I jotted down that night in my journal, because it was just too outrageous to forget. "Clear your head," he said. "Sell everything. Start over." Lattanzio said he would then teach me, as he had taught his traders, how to make trades, generate commission, and put the industry to work for me. He said I could lean on him, lean on his trading desk, and trade myself back to even.

He was good to his word. We cleared the sheets the next day, staunched the bleeding at 9.9 percent, and changed the business model to the one that Lattanzio used on his trading desk. Lattanzio demanded I learn from the people on the desk because they could teach me everything I needed to know.

I wanted to meet those women on the desk too, mostly because there were four of them, every one great-looking and apparently single. I told my assistant, Marilyn, that I would do anything I could to meet the one on the far left side of the horseshoe desk. Marilyn solved the problem; she asked me to get her a Diet Coke at the same time she had told Karen Back-fisch that there was someone who wanted to see her in the kitchen, a shrewd bit of match-making that seemed, at first, to backfire. We couldn't have been more different. I knew I was a huge turnoff to Karen, with my $2,000 monotonously blue Sills suits, white shirts, and red ties, just like I wore every day at Goldman. Her first question when she realized that she had been set up to meet me was, "What's with the suits? Nobody cares what you look like. People just care about your performance now. You're not a broker." It was clear that Lattanzio had shared with her my miserable performance. I told her that Lattanzio said that I needed to learn and that he said I could learn from her.

My first meeting with the woman whom the Street would come to know as the Trading Goddess was in my little office down the hall from the trading desk, and it was all business. First she asked me what I was doing. I showed her my positions, how we owned some Heinz and some Alcoa and some General Mills and American Stores and a dozen other positions. She asked me what I knew about each one. I told her that I thought it was important to have some stocks from the food sector and some from the cyclicals and some drugs. "That's just portfolio manager talk," she said. "In the hedge fund world it doesn't matter what you are overweighted in or underweighted in."

Then she asked again what I knew about the stocks. I started by saying that the Goldman metals analyst liked Alcoa and the Goldman food analyst thought Heinz was good. "Those people are idiots," she said. "They can't make you money, and they know nothing." I told her how mistaken she was, that Goldman had the top analysts and that they were money-makers.

But she knew everything about them, much more than I did, and she demonstrated that by reeling off how much those analysts had cost Stein-hardt.

She explained to me that I should never take a position unless I knew something that no one else knew. I told her that was inside information. Not at all, she said, you need a legal edge. I said I had no idea how to get that edge. No worry, she said; she would teach me.

She then told me her story. After working as an assistant vice president at Lehman Brothers, helping out portfolio managers, her boss had been hired away by Steinhardt four years before and he offered to take her with him. Within one month he left the firm. Karen, who had graduated from the State University of New York at Stony Brook, out on Long Island, and had no graduate school experience in business, didn't know what to do. She had just taken an apartment in Brooklyn Heights and now would have to move back in with her folks in their house in Elmont near the Belmont Raceway on the Nassau-Queens border if she couldn't make the Steinhardt job work. Steinhardt said she would have to leave unless she wanted to fill a slot as an assistant trader on the trading desk. Like me, Karen knew nothing about trading, but she was hungry and wanted to hang on at Steinhardt, where the pay could be huge if you could deliver. Within a few months she was making $20,000 a day, day in and day out, becoming one of the original day traders, who could make money by simply watching and responding to the movement in stocks.

How she did it was by gaming Wall Street, trying to anticipate moves of analysts before they were made, and placing big bets on the direction that analysts were going to go. That way, she said, you always had an edge, you never owned anything idly, and you always had an exit strategy.

I said that's all well and good but no analyst is going to give you a call before announcing his position. You can't get analysts to tell you what they are going to do beforehand.

Of course, she said. So what you had to do was make dozens of calls to brokers and analysts every day to ask them what they thought of stocks. She said you looked for situations where the analysts were growing more positive and you then fed them positive information that you got from others. You pitted them against one another. You told them that someone else was going to upgrade. If you could be sure they were warming up to a story, or if you caught them on the phone before they had told their sales forces that their earnings estimates were too high or too low, you might have something. You didn't move, though, until you were fairly sure that you were about to catch the upgrade or downgrade.

Karen explained to me that the analyst game was a game of sponsorship. Analysts like to get behind stocks and bull them. You have to get in on the ground floor when they start their sponsorship campaign. Sponsorship, she said, means levitation. If you can get in early on a sponsorship campaign for a stock, it is like buying a P&G product that is going to get pushed by Madison Avenue. You know it is going to fly out the door. If Merrill is the sponsor of a stock, it could be good for 5 points. If Goldman sponsored something it could be good for 10. You want to buy something and flip it—sell it immediately—into the sponsorship. That's the only sure thing on Wall Street.

When I asked her how we could find out about all of these wonderful things when I was just a little hedge fund manager, she said one word: "commish." I told her that I did all my commission business, or as much as I could, with Goldman Sachs and that I promised that I would keep doing that. She said if that was the case I might as well go back to Goldman Sachs because I would never make a dime in this business. Commissions, she explained, determine what you are told, what you will know, and how much you can find out. If you do a massive amount of commission business, analysts will return your calls, brokers will work for you, and you will get plenty of ideas to make money, on both a short- and long-term basis. She said it would be enough for Goldman that I kept my account there—they would be happy if I borrowed money from them to buy stocks, a regular practice for hedge fund managers—but that I had to do business with everyone and just forward the reports to Goldman. Commissions greased everything, and until I learned how to trade, and trade constantly, I would never be taken seriously by any salesman or analyst.

She had built up a Rolodex of good brokers who would make calls and generate ideas for her. She also explained to me how she traded "flow." When big accounts come in and buy or sell stocks, invariably they move the stocks in the direction of their trading. For example, if you sold two million shares of a stock such as Georgia Pacific, as Karen had recently, you would knock it down in the process, in this case, from $26 to $24. Once your selling is finished, the stock would lift as the supply dries up. "Your goal," she explained to me, "is to buy the last 200,000 shares and trade out of it into other buyers who want to take advantage of the decline." She said that the real way to make money in this business was to combine all three: trading, sales, and research, which is what she did every day. She would do enough commission business that she would know who was down to "tag ends" on a big sell order, and she would also know whether any analyst might be on the verge of recommending Georgia Pacific, to continue the example, by keeping track of all of the analysts' buy suggestions at every firm. Like a good card player who knows when to bet the most amount of money on a good hand, she might be tempted to buy the last 500,000 shares of a Georgia Pacific seller if she found an analyst who was excited to know that the stock had been knocked down by a big seller and who also thought the stock was cheap.

I told her that it seemed a labor-intensive way to make money, to keep track of so many stocks, to keep track of the supply, and the demand, and the analysts. "Do you have a better way?" she asked. "You just want to buy stocks because you think they are cheap or something? You want to be at the mercy of the market? Be my guest. But you will never make it as a hedge fund manager." You need to do a couple of million dollars a year with *each* broker to be able to get in touch with the analysts and have the dialogue you need to learn of potential sponsorship campaigns. And you need to do $3 to $4 million with your best brokers so you can get their most important calls. She didn't seem to care that I was only running $6 million. "If you know how to trade, you can generate $6 million with $6 million." And you will get every tag end call you need to make money. It seemed hard to believe. Little did I know that a year from then I would be doing just that, and getting the calls that I needed to do as well as Karen said I could.

The genius of Karen was that she didn't care what the market did, she played individual stocks. And she didn't care about the stocks beyond what would happen to them in the near term because that could be gamed. She was from the church of what is happening that morning. She could like them or hate them on a dime. She could fall in love with a semiconductor stock in the morning and then hate it in the afternoon, going long, selling, and then selling short and covering on the way home if she learned that a firm might change its view on the group.

She even had a game plan for me. She said the missing piece of the puzzle was what the companies were saying themselves. She said if she could combine her trading and brokerage research intelligence with what the companies were saying at meetings and in one-on-ones—private meetings with individual investors—we could make a couple of points a day, day in and day out. And if I could find a company that was more positive on its outlook than her analyst network was, then we could make a fortune anticipating upgrades and downgrades.

Both of us were, initially, reluctant to let anyone know that we had mutual interests. We would pass notes within pieces of Wall Street research to each other in the halls. But we kept it a secret; Lattanzio hated any of his women on the desk getting close to any of his male traders. The women were part of a club, *his* club, and he didn't want any stray cats joining.

It was a profitable relationship from the beginning. I could now see companies better, get the measure of what they were saying, and then bounce my thoughts off Karen's network. And it wasn't long before I suggested in one of my notes that we meet out of the office to discuss our work together. As the relationship started with business it wasn't as easy as I thought for either of us to switch out of a business mode. On our first date, as we walked across Third Avenue at 36th Street to Rio Grande for some Tex-Mex, I said there was something I had been meaning to ask her. "What?" she said. "What do you think of Compaq here?" I asked. Amazingly, she didn't skip a beat. "Trades to $30." That would be a good move; the stock was only at $26. And, I said, how about Tandem Computer at

$18? "I would short it to $15." By the time we got to our table, I think I knew who I was going to marry. I was so confident that I told her. She didn't even flinch. I had met my match. We would be engaged within the year.

From then on we worked as a team, calling each other all day from our two different funds, helping each other out as I battled the market alone once my founding partner got fed up with the volatility—and no doubt my reliance on Karen—and went back to Goldman. (Cramer Levy Partners quickly became Cramer Partners.) During that long summer, Karen decided to leave Steinhardt to spend time at another fund, but we had pretty much decided, even while we were dating, that we had a chance to work together to make real money, using exactly the method Karen outlined. In September I had brought the fund back to slightly above even from those depths in April, which was not bad. The market was up 18 percent for the year, but much of that gain, though, happening before I had even started my trading in April.

In October of 1987, though, I could tell that things just weren't right. Many stocks were beginning to give up gains that they had put on for the last two or three years. Analyst recommendations weren't working. Sellers frequently overwhelmed buyers by the end of the day, with the market ending considerably lower than it began. The market had become too crazy, too weird, too out of control for me to make any money, the first time since I had started picking stocks eight years before. Karen noticed it too at the firm she had moved to, which was beginning to lose millions every day just by owning big capitalization growth stocks, the exact area that was starting to get hammered. But her fund wouldn't listen to her calls that the market was going to crash. She insisted that I move out of everything, that I take aggressive action. On October 10 of that year Karen set up a meeting with Michael Steinhardt—she'd left him only in August and still spoke with him frequently—to tell him about her reservations about the market. She urged me to come along. "I think we are going to crash," she told Michael. He was, however, extremely bullish, which was quite a change from his normally ursine manner. But he trusted her judgment as a trader and said that if she felt like this and I felt like it, that we should completely cash out, go 100 percent into cash. That was an almost unheard of strategy at the time, selling everything because you didn't like the market.

As the market went from 2,800 to 2,400, Karen grew increasingly adamant that we were going to crash harder than anything either of us had ever seen. I went into 100 percent cash shortly thereafter, with Karen on the phone insisting every afternoon that I make more sales even though I was selling into a really crummy market. She insisted I liquidate every position, she was that certain it was going lower. And she insisted I make some bets against the market, even though I pointed out that going into cash already was a big bet. So we shorted some of the drug and waste management stocks, making sizable bets against them. In the week before the crash, the worst week ever in the stock market, I covered those shorts for a huge profit. At the time most analysts were still extremely bullish, telling clients that this was simply a huge buyable dip, that we should put some of that cash to work to catch the big bounce that would be expected next week. I called Karen. Not on your life, she said that Friday when the market had shed 100 more points to take the Dow down to 2,200. "We crash Monday. We crash huge." She repeated that prediction to everyone that weekend at the wedding of my friend and former Harvard Law classmate and now New York Attorney General, Eliot Spitzer, to Silda Wahl, just in case you think that this was one of those private epiphanies like so many of the other alleged great calls of the last twenty years that gurus were supposed to have made.

On Monday the market dropped 508 points, the worst drubbing in history. And my fund was 100 percent in cash. It remains the best call I have ever seen. And while my partners never knew where it came from, I can say it unhesitatingly, if it weren't for my fiancée, my firm would never have survived the crash. Instead, we became known as the hedge fund that was positioned perfectly for the Crash of 1987, and we never had to do another thing to raise money again. In fact, we had to be tough on people to make sure we weren't overrun with money. From that moment on, if you wanted to come into my fund, like some sort of elite country club, you had to be nominated by an existing partner. Only that way could we control the money flow into the fund. It was an important reason why we compounded at 24 percent after all fees for the next fourteen years.

Four weeks after the crash I asked Karen to marry me. What started as an office romance had blossomed into something that this thirty-two-year old bachelor couldn't imagine: an engagement. We were to be married one year later, with Marty Peretz, the man who helped me the most in my business life, and my closest friend, serving as my best man.

And in February, 1988, Karen joined Cramer Partners.

CHAPTER 4

Building a Hedge Fund

Cramer & Co. had a terrific 1988 and 1989. Then in 1990 Iraq invaded Kuwait and the market trembled. From the moment that the market collapsed following Iraq's invasion, Karen had been extremely negative on stocks. She had been shorting, betting against every stock, especially financials and retail stocks. Although she called herself a technician, meaning that she looked at charts and divined from previous patterns how the market would behave, she was actually driven more by obvious fundamental events than most technicians were. For example, she was so negative about banks because she witnessed the closing and boarding up of all the S&Ls in our neighborhood in Brooklyn. Her negative view of the Dayton Hudsons and Mays and Best Buys came from her trips to empty malls.

Now that we were working side by side, each a 50 percent owner of Cramer & Co., her negative outlook suited me fine. I hated the stocks she hated. As the index dropped from 3,100 to 2,300, I grew even more negative, worried that the country wouldn't pull out of its tailspin. I thought we had a recession and an inflation problem; a banking system that was teetering; and a budget deficit that was mushrooming out of control. When you overlay Iraq's destabilization of the world economy on top of that, you had a market that, I thought, could take out the lows of the 1987 crash.

Karen didn't care about theoretical underpinnings of what drove the market to various levels. She cared about what made people buy and sell stocks. She understood the market viscerally. If you could tell her what made people feel better, what put them in a better mood, she would tell you where the market was headed. She would anticipate higher prices. Because she had worked at the big-money firms, Karen knew that big money was human. It was a beast that if let loose by events would buy everything in sight. The beast didn't care where stocks had been or how high they moved; it just wanted to buy.

We kept our bearish bet right into the end of 1990, finishing well in the black because of our pessimism. I kept insisting that the fundamentals were still deteriorating, and we should stay short, stay negative, particularly on the retailers. Karen, however, would hear none of it. She made us cover our shorts in the last weeks of December. Then when I wanted to put them back because of negative data, she insisted on playing endless rounds of blackjack and gin in the office. When I urged her to buy puts, or bet negatively, on the market, she picked up the phone and started ordering from holiday catalogues.

Finally, when she could take my badgering no more, she booked us into the Hyatt on St. John in the U.S. Virgin Islands, pausing as she made the reservations to ask me when I thought the United States would attack Iraq, an attack the president had made clear was in preparation. I told her that January 15 seemed likely, so she put us on a return flight to New York on the 14th. That would leave plenty of time for buying, she said. Why would we buy, I asked, exasperated with her cavalier dismissal of the gloom surrounding all the markets in the world.

Because, she said, we would win the war and win it with a minimum of casualties. That would change everything, she said. I reminded her about the recession, unemployment, and the teetering banking system.

She didn't even bother to respond. She also ignored all her technical charts, which were screaming downturn. That too would change with the war, she said.

When we returned from St. John, the bombing began. Karen had levered us up huge, borrowing a giant amount of money to buy everything in sight. I sat dumbfounded. Sure enough, within a few weeks consumers came back with a vengeance, feeling better about themselves than they had in years. It didn't hurt that oil prices plummeted and stayed low, or that banks were able to use the Fed's lower interest rates to rebuild their balance sheets. The market started its historic rally that coincided with the longest peacetime expansion. We made tens of millions of dollars during this rally for our partners at Cramer L.P.

At the end of 1990 we learned we were going to have a child. We were going to be a family, taking up all the available room in our one-and-a-half-bedroom at the corner of State and Hicks in Brooklyn Heights. For Karen, that meant retirement, as she began immediately to groom a new successor for her trading job. Against her recommendation I had chosen a homeboy, Seth Tobias, from Philadelphia, the broker who had been most dogged in pursuing business with us. Karen didn't trust Seth, but I knew I had to have someone who hustled working with me to continue the commission generation we needed to get the calls coming. For the next seven months she trained Seth in the finer ways of how the job worked. She was getting ready to have the baby in July, and she felt certain that by June Seth would be ready to take over. He sure was; in fact, he was so ready that one day he came in and said he had taken a new job. "Huh," my wife asked. "With who?" When Seth answered that he was going to work for Mark Howard, Karen's old boss who had left Steinhardt seven years before, she hit the ceiling. She told him to get out right now. "We'll box your things, and then we will throw them out," she said, escorting him to the door.

I was sheepish about it; he had been my guy and my wife had been right. She turned to me and said that retirement was now out of the question. She stayed working and worked until July 12, 1991, when her water broke in the midst of a big over-the-counter trade she was working with Merrill Lynch. Trading Goddesses don't go easily. After Cece was born, Karen stayed home for four months, and then reluctantly came back to work, but began the more formal task of building a staff so that when we had our second child she would no longer have to go to Cramer & Co. anymore.

For a couple of years there, things were actually normal. I would spend all day researching companies, and my wife would trade. My firm grew in size. Karen hired other traders and a research director, a senior guy she had known for many years in the business. In 1992, I hired a summer associate from Columbia Business School who had gone to Wharton undergrad, Jeff Berkowitz. He was so brilliant right out of the box that at the end of the summer I fired my research director, named Jeff the director, and got Columbia Business School to let him finish his degree at night and on Fridays.

That's when we pioneered our formula for making money every single day, day in and day out, while we also worked to have long-term capital gains. We developed a style that consisted of figuring out what would be hot, what would be the next big buzz. We became merchants of the buzz, getting long stocks and then schmoozing with analysts about what we saw and heard that was positive. Or we would get short stocks and talk to the analysts about the negatives. We would work to get upgrades or downgrades because we knew, cynically, that Wall Street was simply a promotion machine. We recognized that analysts existed to promote stocks, typically the stocks their companies brought public, in order to get those stocks higher. Sometimes they worked to get them higher so they could do a secondary underwriting. Sometimes they worked to get them higher so they could get some sort of financing, a debt deal, a convertible bond. And sometimes they pushed them because, heck, their job was to push stocks. That's what they did.

We had it down to a science by 1992: my wife would pick stocks that technically looked ready to go up, or she would keep track of merchandise to see what was down to tag ends. She would then generate a list of stocks that could move quickly on good news. Jeff would then go to work calling the companies trying to find anything good we could say about them. I would call the analysts to see if they were hearing anything. When we found a stock that looked ready technically to break out, or where the supply had been mopped up, and Jeff found out something positive at the company, and I knew the analyst community didn't know anything positive, we would load up with call options and common stock and then give the good news to our favorite analysts who liked the stock so they could go do their promotion. That would get the buzz going and we would then be able to liquidate the position into the buzz for a handsome profit.

To get this right we had to make hundreds of calls to every conceivable company and analyst in dozens of industries. We would sit there, dialing for dollars until we had our sure thing, meanwhile with my wife trading every day to generate the nut, the daily overhead. I can't tell you how exhilarating those days were. That was when I began to make hundreds of trades a day to generate enough commission to continue to be able to get the callback from the analyst promoters. It was also when I started going to work at 5:00 A.M., because in order to do the homework, to stay up on all the industries, I had to read a stack of annuals and research two feet high virtually every day.

Every night we would go out with Wall Streeters and talk the market. It was nothing but stocks, stocks, and more stocks. My goal was to know *every* stock so that if my wife said, "Phelps Dodge looks right here," I knew who the four key copper analysts were and could get them on the phone immediately because of all of the trading my wife had done with their firms. Jeff developed a Rolodex at the companies within a year that I couldn't believe. Given our knowledge base and his hustle, there wasn't a chief executive officer or chief financial officer he couldn't get on the phone in minutes. By his second year, when the stocks of virtually any industrial or technological company dropped by more than a point or two, these chieftains would call Jeff and ask *him* what was going on. Karen would then check with ten trading desks to see if there was a large seller. I would check with the analysts to see if anyone was saying anything competitively and we would get back to management immediately with an answer. It was all part of the homework, the everyday checks we did to see how companies were doing. We wanted no guesswork.

As long as we didn't call during what is known as "quiet period," the last four weeks of a quarter, when companies couldn't reveal anything lest they give away the quarter and under SEC regulations make us "insiders," who then couldn't trade on it, we were coining money. Over time we developed a list of chief executive officers we believed in, who we felt confident would deliver, whom we were enamored of, regardless of the industry. We discovered time and again that the right chief executive officers would pull their stocks out of tailspins promptly. The wrong chief executive officers regarded themselves as helpless victims of the stock market. The right chief executives would zero in on the problems that we identified. The wrong ones would act as if nothing could be changed or the problems were a fact of life. We also discovered that the chief executives who followed their stocks as a matter of course and cared about shareholders and shareholder value were a breed apart. They were competitive to a fault, disliked anyone who knocked their companies, and took everything said about their stocks personally. The ones who could distance themselves or not take it as a life-or-death experience, who didn't care about a decline of a couple points, those we culled or marked as shortable, meaning that if we had negative news we were confident we could "put the stock out" and not worry that we would be hurt by an upgrade or a rising stock.

It was the perfect indicator and one that still works well to this day. It is the biggest determinant of stock price gains over time, yet it is something that almost all of the Wall Street promoters and analysts are blind to because their "rigorous" methodology handcuffs them into worrying about a stock that was "cheap" statistically, something we could have cared less about. We wanted stocks with buzz, with chief executives who were managers of both their businesses and their stocks. Those combinations began to produce fabulous returns for my fund and we quietly grew over time. We worked relentlessly, but I wanted to keep the thing mom-and-pop, to make the most money with the fewest people. And I wanted to have a good time working with my wife and Jeff.

The rigor with which we approached the business still defies what most people are willing to subject themselves to. I never found another firm that played the game like we did, with hundreds of calls to firms, analysts, brokers, all backed up by trips to the companies and massive commission dollars to get the trading edge we needed. We were the only firm I knew that actually attempted to make money every single hour we were at the office. We hated to lose money so badly that we used to get off the desk and literally go over every position every hour. My wife would rip down the position sheets, in a dour cadence that drove us crazy. "Alcoa, why are we long it?" "Bethlehem Steel, what's the deal?" "Chrysler, what's the story there?" "Dean Foods, why do we own it?" And we would have to answer each time why we liked the stock. My wife called this the "Discipline over Conviction" style, and it forced us to focus *every hour* on what was going on with the stocks. If a stock was down a half dollar she would grill us. Or she would say that if we didn't get more information about why the stock was down a half point she would sell the position out from underneath us unless we knew more. We used to call people over and over again to find out why a stock moved up or down a half just to please Karen and keep the position on our sheets. Jeff and I would dread these meetings but they kept us from ever having big losses and gave us the conviction we needed to stay long regardless of what the overall stock market was doing. It also kept us from having too many positions on the sheets because no one could take Karen's scrutiny for too long unless he really loved the stock. We would be drenched in sweat every time we got off the desk. Sometimes Karen would threaten to sell something simply because we hadn't checked in with someone. Sometimes she would sell a stock because she didn't like how it "acted," and we would have to argue vociferously to put it back on.

The terror of Karen's tongue and the embarrassment of her selling out our positions kept us humming and profitable beyond what I ever thought could happen. There was no room for mistakes. You lost money and Karen would break out cards and play solitaire while she went over the portfolio. If she thought you were doing a poor job, and weren't trying hard enough, she would pore through her Lands' End and Kinsman catalogues, placing orders to them, instead of placing orders we wanted. And if she really thought we didn't know what we were doing, she would sell out our positions when we went to the men's room. We wouldn't notice until she updated the position sheets at the end of the day. It was a humbling experience, one that made you dread going to the gent's. Our model, our method of operation was so rigorous and severe that it kept driving us back to stocks where we trusted the chief executive officer not to screw it up; the penalties for his screwup would be too harsh to tolerate. We didn't want to look bad, if only just to please my wife at those root canal review sessions. The heat was just too great otherwise. It was brutal. It was vicious. It was rigorous. It was intense. It was heaven.

How intense was it? How about the pressure I felt the day Emma, our second child, was born, May 17, 1994. The Federal Reserve had been on a tightening rampage that year. We felt the only way to make money was to short stocks, because they eventually had to go down, to react to those waves of Fed tightenings. We were beside ourselves when, each time the Fed tightened, it hinted that it might be done tightening and the market would go up.

I had wanted to square off all our positions when my wife went into labor, but we couldn't. I had this premonition weeks earlier that the market was going to rally big just when my wife was about to deliver, but it seemed too ridiculous to come true for this tradeaholic. Karen was supposed to have the baby the week before the Fed meeting. But as day after day went by and nothing happened, the premonition was looking more and more like reality.

Finally, on May 17, the doctor induced Karen. At 2:11 on May 17, the baby's head appeared. At 2:12, a frantic Jeff called me on my cell phone while I was trying to help the doctor coax the baby out, and said he didn't know what to do, the Fed had raised rates and the market was ripping and our shorts were killing us. I said it was an inopportune time. He said, of course it was, but we had to do something. The doctor looked at me and asked me what was wrong. Then Karen looked at me and asked what was wrong. The only person who didn't ask me what was wrong was Emma, who popped out while I fielded Jeff's questions about our Alcoa and Dow Chemical shorts. I told Karen that Jeff was on the line talking about how the Fed hiked rates and we were being squeezed. The delivering doctor then turned to me and said, "Hey, where are rates going?" As I was about to answer him, Karen blurted out, "I can't believe this. We just had a baby and you clowns are standing around talking about the market? Tell Jeff to go figure it out himself." Jeff overheard and rang off. The damage had been done. I apologized profusely, but Karen was furious. "You better get your act together," she said. "There are some moments when you just don't talk about the stock market and this is one of them."

I could only shake my head. My mom's death, Emma's birth, no getting away from it. I still hadn't found that moment when it wasn't right to talk about the stock market.

CHAPTER 5

SmartMoney

We finished 1994 in the black, despite some nasty reversals that decked a lot of other hedge funds, including the collapse of Mexico's finances and the destruction of Orange County's municipal treasury through the poor use of derivatives. We never made use of these derivatives, which are simply fancy bets on the direction of interest rates that involve huge leverage, or borrowings from brokers. We always just bought stocks, options, or bonds, and kept the business simple, which kept us from overextending ourselves and blowing up, like so many of the other hedge funds that had since started running money.

Despite the okay performance, the hedge fund wasn't the same for me; it wasn't fun, because Karen didn't come back to work after Emma was born. Karen had done so many things at the firm—all of the office management, the hiring, the firing, the managing of the complex web of sales and trading relationships, known as our "coverage," the maintaining of the firm's finances, and, of course, the spontaneous, daily moneymaking that came from her ability to "read the tape." Put simply, no one could meld the research calls brokers made every day about individual stocks with the flow of stock available through big institutional supply and demand, and come up with good trading ideas every single day. When she retired we had to replace her with five people: an office manager, two traders, a trading assistant, and a research assistant. We went from being this terrific, profitable mom-and-pop shop to being a company with a payroll, personnel problems, and a nut we would have to make each year because we were responsible for the welfare of other employees. Gone was our ability to take the firm wherever we were. We could no longer trade out of our Bucks County farm on Thursdays and Fridays, as there were too many people left out of the loop in the New York office. To me, without Karen, we simply seemed like every other hedge fund and I felt the loss of something special acutely. It became a job.

Karen had handpicked a worthy successor, a former sales trader from Lehman Brothers and Goldman Sachs, to run the trading desk. He could execute the trades I asked him to, but he just didn't have Karen's creativity when it came to making money on a daily basis. Also, with Karen running the desk, I didn't have to say or do much about the actual trading of stocks. We would agree, off the desk, what we would have to do, and then I didn't have to tell her anything else, which broker to use, what price parameters we would accept, or when we had to finish selling. She had a better sense than I did on all of the trading mechanics. With our new trader, I had to be much more involved with every trade. I had to negotiate more, and, in many cases, I had to pick up the phone myself and do the actual trading rather than give the orders to my desk, because I was not happy with the way the trading was going.

I didn't think we were making enough of the incremental money on the going in and out of stock that Karen always made. Under Karen, I always thought we did better, got a little better price, saved a little extra money, and I was determined not to lose that edge, even if it meant taking huge amounts of time away from idea generation to focus on the execution of trades. Trading generated massive stress, because you don't just place orders when you are buying and selling hundreds of thousands of shares at a clip. There is give and take. There is negotiation over price. There are events that can occur, news that breaks either about the stocks (upgrades, downgrades, earnings) or about macro events, like Federal Reserve or Treasury actions, or just straight-out world news that can instantaneously derail whatever trade you are working on at the moment. Karen had made it look so easy. I had no idea what a tense and weary game it was every time you wanted to move a sizable piece of merchandise. You needed vigilance—an ability to spot when you are being ripped off or abused by a trading desk trying to get its way with you.

Nobody screwed with Karen. I always thought we got the identical treatment that brokers gave even the biggest, most powerful firms, like Fidelity or Janus or Invesco. She knew how to reward good investment calls by pouring on commissions. She knew how to "pull the wire," meaning terminate a trading relationship with a firm that she felt had betrayed us or not done a creditable job. Now, I often felt we weren't getting the best for all of those millions of commission dollars we spent routinely. Most important, trading had always been a profit center for the firm. Karen had her own profit-and-loss statement; we always kept track of who was making the money and who was responsible for positions because there can be no discipline if everything is owned by the group, instead of by individuals.

That was all changed now. The trading desk under the previous head trader left me doing too much work. Karen dropped in occasionally to be sure the operation was running smoothly, but her heart was no longer in it. She said she couldn't imagine, now that we had so many good years under our belt, why both of us had to work, and she enjoyed the luxury of taking some time off. She threw herself into finding a town for us to live in now that our eldest was ready for school. We were both public school enthusiasts, and we ended up choosing Summit, New Jersey, for its great elementary schools and its proximity to our office.

The whole time I was building the hedge fund I couldn't kick the writing habit. I yearned to have my own newsletter, to tell people what I was thinking, because, beginning with the 1991 turn in the market, I wanted to be invested in American manufacturing, a sector I had studiously avoided for most of the last decade. For much of the 1980s, I was convinced that the only place to be was in safe stuff: the drugs, the foods, the movie stocks. I loved Philip Morris and Heinz and Kimberly-Clark. Most of that was out of fear of the Japanese. I know it is hard to recall how dominant the Japanese were then. Now they seem like such a hapless bunch of old cronies and bankrupt artists, early state capitalists at best. But, at the turn of the decade, I began to get rumblings from the companies that I dealt with, whether in technology or aerospace or finance or plain old industrial hardware companies. For a decade Japanese companies had been taking it to us, taking share, buying companies, dominating markets, and running us out of profitable businesses.

It got to the point where I would feel safer owning a Heinz than an Intel because while it was possible that Intel would not be an important semi-conductor company at that moment it was inconceivable that we would be pouring Mitsubishi Ketchup on our burgers. It was during this period, before our children were born, when I was free to visit companies in all sorts of businesses, that I could see America was having a resurgence in manu-facturing. At first it was just anecdotal. Caterpillar takes a little share from Komatsu. Intel comes up with the 286. Sun Microsystems workstations pop up on trading room desks. Applied Materials wins a couple of semi-conductor contracts. But by the end of the 1980s, I was certain of it, so cer-tain that I went on Charlie Rose's television show on PBS and suggested that people short the Nikkei (Japan's stock market average) at 38,000 and buy the Dow Jones at 3,000 and keep that trade on until they cross. (I still haven't changed my view, and we have just crossed averages!) I was fa-natical about writing about my point of view. I wrote pieces for *The New Republic* about the resurgence of American manufacturing, and I penned a weekly column for a chain of legal periodicals, but I had no place to go to talk about what I thought could be a multiyear comeback by industrial companies.

That's why *SmartMoney,* a new opinion magazine about stocks and per-sonal finance, seemed so right for me when the *Journal* approached me to help create it in 1990. Along with Jim Stewart and Steve Swartz, then page one editor of the *Wall Street Journal,* we set out to change the way journal-ism covered the stock market. They, along with Norm Pearlstine, wanted a real live money manager to write. They didn't just want an "as told to" money manager and they didn't want an interview. They wanted me in the trenches, writing about what I was buying and selling. It had never been done before and it seemed like the most exciting job in the world: a market commentator just like a political commentator, taking a stand and defend-ing it in print. I was going to put my mouth where my money was.

I couldn't have been more excited. A chance to be a journalist and a trader. A chance to write about my views that American technology was coming back, and that a giant bull market was around the corner. At the time, the notion of a new magazine in the category seemed laughable. *Money* dominated the personal finance category and whatever it didn't have, *Kiplinger's* owned. But I knew they were vulnerable because neither was capable of doing anything except writing over and over again about how to retire on $47,000. They accepted every bit of the conventional wisdom of the hour. For me, the incentive was bigger than I let on. I always blamed Frank Lalli, my editor at the *Los Angeles Herald Examiner,* for his merciless treatment of me during my tough times in Los Angeles. Somehow he had ended up as editor of *Money* magazine fourteen years later. Okay, I am a grudge sort of guy. Here, with *SmartMoney,* was a chance to show him up, to show who was the better journalist. I loved it.

It had become an unfriendly grind at work, where, as I've described, I had to spend a great deal of time actually running the place instead of looking for good stocks, which is all I ever really wanted to do anyway. I took solace that year, not in the performance of the fund, but in the writing I began doing for *SmartMoney,* explaining the market to others. The magazine had turned into a huge success and I enjoyed being a part of the celebrity of it. But at the beginning of 1995, something happened with my writing that I still can't believe occurred, something that changed forever how people viewed me. I got caught up in a trading scandal that rocked *SmartMoney,* my money management firm, and just about everything else in my life. I had written an article that didn't properly disclose my stock holdings, something that didn't sit well with the agency that regulated my fund, the Securities and Exchange Commission, which was founded on the notion that disclosure is paramount when anyone talks about stocks. The dropped disclosure happened when I wasn't paying attention. I had now been writing my column, "Unconventional Wisdom," for three years, and we all got pretty lax about the way we handled the disclosure of ownership positions. That was the real nugget of the scandal.

At the end of 1994, my *SmartMoney* editor, Steve Swartz, had asked me to write an article about small capitalization stocks I liked that lacked Wall Street research coverage. So I wrote a piece about four "orphan" stocks that I had been buying aggressively at year-end. They were tiny stocks that I thought represented value because they weren't being promoted or sponsored by any firm. That in itself wasn't smart. You should never write about small stocks you can impact easily; it is too fraught with ethical problems. But what really hanged me was that *SmartMoney* left off that little box at the end of the article that should have said, "Cramer & Co. had big positions in these stocks." It didn't matter that I said I "loved them" in the text, and had been buying them, the Securities and Exchange Commission, through informal regulation, insists that managers disclose ownership at the end of any article they write, especially when the ownership was "reportable," meaning greater than 5 percent, as mine was in each of the stocks. The government doesn't want people saying nice things about stocks they own without the public knowing that the writer could benefit from any increase in price that the article causes. I had now violated that informal agreement that publishers have with the government. (As a writer who bought and sold stocks for a living I was an anomaly in the world of magazine publishing.) And, to make matters worse, I was sure someone would think that I was taking advantage of my power to move the stocks to levels where I could then sell them at a big profit—*even though I had no intention of selling.* That would be a pump-and-dump scheme, a federal crime where a promoter touts a stock and then uses his own hype to blow the position out to the unsuspecting buyers (think Enron). The government would certainly have brought that case against me if I had sold the stocks when they were at the peak. But I hadn't.

All four stocks, low-single-digit equities, jumped between 30 percent and 50 percent a few days before the article had general distribution, meaning whoever got the magazine first went in like gangbusters to buy the stocks. At first, I was titillated by my apparent power to move stocks. I thought, Holy cow, can you believe that my little *SmartMoney* article moved up the four little stocks that I had written about in the February 1995 issue? Could it really have been my column moving up Smith Environmental and Hogan Systems? Was my "Unconventional Wisdom" really behind the giant moves in UFPT and Rexon, two stocks that had been doing nothing for years? After writing hundreds of articles about the stock market in the last six years, had I finally arrived as someone who could impact the markets? I didn't know whether to be proud that my column had that kind of impact, or embarrassed that people trusted me so much to pay up absurdly for stocks that anybody could figure would soon go back down, or worried that I would be prosecuted for hiding ownership and pumping up stocks to dump them eventually at higher prices.

Immediately, I called Swartz and told him that my column moved the stocks and that perhaps we could get some reporter from Dow Jones to call me so I could say, "Whoa, don't bid these up like that, they will just come down when the hype is over." Steve thought it was amusing too, but didn't think it warranted bothering anyone. I told him my many concerns. He checked with the folks at Dow Jones, and he told me that no one there thought I had even played much of a role in moving the stocks to begin with. They must have thought I was an egomaniac about my own column's prowess.

None of these editors could figure out why I was so worried about moving stocks higher, anyway. Yet, the more I thought about how these stocks had flown, the more I worried that the readers would overpay for these stocks. More important, I now faced a serious dilemma: I would be hanged by the public if the stocks stayed up and I tried to sell them, or hanged by my partners, the people whose money I was running, if these stocks went back down and I *hadn't* sold them. I knew these kinds of moves off an article couldn't be sustained.

When no one from Dow Jones felt motivated to correct the record about the stocks, my second move was to call my lawyer, Bruce Birenboim, a partner at Paul Weiss. I told him that I owned stocks that had just jumped a couple of million dollars because of an article I wrote. Not a large amount when you are running more than $200 million, but nothing to sneeze at. What could I do? What would happen to the people who paid above-market prices and then sold them lower a few days later?

Bruce is the best lawyer in the world. He senses trouble from a planet away. He called me into his office immediately for a talk about the article. Unlike the people from Dow Jones, he knew there would be a huge fracas and an investigation about this article. As someone who had negotiated my contract with Dow Jones, a contract with a ton of safeguards to prevent any charges of pumping-and-dumping, he first wanted to know what happened to the disclosure box at the end of the article that was meant to state that I owned the stocks I had written about. I told him I had no idea, that we had all become lax about this stuff. "Oh, that's just great," Bruce, ever sarcastic, said. "Just terrific. Great job, Jim."

Without that protection, he explained, people will think that I hid my ownership. I told him, if you read the article it is clear that I owned the stocks. I also thought my contract would protect me. He told me it didn't matter, the press would have a field day with this. He told me to prepare for an ethics firestorm that would most certainly singe if not immolate his favorite client.

I left the meeting shaken, thinking, Oh my. No one had ever challenged my ethics. I had been the proverbial Boy Scout, never breaking any laws, never even getting a parking ticket. I had had nightmares about overdue library books. I was Little Miss Goody Two-shoes. When I got home that night I couldn't even look my wife and kids in the eyes when I warned them what was about to occur because of some stupid article I had written. A few days went by and nothing happened, and I felt like I had been the ultimate paranoiac. Life proceeded normally. Maybe I was worried for naught? Maybe I was home free?

And then I got a phone call from Howard Kurtz, the media reporter for the *Washington Post*. He said that he was doing an article about how I had used my *SmartMoney* column to make myself rich. Oh God, I thought to myself. I write because it is fun, because I like it. I have never made a dime off my writing. And rich? Because a couple of my stocks jumped for a couple of days? That's rich? Sure I was rich, but not because of some huge scheme to write about stocks and profit from those writings. I explained to him that the stocks had already started coming down, that I had sold nothing, and that I had never in the history of all my writing ever moved a stock. I said I regretted writing about small caps, but that I hadn't been the one who left off the disclosure box. Didn't matter what I said; the long knives were out. I could tell that Kurtz had decided to make me financial public enemy number one for this *SmartMoney* piece, the man who betrayed the readers for his own self-interest. The man who wrote not because he liked it, but because he could move stocks, generate performance, and get rich off the unsuspecting public.

Kurtz's article appeared on the front page of the *Washington Post* on February 10, 1995, the day of my fortieth birthday. Kurtz had tallied the gains on each stock in the "orphans" column at the maximum moment and put the winnings at $2 million for my firm. The piece dripped with innuendo, including quotations from a top editor at competitor *Kiplinger's* that I had sold the stocks and bought BMWs with the money, even though Kurtz knew I hadn't sold any stock into the article. I was burning. Bruce had been right. The firestorm had begun and I didn't have the tools to put it out. I didn't even have a garden hose to wet the rest of my family down.

I knew the government would come calling soon after Kurtz's piece. This type of article was meant to spur an investigation, and I knew one was coming. I also knew the rest of the media would have to follow up on Kurtz's attack on me. It was too juicy a story: hedge fund manager uses column to bang readers for big bucks.

Even though it was before noon on a Saturday morning, I poured myself a giant shot of Johnnie Walker Black, called Bruce, read him the article, and shouted out all my terrible thoughts to him. Good lawyers are like shrinks; Bruce overnight became my chief psychiatrist. To me, I was done for, headed for the concentration camp of pump-and-dumpers, a finished man, disgraced: Going to lose my fund. Going to lose my house. Going to lose my family. All because of this stupid article. Bruce was so worried about me that he summoned Arthur Liman, the prestigious criminal lawyer who had headed up the Michael Milken defense, to call me at home that Saturday afternoon and tell me that this is just a "hangnail" and I had nothing to worry about. The firm would take care of me. Easy for him to say, I said to myself. What did he do for Milken?

As the afternoon dragged on I became more and more distressed about the article and the pending nightmare. Between repeated calls to Bruce I downed almost the entire bottle of Johnnie Walker. Take a shot, call Birenboim. Take another shot, call Birenboim back. That's how I passed the afternoon of my fortieth birthday. Each time I would recite the litany of terrible things that were about to befall me. Each time Bruce would attempt to parry it to no avail.

My wife told me that to get my mind off of it, she had set up a dinner with my sister, Nan, and her husband, Todd Mason. I could not think of a worse prospect. I didn't want to leave the house. I didn't want to ever leave the house again. I didn't want to be seen by anyone. "They'll think I'm another Boesky," I kept repeating.

She told me not to be ridiculous, that this would pass, that nobody had even seen the article, and that we were going out with my family that night, no matter what. That made me polish off the bottle right then and there. Don't drink too much, she warned. Save something for tonight, she kept saying. It was too late, though. I was too far gone.

When we got to Gallagher's a couple of hours later in the heart of Mid-town Manhattan I was in a horrible mood. I could barely look my sister in the eye as we walked into the restaurant. She and her husband were ex-securities lawyers and they knew I feared the Commission, as I should. Next thing I knew, the people at Gallagher's were telling us that we had to go upstairs, that there were no tables downstairs. I was furious, livid, de-manding we go somewhere else. I said I would not be sent upstairs. I wanted to know how we could pick such a restaurant that would, on my very-not-special-fucking-fortieth birthday, make me go upstairs where the losers ate. Karen told me to shut up and led me upstairs. I turned around midway. She grabbed me and then pulled me up and into a dark-ened room. When the lights flipped on, every single living friend I have ever had burst out with "Surprise!" Next to the crowd at the overflowing bar was a giant mock cover of *SmartMoney* with the headline "Cramer's 40th: It's All About the Hair," which I had been consistently losing for years. As soon as I saw it, I thought about the orphans article, and I broke into tears. The confluence of all of those who were there to celebrate, but who also knew that I had gotten myself in big trouble because of my writ-ing, was just too much for me.

I don't recall much else, other than a switch to Absolut and another pounding of five or six drinks and then a sit-down, between Marty and my wife, with Jim Stewart standing up to the right of me as the toastmaster. Each guest took a turn roasting me. My college roommate John Spritz had brought a phone with him and said it was the same phone I had thrown at him my sophomore and junior years and he wanted to know if anyone else had ever had a phone thrown at him by me. Three quarters of the hands in the room went up. I remember Jim Stewart toasting me as someone who people wanted to love, in spite of myself. Then I went blank as my sister and my dad both talked about how I wasn't the ogre that I made myself out to be. Seated next to me was Marty Peretz, who was preparing to make some remarks.

It was right about then, between my sister's toast and Marty's, that I began to throw up. First, I did it into my hands, trying to cover my mouth. Then it was under the table, then on my shoes. I kept asking Karen if it was really obvious, and whether I was being discreet. Then I threw up on Marty's pants and Karen's dress. Finally, while toastmaster Stewart took a brief break, Karen shuffled me over to the back stairs of Gallagher's, where I threw up an avalanche of puke that cascaded down the stairs.

Karen talked Jimmy Manfredonia, a trader from Merrill Lynch, into giving me his shirt because it looked like mine. An hour later I had finally stopped throwing up, but not after at least a half-dozen people had been pelted by my projectile vomit. Happy birthday.

Somehow, I rallied enough to reprise Lou Gehrig's "Luckiest man on the face of the earth" speech before being whisked home to avoid any further humiliation. But it was a night that pretty much epitomized my first forty years on the firing line of life. If it hadn't been on tape, I would have never remembered a thing, that's how blotto I was. Six months' worth of elaborate planning by my wife to create the greatest surprise party, and it gets overwhelmed by my own panic in the face of an investigation that I knew had to come. And all for what? For the need to tell others about the market? For the celebrity of writing? For what?

Hunting season on Jim Cramer began the following Monday, February 12, 1995. I had written dozens of articles criticizing the ethics of everyone from mutual fund managers to brokers to financial journalists. I had never hidden my contempt for much that went on around me on Wall Street. As long as I kept my nose clean, I didn't have much to worry about, despite all of my rock throwing. Now I had done something wrong, and those whom I had criticized, chiefly Dan Dorfman, the peripatetic hype artist at that time working for CNBC, and Frank Lalli, my old nemesis now at *Smart-Money*'s archrival, *Money* magazine, were about to have a field day with me. Unless you have been caught up in one of these media spin cycles, you have no idea what it is like to be trapped in the big television-and-print wringer. I was about to experience it with all of its ramifications.

For years, in my columns in *SmartMoney* and before that in *Manhattan Lawyer,* I had criticized Dorfman, the hoarse-voiced newspaper columnist and radio commentator, for bagging, gunning, and liquidating, Wall Street shorthand for fund managers who would buy stocks in great quantity, "bagging," then craft takeover rumors and give the rumors to Dorfman to repeat, or "gun" in his columns. Then the fund managers would "liquidate" the positions when Dorfman went public with the bogus takeover plans. For years every hedge fund trader in New York knew the easiest way to get out of a bad position was to call Dorfman and tell him that Coke was going to tender for the company or that Exxon was on the prowl for the sucker position. I know many managers who made their whole year by buying up some crummy stock, then buying calls on it, gunning the stock and then leaking it to Dorfman with some made-up story to go with it so they could sell the stock into his report. As Dorfman needed a new story each day, he was easy prey for these folks. I had written repeatedly in many venues that he was not to be trusted because he did hedge fund dirty work. (Dorfman would later lose his job at *Money* and CNBC precisely because he had been used by a PR man who was paid fortunes to tout stocks to him.)

Now Dorfman had his chance for revenge. On his morning broadcast on CNBC a few days after my birthday he called for an investigation. He said that if he had done what I did he would go to jail. Of course, he would, he's a journalist. I am a money manager, though. If a journalist bought stock and then hyped it he would get in trouble unless he had been authorized to buy stock. But my job, as everyone in the hierarchy of Dow Jones knew, was to write about what I bought. That's why I was hired. That's exactly what I was supposed to be doing and Dorfman knew that. No matter; it was too juicy a story. The Dorfman report was repeated several times during the day, including the last time at dinner, when my four-year-old heard it. Now there were two Cramers who thought I was going to jail!

Next, the *New York Times* took a shot at me. It managed to get hold of former managing editor Norm Pearlstine, who was no longer with the *Journal,* to ask him what were the real circumstances behind hiring a money manager to write about stocks. Pearlstine, the man who had formally hired me to write the column about what I was buying and selling, the man who negotiated my contract, the man who wanted a live portfolio manager writing, told the *Times* he didn't know if it was right that I could write and trade. He wasn't sure I had a contract to do so. He wasn't sure if I was authorized to do what I did.

Oh man, that comment to the *Times* really sank me. If I didn't have a contract I was in the same boat as Foster Winans, the disgraced former "Heard on the Street" columnist who, in the 1980s, had bought stocks before he wrote positively about them and then sold them at a big profit. He had been convicted of stealing the information in the articles from his employer and gaining from it. He went to jail for what he did. Pearlstine's comments implied that perhaps I had done the very same thing. Would the government now charge me with doing the same? If you were with the government and you read that *Times* article, you would have to open an investigation. You had to go after Cramer.

The worst outcry, though, came from Lalli, who must really have relished this opportunity to lay into me one more time. Lalli, in his editor's column in *Money,* devoted two whole pages to castigating me, grandly blaming himself for not teaching me ethics when he was my boss at the *Los Angeles Herald Examiner,* arguing that had he taught me better I wouldn't have turned into the unethical swine that I had become. He charged me with putting my interests ahead of those of the readers and he suggested that there should be a solid investigation of how much money I made on the column. He made it clear that *Money* magazine would never tolerate such deceit. He practically begged *SmartMoney* to fire me.

After that drumbeat it was only a matter of time before the Securities and Exchange Commission called to get to the bottom of what really had happened here. A few days after the *Times* and *Money* articles, I got the call from the SEC that they had opened up In Re: Cramer, an informal inquiry to see if I had broken any laws by writing about stocks that I owned. They told me the investigation would be private and discreet and that no one would learn about it.

Of course, the next day, word of the SEC's investigation appeared on the front page of the *Wall Street Journal* with none of the informal inquiry niceties. The article said that the SEC was investigating me for abusing my column to make money. By the time the investigation began, the orphan stocks that had caused all the commotion were all the way back to where they were before the article, and I had never sold a share. But why should that fact get in the way of a really good manager lynching?

The government inquiry initially focused on three issues: whether I was allowed to write about stocks I owned, why I had failed to disclose my ownership, and whether I took money from the companies to write the articles. But as is often the case with the regulators, when they pull you over they also get to look into the glove compartment. Next thing I knew the government was investigating whether any of my employees or family members had secretly bought and sold the stocks. None of them had, as no one was allowed to trade individually at my shop. Then the inquiry escalated into whether I was running the money of any individuals who were not wealthy enough to qualify for a hedge fund, a potential violation of the laws that govern all hedge fund managers.

How could I get off the hook? I asked Bruce. How does this nightmare end? My lawyer then explained the case pretty simply: if Dow Jones would back me up on the purpose of the column, that a money manager was supposed to be writing about what he bought, then we would be fine and the inquiry would just go away.

There was a problem, though. There was always a group of people at Dow Jones who questioned why I was allowed to do what I did. They didn't want managers writing about stocks, they wanted reporters interviewing managers. Pearlstine, who had hired me and negotiated my contract, was gone (and wishy-washy in my defense). Others were far less comfortable with my role as fund manager and columnist.

So Dow Jones decided it had to do its own full-blown investigation of my hedge fund before giving me a clean bill of health. It couldn't just tell the feds that I was acting on its orders, even though I was. And without that clean bill of health, the regulators weren't going to let me go. That investigation, however, would cost me weeks of lost work time, and hundreds of thousands of dollars in legal fees.

Dow Jones at first demanded a timeline of the 120 stocks I had written positively about since the magazine started to see if there had been a pattern of my buying them, writing positively about them, and then selling them.

Over a period of several weeks' time I turned my office into a war room about what I had bought and what I had written about and whether, if ever, there had been any attempt to capitalize on my own writings at the expense of the readers. We traced the history of every stock mentioned in every article I wrote, way back to 1992, with IBM and ATT. We could not find a single situation where I had bought a stock, written positively about it, had seen the stock run up, and then sold it higher into the readers. Not one. It had never happened. In fact, until that orphans column no piece I had written had ever even budged a stock upward.

We were able to piece together a strange phenomenon, though. People were beginning to discuss stocks and investing in forums and groups online. I discovered a Web site where people eagerly sought out my picks because of my record. On this site, several traders who had early copies of the magazine—it had been mailed unevenly around the country and arrived in different regions a day or two ahead of other regions—had posted my picks from the controversial February column, betting that the stocks would run up once the column had wide distribution. Others suggested buying the stocks up and then selling them into any sort of increase a few days later. To me the world of the Web was brand-new, but to these players, talking about stocks and discussing likes and dislikes was already second-nature.

Others had regularly discussed my picks in *The Motley Fool*'s chatrooms. There was an amazing underground of stock-market-philes on the Web who spent phenomenal amounts of time researching picks and swapping ideas. They bought because my column was making them money. I could see that this kind of chatter about my stocks may have had more to do with moving my stocks than what I wrote alone. The Web hugely magnified this little article.

Dow Jones wasn't quite sure what to do with me after I presented the evidence of no wrongdoing. My lawyer, Bruce, and I were demanding that they come out and stand by me in a letter to the government explaining everything about my role in the article. We wanted the *Journal*'s Good Housekeeping Seal of Approval. Dow Jones, however, remained split into the two camps: the camp that said it's fine for fund managers to write, and the camp who thought it inherently dishonest. The contract didn't seem to matter to this latter camp. If I could not get that seal of approval, if Dow Jones didn't admit to the contract's right to write and trade, the government might be inclined to go after me as someone who traded on his own inside information.

It all came down to a heated, tense session at Paul Weiss where the general counsel of Dow Jones and a couple of Dow Jones editors spent a day grilling me, to see if I was worthy of their endorsement. At the all-day interrogation, the editors picked twenty-five stocks I had mentioned in my column over the last four years and asked me again why I had written about those stocks, why I had bought them, and whether I had sold them after the articles appeared. Again, they could find no pattern where I had done such a thing. Because I hadn't. No matter, I couldn't coax that endorsement out of them even after the exercise was completed and the meeting broke up in anger. Finally, when no one could be sure whether Dow Jones would throw me to the wolves or not, Steve Swartz stood up and launched into an impassioned defense of my honesty. He insisted that Dow Jones stick by me. He said he believed in me totally and completely. His solid backing and his forceful stand made the Dow Jones crowd give me that seal of approval.

The next day the Dow Jones counsel crafted a letter informing the SEC that it was the magazine's fault for leaving the disclosure notice off the article, and not my own attempt to hide my ownership position, and that it believed I had done nothing wrong. That letter apparently ended the inquiry in its tracks. Unlike the beginning of the investigation, widely chronicled everywhere, though, there would be no articles about how I had *not* done anything wrong. There would be no pieces in *Money* about how there were no penalties for me. Dan Dorfman didn't report on the conclusion of the investigation, and Howard Kurtz never wrote about it again. Because of the nature of government regulatory inquiries, the government wasn't going to exonerate me for what I did. They weren't, as my lawyer never tired of saying, going to award me the Congressional Medal of Investing. In fact, it was only after Joe Nocera, a columnist for *Time* magazine, wrote an article a month after the inquiry began, saying that it is vital that fund managers be allowed to write about what they buy and sell, that the heat started dying down and I felt comfortable writing about stocks again. Nocera scoffed that a world where no managers can talk about stocks they own and no journalists can own stocks is a world where journalism is not helpful to the average investor. That investor needs the help of pros who shouldn't feel that they are going to be investigated. Nocera's theory, novel in 1995, is implicit in a massive amount of what we now accept routinely on the Web and on television devoted to stocks.

While the government's inquiry of me finally just went away, people I meet in business now remember the scandal as a generic "insider trading" rap even though the outcome produced no indictments, no pleas, and no guilt. Few people seem to recall that I wasn't found guilty of anything; they just remember that I was investigated, and the government doesn't investigate you for doing nothing.

Dow Jones, by the way, paid for a large portion of my $700,000 in legal bills accrued in cooperating with the government's inquiry, for which I am most grateful. The firm also promised me a white paper fully exonerating me for what happened, but I never got it. In a strange way, though, it didn't matter. In two years people would routinely be doing what I was investigated for at *SmartMoney*—owning and writing about stocks—and it would be endorsed by the SEC chairman himself. Arthur Levitt, the commissioner under Clinton, in his final years championed the *Motley Fool* site, sponsored by a couple of brothers with no knowledge of the market who wrote and talked about stocks constantly. Levitt understood that we all became journalists once the Web opened up and anyone could write about stocks he liked. What I did—writing about stocks I owned—seems, well, downright innocent considering the outright touting of stocks on a daily basis that now goes on in popular sites all over the Web.

CHAPTER 6

The Birth of *TheStreet.com*

After the *SmartMoney* fracas subsided, I couldn't get it out of my head that there were so many people online discussing stocks that you could somehow make a business of the dissemination of information about stocks on the Web.

At the office I found myself lingering in the discussion rooms already widely available on the Web. I kept thinking about how natural it was to chat about stocks, how powerful it was to sit in front of your screen and talk real-time with others about your holdings and about prospects and ideas. Whenever there was a break in trading, a lull in the markets, I dove into the chats to find out from real-world people—not analysts—how companies were really doing. Back in those days the Web was so wild that people would go online and talk about their own companies' strengths and weaknesses. It was incredibly easy to find out through the chats what companies were working on interesting things—provided you were willing to accept that people using aliases could be trusted. I weaved in and out of lots of *Motley Fool* boards, places where individuals communicated about stocks, identifying myself only as UPOD, which stands for Under Promise and Over Deliver. No one used his real name online then. Everything was a big exciting undercover operation. I picked UPOD because I had heard the chief executive of Tambrands use that term to describe a philosophy that reflected perfectly how I ran my hedge fund.

I never wanted to promise more than I could deliver. And I always wanted to exceed what was expected. As UPOD I would dart in and out of different chat rooms day and night. I would check the postings that would appear on different biotech and tech stocks I followed. I would ask questions of the participants in each. Was the Gandalf Technologies modem better than the Hayes modem? Was Penril a legitimate company technologically? Did anyone have any feel for how the Biogen MS studies were going? It seems so darned innocent now, in an era where chat rooms have become cesspools of stock promotion and people enter stock boards only to hype stocks and get them moving so they can dump them onto the unsuspecting. At that time, however, in late 1995, engineers from major companies used to swap anecdotes about benchmarking of different technologies and doctors shared results of studies that could impact stocks. You could learn something. And you could do so without the intermediary, the broker, who typically had an agenda other than your welfare.

I couldn't believe the sheer number of people who were coming online to talk and trade stocks every day. People seemed to get hooked on it. The Web seemed like the natural medium for me to communicate with others about my views—faster, simpler, and better.

At the beginning of 1996 I realized that no matter how exciting hedge fund management was, I was in early on what I thought could be an explosive idea: an online newspaper that reported and commented on stocks in real time. Why not give real-time news and analysis for a fee right through the Net? Why not build a small staff of people and figure out a price point that would make us instantly profitable after a doable number of subscriptions? The Net had turned everyone into journalists and stock critics. It turned the stock market into something that was remarkably accessible where you could read about a stock, type in a keystroke, and then buy that same stock for pennies in commissions. Commissions for stocks, once so high that they ate your profits unless you had a home run, became a token part of the trade now that trading was done electronically.

At the time the only professional format where you could learn about stocks in real time was the very expensive proprietary newswires like Reuters, Dow Jones, and Bloomberg. Those news services cost up to $1,500 a month. I wondered, What if you charged them one one-hundredth of that for commentary from me and a couple of other managers who were willing to write about stocks on a Web site from the professional point of view? Wouldn't we have an edge over these other, more expensive services? They only broke news. They had very little analysis and no opinion. Analysis and opinion were the province of magazines and newspapers. But most magazines came out monthly and the lead time between when you wrote for them and when people read your copy was too long. You would have no idea when you were writing what the market might do in the next week, but when you write for monthlies you have to know what is going to happen, or at least pretend to know what is going to happen, three months in advance! You had to be a seer and if you were wrong, there was scrambled egg all over your face the day the issue hit the stands. It would be late summer when I submitted my draft for *Smart-Money*'s November issue. I remember having to write articles *as if* the market crashed in October and then rallied in November during August when the market was going great guns.

Analysis was in short supply in journalism. For the *Wall Street Journal*, the "Heard on the Street" column represented the only place where reporters could speculate on what would happen to stocks, the only place that people would venture to conclude that a stock might go up or down. The papers and the magazines never criticized money managers. There was a virtual taboo on mentioning mutual funds in a negative light, even though so many funds underperformed. Nobody ever knocked anyone in a business that was the largest advertiser.

More important, no reporters and editors were explaining to readers the obvious conflicts of the analysts who worked at investment banks and came on television to promote stocks they helped underwrite. No news organizations were revealing what we managers knew to be true: many recommendations couldn't be trusted because the companies being recommended *paid* for those recommendations through the form of underwriting fees. Investors needed to know who was being paid by a corporate finance client—kind of like a movie critic being paid by Warner Brothers—and who was actually trying to make money as an honest broker of ideas. Who was on the take and who was representing only the customers buying stock instead of the ones who are issuing it? Readers, I thought, would love that kind of fresh information.

Everyone in my business had either a Bloomberg machine or a machine with Reuters or Dow Jones on it *and* a personal computer. What if every personal computer was to get hooked up to the Net? What if everybody who sat at a blank computer screen every day had something to read that helped them make money? What if they could read articles about stocks, chat about stocks, and then buy stocks all with clicks of the mouse or the keyboard? All of the other services cost thousands of dollars a year to get and required massive hardware and software and personal installation. These other surfaces already had claimed their space on people's desktops. But my idea, a feed through the Net of news and analysis that you would pay a modest subscription for, didn't need to battle the other providers because it would appear in the ubiquitous personal computer terminal at your desk.

We take all of that for granted now; it turned out to be what the Net was about. But when I thought of coming up with a product that tied the two together, it was so novel that people couldn't even grasp it. My first move was to take this idea for a new kind of site to Steve Swartz, who had stood by me during the *SmartMoney* orphans debacle. I told him we would call it *SmartMoney.com*—even that seemed like a new idea then! Steve loved it and set up a lunch with Paul Steiger, the managing editor for the *Wall Street Journal*.

Paul's a total gentleman and when I told him the idea, even mentioning that I thought we could give both the wires and the print world a run for the money, he was interested.

I made it clear, though, that unlike *SmartMoney,* where I knew I should have fought for some equity (it was already worth several hundred million dollars as a franchise even then), I needed a couple of percentage points of *SmartMoney.com* if he wanted me to conceive, design, and execute it, that I wouldn't work for salary, because if this one turned out to be big, I would feel like a total idiot. Paul said he would see what he could do and thanked me for the idea.

Within a day the word came back: "no equity." Not going to happen. I would be strictly salaried. As my fund was having an outstanding year, the last thing I needed was another puny *Journal* stipend.

At the time I had no idea what the Web really was other than something that you typed in www for. I was never a computer guy in school, and while I liked using my personal computer as a word processor or to do a spreadsheet, I didn't know how 98 percent of the computer worked.

I did know, though, that you could design your own page for a little bit of money and that my page would be well read given the number of readers I had at *SmartMoney*. If I could get another dozen writers and a couple of business guys, I figured we could get this project off the ground with the money I had made from the hedge fund.

But I knew I needed a partner. One of the reasons I went to the *Journal* in the first place was because I didn't want anyone to think it was my paper, as if it were some sort of personal tout sheet for a hedge fund manager. I wasn't worried about the cost; you could do it on the Web for practically nothing. As someone who had always dreamed of having his own newspaper but had been born too late for that, I had this epiphany: the only really expensive parts of a newspaper are the trees, the pressmen, the trucks, and the distribution. The notion of producing a newspaper online eliminated what would later be known as the "friction" of pre-Web enterprises, friction being the venture capitalist word that justified virtually every Web investment.

So, with this lack of knowledge of how the Web really worked, but with a burning belief that we would find a way to harness the Web to intrigue online stock followers, I turned to the same man who had given me my first break in the business, Marty Peretz. I explained to Marty the business model—subscriptions online, because I didn't think there would be much advertising—and he immediately agreed on the spot to be my partner, with a fifty-fifty split. We right then set out to come up with a team of people to take the vision to reality, even as I had only a few scraps of paper with the ideas of the site on them.

I was as innocent and naive as Bambi when I talked Marty into the venture. Or maybe Bambi's mother. I thought people would pay for money-making information on the Web, and that they would pay more for it than offline because it was real-time! That turned out to be totally wrong. No one wanted to pay anything for the Web even if they would pay thousands for slow hard copy. That's just the way it was. I thought that a personal computer would have enough power to handle whatever we published and send it to millions of people. I didn't know that I would need hundreds of thousands of dollars in hardware alone to publish online. I thought it would be simple to type in a credit card number and be billed for the right to read my stuff. I had no idea that I would have to develop a commerce system from scratch because the Web wasn't as friendly as I thought to the notion of paid content. What a liberal arts dreamer I was!

Given the simplified cost structure I envisioned, and the lack of a budget for anything but talent and a couple of personal computers to host the site, I proposed to Marty that $400,000 max would be all we would need together to pull this project off. In fact, I was so sure that I said I was only willing to put in a total of $400,000 on my end. Marty said no problem, he would stop me out at $400,000 and fund the rest.

Once Marty gears into action he's unstoppable. Once we both get together it's an Indy 500 worth of energy between the two of us, high-octane and massive horsepower. Back then we didn't even have a name for the darned thing. I thought *People'sCapitalist.com* or *TheDailyProfit.com*. All during the trading days in 1996, I kept kicking around dotcom names. Everything was available back then and any time an idea came into my head we simply registered it.

Marty, who had run *The New Republic* for so long, and had become so adept at finding young talent, set up a series of meetings at the Regency Hotel in Midtown New York for people to run the day-to-day of the operation. I was so busy running the hedge fund that I had to leave the personnel matters to Marty. We first tried to grab whoever was running *The Harvard Crimson,* a legacy of the days when I thought that anyone who got that job had to be capable of handling any other. But we couldn't find any candidates from immediate years past who were interested in business, let alone working for a soon-to-be-announced dotcom, at a time when you were still explaining what www stood for, let alone the suffix dotcom. We advertised in some Ivy League papers for more talent, but again came up empty except for a film critic from the *Daily Pennsylvanian.*

Next thing I knew Marty decided to go out of the journalism business and seek consultants to run the place. He brought in a man in his twenties who looked like he could've been my kid, a consultant from Bain by the name of Andrew Drake. The young consultant talked about the Web in expansive ways, big ways, big concepts. Most important, he wanted the job;

we wanted the job filled and couldn't find any other takers. Marty suggested we make him an offer, I said it sounded like the right idea, and we had our first employee. Just like that. We were well on our way, and I do mean this as cynically as possible, to doing lots of the same things that other Net companies did wrong, including hiring incredibly young people with no experience and telling them to go build a company with no real plans beyond a sketchy couple of pages of paper.

Drake then brought in his friend Ravi Desai, another consultant, for us to interview. Desai had the single greatest résumé I had ever seen: summa at Harvard and Harvard Business School, running major projects for Boston Consulting Group in his first year there, a man who everybody we talked to, every check, from the fellow at Schwab to the man at American Express, said how lucky we would be to grab this Desai. So we did. After one quick breakfast meeting at the Regency, Marty and I agreed that Ravi would be the ideal editor in chief, even though he had never edited a thing, and knew little about journalism. We were in too much of a hurry to care. Our first order of business, now that we had the executive team in tow, was to get another marquee player, another name fellow who could drive traffic besides me so it wasn't just *JimCramer.com.*

What we needed was another insider, someone who really got it and could speak for the cool, hip part of Wall Street that we needed. We needed to hire Michael Lewis, the author of *Liar's Poker.* Marty knew Lewis, who had done some writing for *The New Republic,* so he talked with Lewis, who seemed genuinely interested in being part of the team. The next thing I knew it was late spring, 1996, and Marty and I were meeting at my Bucks County farmhouse, with Michael Lewis, Ravi Desai, Andrew Drake, and the film critic from Penn, who had answered our ads in the Ivy papers. Here we were, sitting in the dining room of our farmhouse, with legal pads and black Berols outlining what our mission was and what it would be. We knew there would be doubters, but we knew that we were early and we had a chance to make something happen before others. We were, in the parlance of the day, "first movers, with first mover advantage."

Lewis wanted 5 percent of the operation. He needed to be coaxed, however. Marty and I took him outside to talk. As we walked past the swimming pool, toward the unplowed cornfield, Marty explained to Lewis that he could get 5 percent of the enterprise for a reasonable amount of work, perhaps a twice-a-week column about the market. With that, Lewis said he had had his doubts about the Web and about our enterprise but we had resolved everything to his satisfaction and now he was ready to become a dotcomer and looked forward to helping make the venture great. He was on board for 5 percent, ready to roll up his sleeves and get cyber-dirty. Once we had him, I said to Marty later, I figured we could take the world by storm. Marty was equally confident, although he felt that the 5 percent was a lot to give. "Not with him writing regularly," I assured Marty. We left the farmhouse that day confident of the prospects of our venture, because now we had the hottest business columnist in the world, for a 5 percent equity stake. I was, it turns out, wildly premature about everything, most particularly our star writer whom we thought we had just sewn up with a handshake.

I never spoke to Lewis again after that weekend. Heck, I never saw him again. He didn't return calls. He has subsequently denied any involvement in the project and has been a sworn opponent of our work ever since.

Very strange. So very Web, where contracts were made to be broken and handshakes were totally meaningless, just a simple spreader of another guy's germs. It was emblematic of the problems that would soon plague every aspect of our new Web business.

Lewis did, however, contribute something concrete: a name. While we sat around the dining room table, kicking around URLs, he suggested that we call the company *TheStreet.com.* We liked the ring of it immediately; it captured the wiseguy essence of what we were meant to be about. We all agreed it was good, and we set about claiming the name the following Monday. Of course we had to buy it from someone who was hoarding a whole bunch of highway names, such as *The Boulevard, The Avenue, The Street,* and *The Road.* We paid $5,000 for *TheStreet,* explaining that we didn't care which street we picked—we didn't want the owner to know we were going to use *TheStreet* to mean Wall Street, lest he jack up the price—and the venture's name belonged to us. We were now truly off and running before the summer of 1996. We also, at that fated Bucks County meeting, targeted November as our launch come hell or high water, because we were so afraid that others would catch up with our concept and our game.

Ravi and Andrew immediately decided, even before we had a fleshed-out business plan, that we would need to establish ourselves among the venture capital community. They told me that you had to do that, because there was no telling how much this venture would ultimately cost. I readily agreed and they asked me to fly out with them for the obligatory trip to Sandhill Road in Palo Alto, where all the prominent venture capitalists have offices.

It was a total disaster. Nobody wanted to see us. We shuttled from one office to another and were simply waved right through without so much as a comment. The only substantive meeting we had was with Kleiner Perkins, renowned as one of the top VC players. I had used my old *Los Angeles Herald Examiner* ties to get a meeting with Will Hearst, the new partner in charge of new media. Hearst dismissed our efforts, saying that unless you were going to be involved with hardware for the Net there was no future to it. He warned me not to spend any more money on the site, that it would eventually just fall by the wayside. He laughed at our business plan, to make money with subscriptions, and suggested that we do something else with our time.

We flew home silently after that meeting, wondering if we had even a clue of what we were doing, or why we were even doing it. Ravi told us not to worry, though. He had other tricks up his sleeve, he was just beginning to do battle, and if I could keep our name in lights for a while with television appearances (I was beginning to appear regularly on *Good Morning America* and CNBC to offer insight into the markets) the VC money would be thrown at us in the end. Ravi rekindled my spirits, although I think Drake already knew he was way out of his league, and we vowed to make Marty's and my money work harder and better, so we would not need venture capital until much much later in the game. I remember telling Ravi that he was so right, and that when they came after us I would punish the most arrogant ones by making them pitch their wares to me and then turning them down, as we had just been turned down. It would be sweet revenge, I told myself. And what the heck, I was having another good year, I had plenty of money to fund the operation. How much more could it really cost me before we broke into the black? Another million? Maybe two million? That wouldn't be a problem, not with the numbers I was putting on at the hedge fund.

I've always been a manic guy. Not manic-depressive, just manic. Fired-up. Ready. Everybody in the business knew I was shot out of a cannon each morning. I was always first to arrive at 85 Broad Street, the headquarters of Goldman Sachs, gleefully turning the lights of the 28th floor on, hating it if anyone got in before me. It was no different when I left Goldman four years later to start my fund. In the first years of the hedge fund, I couldn't even wait till my wife would come in at 7:00 A.M. I left our Brooklyn Heights apartment seventy minutes before she did. Always too much to read, too much to do. I liked to hop on the subway from Clark Street and get there at 6:00 A.M. to get a jump on everyone. That way I could read the papers and be up to speed when the wires started manufacturing that day's news feed that was the lifeblood of trading. The wires didn't start until 7:00 A.M. back then, which seems quaint now, as if trading had a civilized beginning and a 4:00 P.M. closing time. Back in 1994, trading around the clock would have seemed like some sort of science fiction plot to kill guys like me.

I pushed up my arrival time another hour to beat the traffic when, in 1994, Karen and I and our two girls moved to the New Jersey suburb of Summit. For me, the earlier the better, because of my sleep problems. I had never needed much sleep, taking what I could to get by. In college I would regularly go two days straight without so much as a nap after a long night of Yuban. It came naturally to me. I hated missing a press run at the *Crimson,* and nothing gave me more satisfaction than going to classes, then going to the *Crimson* in the afternoon, banging out a couple of stories, editing the product, proofing it, pasting it up, putting in on the press, and then delivering the paper across the campus, only to finish in time to attend another day's classes. If I had to grab some sleep, the four hours from 5:00 A.M. to 9:00 A.M. gave me all of the energy I needed.

Not long after I started running money, I reverted to those same hours, but not in a fashion I would have preferred. I simply couldn't stay asleep past three. No matter what I did, no matter how late I went to bed, no matter what I took, Sominex, cabernet, Bombay and tonic, didn't matter, I would sit up, eerily awake every night at 3:00 A.M., sweat pouring from every pore. Jeez, it's dark at that hour. And nobody to talk to at all. Once up, all I could do was lie there and be paralyzed by the poor trades I had made the day before or the potential for great trades I could make the next day. I would roll on my stomach, press my head to the pillow, and think about the money I had lost if I had traded poorly, or the positions that had gone against me even if I had traded well. What good would it do to go over the good trades? That couldn't make you money.

Eventually, after a ritual hour of bogus attempts to fall back asleep, at 4:20 A.M. I would give up and find myself on the treadmill in the basement. Bleak existence.

The Net changed that. Now I knew what to do when I couldn't sleep. I would get up and read and enter message boards, go to the Web sites of all of the newspapers around the world, and plan what our Web site would look and feel like. I would spend from 3:30 until dawn working on designs for what would be *TheStreet.com* and then shift to my day job of trading until 4:00 P.M., when I would once again start working online, taking a break for dinner before reimmersing myself in a night of e-mail and planning.

What else was I supposed to do? How else was I to get everything done? How else was I going to learn to use the computer, which, like many others my age in the early 1990s, was something done by my assistant. As a trader, I needed to be devoted 100 percent of the daytime to trading, to making money. The style of money running that I used required maximum concentration. If you are trading the tape as I did, looking for news that I could process faster than anyone else, how could I think about what the Web site would look like during the day? How could I get anything done on it?

Until 1995 I didn't even know how to get online. But from the moment Marty and I decided to go ahead, the project struck me as something I just had to do. It was something I felt I had to make successful. After writing for so many entities for so many years, and being paid far less than what I brought in to them, I knew I had to do what I described to a skeptical Karen as "this Web thing." Karen warned me that I was taking on too much. She also was saddened to see that, once again, Marty and I were back in that crazed mode where we were working around the clock together. She also urged me to keep track of what these young hires were doing. She didn't trust them at all. I told her not to worry, that we could run the whole *TheStreet.com* from some unused space down at the end of the hall of my office, at 100 Wall Street. That way I could keep an eye on what was going on, to be sure that we weren't spending an arm and a leg on the thing, and that it would be as barebones a start-up as you can imagine.

My wife and I had always run a frugal firm. We didn't hire unless we knew that we could pay the person out of our own pockets if we had a bad year. We didn't like to waste space. For the first four years of our firm we *borrowed* space—not rented, just borrowed—from different brokerage firms such as New York and Foreign Securities (now defunct) and SG Cowen in return for commissions. When we finally decided enough free-loading, Karen put us in a bankrupt failed residential condo project down-town next to a homeless shelter and right above a steak joint for a measly $12 a square foot. She outfitted the whole place with used furniture and tried to keep all expenses including out-of-pocket expenses, to no more than $2,000 a month. She wouldn't even allow the company to have a credit card for fear that we would abuse it. I would complain that if any of our rich clients came by they would be mortified, but she insisted that our frugality was exactly what they should want.

And when the stink of the grease from the burgers at Delmonico's finally overpowered our research director, Jeff Berkowitz, who repeatedly complained that he couldn't think for the smell, and one of our employees was beaten up on our street on the way home after working late, Karen agreed in 1995 to upgrade our offices to the recently vacated space of a failed Singapore bank at 100 Wall Street. I was shocked at the prestigious address she picked and blown away by the minuscule $14 a square foot price she had negotiated, which was much cheaper than anything else around it. Until she told me that the space was available so cheaply because of an asbestos problem. "What the heck, last time I looked neither you nor Jeff were pregnant," she would say whenever anyone questioned the choice.

My intention was to have the Web project run with the same level of frugality that dominated the hedge fund.

Which is why I was shocked, after two weeks with Drake and Desai ensconced in the back of my office as it got organized, that they already had more people working for *TheStreet.com* than worked for Cramer & Company. No matter, I figured, heck, maybe Drake and Desai knew something I didn't. To be honest, and despite my assurances to Karen, I didn't pay enough attention to the company once we picked the firm's leaders, as I was busy with the buying and selling of stock every day. I had paid scant attention to both of them when Marty introduced them to me.

Now I was forced to see them every day as they came to work at my office.

Drake was a tall, good-looking white kid—I kept saying, Man, is this guy white—with tortoiseshell glasses and a way of speaking that made me think he was General George Marshall when he uttered something. Drake impressed me as one of those Gentile folks who seemed like he could have been in the State Department if he had chosen to be. I could barely remember a thing about him after we hired him, other than that he seemed entirely inoffensive. He was all classic American suits, smiling, with a shock of blond hair hanging down and a level of surety that John F. Kennedy would have envied. Drake said he saw the future of the Net. He knew where it was going, and how we were going to get there. His qualifications were that he had guided in his short consulting career several major Fortune 500 companies toward a path of glory. He assured me that he was tough as nails, although at first glance I wasn't so sure. He told me that the Web was his forte, he lived and breathed it, which was good, because I was still trying to insert my computer's phone jack into the wall without taking out the regular phone. He had a sense of calm and a sense of entitlement.

"Very likable guy," Karen described him upon meeting him soon after he was hired. "Has no idea what he is getting into."

That was okay because I was less interested in the business side than the editorial and that was Desai's department. Desai, the man we were really banking on—he was, as they say in law school, sui generis. Marty paired himself with Drake and stayed close to the business side. The man I paid attention to was Desai. But our first meeting, after Marty had blessed him, was not auspicious. I was expecting an Indian Henry Luce after the way Drake had built up the guy. You never heard Desai's name mentioned by Drake without being bracketed by the words "genius" or "brilliant."

Desai, he said, would have been a poet if he didn't want to make money so badly. Money was in his blood, Drake said, the perfect combination of thinker and doer. Before I met him I had already heard from Drake that Desai practically invented the American Express tiered card structure—before he was twenty-five! Express's Harvey Golub wouldn't make a move without talking to this guy, Drake would say. Desai, apparently, also had the ear of the top people at Schwab, the giant discount broker. One of his recommenders appeared high up on the Schwab masthead as the strategic planner for the company. Schwab and Express, the two biggest and most important outfits in America, and they love this guy? How could one guy exist with such credentials?

So I barely focused on Desai the first time I met him. And it was why I was unwilling to question the massive amount of hiring that Desai started right from the get-go. In retrospect, I didn't pay nearly enough attention to him.

I also couldn't afford to be too invasive. Bruce Birenboim, my lawyer, warned me that if I didn't want to get in trouble with the Securities and Exchange Commission again I would not be allowed to know the day-to-day operations of the company, lest the Commission think that I was using *TheStreet.com* to move my stocks higher, as they thought I might have with *SmartMoney*. We went so far as to ask the Commission what relationship it wanted between me and *TheStreet.com*. The answer came back quickly: they wanted us to be very separate, with me able to criticize the operation only retrospectively. There could be no regular contact between the organizations without genuine trouble for my moneymaking hedge fund. I was pleased they let me be involved at all.

My wife saw the Commission's qualified go-ahead as something else entirely. She said that in the wrong hands, in the hands of people I did not know, this company could become the veritable black hole spending our hard-earned dollars. I would be writing checks for people I knew nothing about, who were not under my control, who would do anything they wanted and who would not only be free of my influence but could run amok undetected. "It could be a rogue operation," she predicted. "They could end up hating you and trashing you. They could end up hurting us. And you can never go and see what they are doing with the money."

I told her how silly that was. There was no "they" and "us." We were in this together. I said the SEC merely wanted a "Chinese wall" between us about articles that were about to come out, but everything else was pretty much fair game for me to monitor.

Karen's view turned out to be spot-on. Ravi, Andrew, and Jamie Heller, the firm's third hire, a lawyer by training, took the SEC's guidance to mean that they needed to be completely independent of me. They didn't want a Chinese wall, I joked to Marty Peretz not long after they had decided they had to move crosstown to be separate from my offices. They wanted an electrified fence with claymore mines, searchlights, and machine gun posts, all to protect themselves from me.

Nonsense, Marty insisted, we could go over there all the time, check things out, see how they were doing. We could follow Ravi's and Andrew's every moves and we would know everything about the operation except what stories they intended to write.

By the fall Drake and Desai said they were busy running the company and that they would brief us roughly once a month at the Regency Hotel about all they felt they could tell us. I wanted more information, but it was clear that they weren't going to give me any. Heller, the lawyer turned journalist, made it clear before a single issue of the site came out that I was to have *no contact at all* with anyone but the principals from the business side. I would have to get an appointment—get permission—to visit and it would not be given easily or automatically. Neither Drake's team nor Desai's were allowed to speak to me from the day that they moved, instead viewing me as someone who should *only* be promoting the venture and no more. My wife's paranoid view of the operation seemed to be coming true.

Worse, when we went to the Regency the first time to review, we learned that the venture had already blown through all of the $400,000 I had put in. It needed more, much more, and if we wanted it to get off the ground we would regularly have to infuse the company with $250,000 each meeting at the Regency, Drake told us. Marty explained, gently, that he could not backstop me as he'd intended given how expensive this operation was going to become. I would have to continue to fund the company with him. Every assurance I had made to my wife, from the amount of loss we could be exposed to, to the oversight I could provide for that money, was by October of 1996 obliterated. Our monthly meetings became absurd: they would tell us all was well, we would hand over my checks, and Marty and I had no idea what we were getting for our money. It was the very black hole of expenses my wife feared.

CHAPTER 7

Dow Jones Again

Inevitably when people at the *Wall Street Journal* talk about what I wanted to do with *TheStreet.com* they couch it in terms of revenge, as if somehow the scars of the *SmartMoney* investigation never healed. They think that because when I left *SmartMoney* at the end of 1995 to become the "Bottom Line" columnist for *New York* magazine, I soon began to agitate against the way Dow Jones was being run.

In early winter of 1996, while we were vacationing at Hershey Park, I received an extraordinary call from Eric Breindel, whom I had run against at the *Crimson*. After I became president, Eric was the editorial chairman. We became good friends, and stayed that way. He had been one of my first clients at Goldman Sachs and we enjoyed a good social relationship. Breindel, at the time of the call the editorial page editor of Rupert Murdoch's *New York Post,* wanted to see me because he didn't know whom else to trust.

Murdoch, who had been Breindel's closest friend for more than a decade, wanted someone who knew Dow Jones cold and could be trusted to keep his mouth shut. It was typical Murdoch. At the moment Breindel called, I had been taking in some of the rides on a beautiful Sunday morning. The hotel tracked me down and informed me that there was an urgent message from Breindel. I hadn't spoken to him in months.

How comfortable was I with the fundamentals of Dow Jones? he asked me when I returned his call.

I said I closely followed the company as part of my research. I knew that Dow Jones, if it were to close one of its money-losing divisions, Telerate, a dispenser of information about bonds that was getting killed by Bloomberg, and put the resources into the Internet, could become dominant there.

"Terrific," Breindel said. "Can you come in?"

Sure, I said. "When?"

"Today. This afternoon. Rupert wants to see you."

I knew Eric well enough to know that he wasn't kidding. I repeated the question aloud, and my wife came running into the room. "Don't you dare," she mouthed. "Don't even think about it."

I explained to Eric that it would have to wait until the next day, after the markets closed. "Fine," he said, in a way that expressed disapproval but made it clear that I better be there, with knowledge, because Murdoch had plans.

The next day, I went back over the Dow Jones financials. They were losing hundreds of millions a year trying to save this Telerate division. If you could close Telerate and take just a tenth of those resources and make Dow Jones the destination Web site for the do-it-yourselfer, the result could be an Internet play that would be bigger than anything else out there.

At the beginning of 1997, people still thought we at *TheStreet.com* were crazy to take on Dow Jones and Reuters. (Roughly two months into operations, we were doing about a dozen stories a day.) I, frankly, didn't care. I was thinking about the stock market, and how it was becoming the national pastime, a pastime where if there could be one destination site for information and for trading it could be worth more than any other site out there, including Amazon, which was already being valued in the billions of dollars by a willing-to-believe stock market. I wasn't sure we at *TheStreet.com* could do it, but it would be a slamdunk for Dow Jones. Remember, this was before *Yahoo! Finance* even existed, before the explosion of online trading, just when people had discovered Amazon and recognized the Net as a place to buy and sell things—including stocks.

That would be the play for Murdoch, I thought.

At 4:45 P.M. Breindel ushered me in to meet the man himself. He introduced me as the only person he would trust with his money. Murdoch seemed impressed but wasted no time getting to the point. "I want to buy Dow Jones, how much should I pay?"

I mumbled something about how Dow Jones had two classes of stock. But then I figured, you know something, you don't get to be Rupert Murdoch if you haven't figured out garbage like that. So, I said, "Seventy-three." (It was trading in the low 40s at the time.)

Murdoch loved the certainty and he smiled. "Why seventy-three?" I gave him my plan, concluding with, "And if you closed Telerate and applied the money that they were pissing away to the Net, you could bring Dow Jones Interactive public a year from now and pay for the whole darned thing."

Okay, Murdoch said. "How do we make it happen?" He looked at Breindel, who looked at me. I pulled out the Dow Jones proxy, and circled the names of the people whom I thought if he contacted, he might be able to convince to take a $73 bid. I told him it was worthless to go through the lawyers involved in the family trust, because they didn't have a clue about what was ailing the *Journal* and were just high-paid rubber stampers. Individual letters should go to these board members conveying the bid right to them and telling them that you will preserve the paper as a sacred trust. "Especially the editorial page," Murdoch said, with a loud laugh and a nod to Breindel. Murdoch seemed concerned, however, that if he moved on the *Journal,* the company would turn to either the Washington Post Company or GE rather than have him take it over. "Jack Welch wants the *Journal* very badly, so we'd best move fast," Murdoch said. He then asked me a question about interest rates—I said they were going lower—and then, in a pixie fashion, he jumped up and ushered me out.

Three months later, the stock had dropped 10 percent, Breindel had taken sick—he would die of a liver ailment not long after—and I never heard from Murdoch again. So one day when 200,000 shares of Dow Jones came in for sale on the trading desk, and the broker on the trade told us that there was a big seller in the marketplace that could knock the stock down fast, I got interested. A few days and another 5 percent later, with the stock now in the mid-30s, I pounced and took down several hundred thousand shares.

The stock took a hit almost immediately, so I bought another 200,000.

It was and remains my style to buy more as a good stock goes down, and Dow Jones certainly qualified as that.

It dropped a point again almost immediately, and I bought more, to where it became my largest position.

Fortunately, the stock found a bottom when the seller, a large mutual fund, at last finished dumping the stock at $33. I doubled the size of my position for the firm, bringing us to a million shares. I had backed into a giant slug of Dow Jones, and now I had to do something about it. If Murdoch didn't see the potential, at least I could show the marketplace what could happen if Dow Jones were to stop spending recklessly on Telerate and instead focus on the Internet.

I called the investor relations department of Dow Jones to get a meeting with management to talk about the changes I favored. Instead, we were able to join an already scheduled analyst meeting. The meeting, in some nondescript board room at the Dow Jones headquarters, seemed routine. Until I opened my mouth and asked Peter Kann, the chief executive officer, whom I had met several times before when I worked for *SmartMoney,* why he didn't deep-six Telerate and save the shareholders' fortunes. Kann smiled, he laughed, and then he suggested that Dow Jones Markets, the new name for the beleaguered Telerate division, was doing just fine.

Wrong, I said. It was doing terribly, and I thought it vital for the company to close Dow Jones Markets, take a big charge, and move on—*or the company would be taken over by someone else who would do it.* Kann smiled again and said he would think about it. The totally unflappable Pulitzer journalist was also a totally unflappable chief executive officer who viewed my suggestion totally unflappably. In other words, he dismissed me with charm, as if I were just some noisy guy trying to make a few bucks in the stock. (Hmmm, I guess we all played our roles well.)

Knowing that I couldn't get to first base with Kann, I then tried to contact all of the members of the board, warning them about the huge losses that Dow Jones Markets was generating and how the losses were bringing the stock down to a price that made it attractive to others.

The caretaker lawyer in charge of the trust sent me a thank-you letter. I could have sworn it was a form letter. How many shares did I have to buy to get these guys' attention?

I bought another couple hundred thousand shares soon after the discouraging Kann meeting and the rejection letter from the lawyer in control of the trust, betting that I could make an impact at the upcoming annual meeting.

Annual meetings are pretty much a joke in this country, a painful show day that every major executive dreads as a total waste of time. The annual meetings are open to the smallest shareholders, and the smallest shareholders believe that owning stock is like voting in a democracy. Routinely, the same gadflys come to the meetings and ask silly questions that have no bearing whatsoever on business. All the chief executives rue these regulars and try to make jokes with them as they ask their inane questions, but there's no stopping this torture.

This time, though, the annual had a different mixture. Both my firm and Mutual Shares, the firm of Michael Price, a renowned value investor who had just helped force Chase to merge with Chemical Bank by carping publicly about how Chase wasn't doing enough to bring out value, had taken down huge chunks into this sickening swoon.

Both of us had been interviewed extensively by the media about our respective stakes—Price had, unknown to me, been buying alongside us and had taken down an even bigger stake than I. The media wanted to hear what we had to say about Dow Jones even if the board didn't. At first, in the crowded April meeting, we had to listen to the gripes of the nuisance shareholders, and then Price's people and I asked to be recognized. I made my pitch short. I said that Dow Jones Markets was a black hole that if it weren't shut down could cause the company to lose billions of dollars and its independence. I said if it did close Dow Jones Markets, the stock would vault into the 60s and we would all do well. The company had to act to preserve its crown jewel, the *Wall Street Journal*.

Kann looked at me, again unflappably, and said that he understood my view but that Dow Jones Markets was here to stay. He thanked me for my input. A few minutes later Price's representative said basically the same thing as I did, arguing that the company's earnings per share, the only gauge that matters to the Street, would improve dramatically without the ne'er-do-well division. More unflappability from the chief executive.

I left shaking my head that giant shareholders with stakes in the hundreds of millions of dollars could just be dismissed as being plain wrong about something that was so clearly terrible for the fortunes of the company.

Then again, I knew that shareholder democracy meant only that I should vote with my feet if I didn't like what management was doing. Fortunately, the press had made enough of a to-do of our stand that other institutions had been drawn into the stock and it had risen, dramatically, in the weeks after the annual meeting to the high 40s.

Unfortunately, management insisted on telling the analysts on Wall Street that neither Price nor I knew what the heck we were talking about.

Internally, Jeff Berkowitz, my partner at Cramer & Co., was pressuring me to lighten up the stake, given management's total intransigence. "Give it up, Jim, we've got the good gain," he would say. "We are hedge fund managers, not shareholder activists."

Not until I was absolutely sure that management wasn't about to listen to me, I said. If it did listen, and close the division, the gain we had so far would be chicken feed.

I agreed with Jeff, however, that we had to think of our partners at the fund first, but I wanted to check in with Dow Jones once more to see if our pleadings were making any headway behind the scenes. I called Kann, but got his functionary, Dick Tofel, a man who was in my class at Harvard and had edited the weekly *Independent.* He either had a grudge against me or just didn't like me, and he had been one of the people in the *SmartMoney* uproar who had done his best to obscure the fact that I had a contract that allowed me to write and trade.

Tofel told me no one at Dow Jones was taking my view seriously because Dow Jones Markets was an integral cog in the corporate engine, and that while my antics might have made good headlines, they weren't going to mean a thing internally. I told him that I would most likely dump my stock if there was no chance that Dow Jones Markets would be shut. I said I would hate to see the division closed and the stock skyrocket right after I sold the stock. He told me that wasn't going to happen.

Over the next few days we offered the stock, and repeatedly, large-quantity buyers took our offerings on the wire, meaning that the merchandise was snapped up without any resistance. The stock walked right up through the high 40s, even as we put out 100,000 shares a day.

We racked up a multimillion-dollar gain over the course of just a few months, but it gnawed at me for weeks on end that the stock took my sizable position without skipping a beat. That never happens unless something big and positive is going to occur and someone knows it ahead of time.

No wonder. In a couple of months, Dow Jones did exactly what I suggested, shutting down Dow Jones Markets and taking a huge charge.

While I made $5 million on the trade for the fund, if we hadn't been talked out of holding the stock by Tofel, we would have had a $30 million gain.

That made me angry, a lot angrier than whatever Dow Jones might have done to me during the *SmartMoney* incident. But given the way companies treat their shareholders, all I could do was marvel that these folks managed to get me out of the stock and do exactly what they needed to do to get the stock close to where I suggested Murdoch pay to buy the whole company.

CHAPTER 8

Desai

Not long after Desai took the editor in chief job at *TheStreet.com,* I found myself brainstorming with the man over a dinner at Annapurna, in the Indian section of Midtown Manhattan. He meticulously traced out our timeline and our recruiting strategies. He revealed a precise timetable that would have us up and running by November 1996.

We would build our business, he said, on four key blocks: Disney, because its unit ABC, which had recently started *ABC.com,* needed good business news that we could provide in return for their eventually hosting our site; Charles Schwab, which would be interested in buying subscriptions from us because of Ravi's extensive contacts with top people at that firm; Fidelity, the giant mutual fund company, which, he assured me, wanted to be a part of our operation in return for my writing for *Worth,* the financial magazine which at that point they owned; and America Online, which he intimated to me was incredibly interested in paying for a feed from a legitimate newsroom for its fast growing financial section. Each block would provide us with ready revenue and a chance to be profitable virtually overnight. Desai assured me that all of these enterprises wanted copy from a Net company that captured the excitement and the attitude of the stock market.

Disney, Schwab, Fidelity, AOL. Could it get any better? Could there be four more important elements to a new financial services business? I was dazzled by all he had accomplished in just a few short weeks. We were, as

I remember telling my wife when I got home from the thrilling dinner, well ahead of schedule even though we were spending a great deal of money. It was my first real insight into what *TheStreet.com* was up to now that it had moved to 2 Rector Street, and I was thrilled for the update, especially given that Marty and I had each spent about $500,000 before we launched.

Of course, the night had not been without tension. Ravi seemed so excited that he could barely speak without stuttering, something that had seemed to be a bit of a problem in our first meeting. It was clear to me now that he had a severe stutter. And when I tried to crack his exterior to find out more about this whiz I was dealing with, he cloaked all details of his personal life in secrecy. He promised, though, that when we were launched and were on our way, there would be plenty of time to discuss such pleasantries. What did Desai need me to do? Simple, he said, with a bit of a stutter. "Be ubiquitous."

And how, I asked, could I do that and run the hedge fund?

Simple, he said. Go on whatever television program you can, and mention that you are from Cramer & Co. and *TheStreet.com*.

For the next month Ravi solidified all that he promised. He set up key meetings with Schwab to demonstrate the prototype of the Web site. He coordinated discussions with a brand-new Web hosting company called Starwave, which was owned by Seattle billionaire Paul Allen in partnership with Disney. Starwave handled ESPN's Web site and was going to host *ABCNews.com*. We would become *ABCNews.com*'s business section, giving us some instant imprimatur. He struck a deal with Fidelity's *Worth* that he told me would bring Fidelity's mutual fund guru Peter Lynch as a regular contributor to *TheStreet.com* once we rolled off the cyberpresses. I just had to do a few pieces for them. We had held a couple of meetings with America Online to figure out how much they would pay us for our articles, and whether they wanted to "greenhouse" us as part of their venture capital work—which meant that they would stake us with capital and nurture our own business, which they would own a piece of.

While Desai was juggling all these difficult relationships he was also building a newsroom, centered around a fellow by the name of Dave Kansas, who wrote market commentary for the *Wall Street Journal*. Kansas, just a few years out of Columbia Journalism School, didn't seem too eager for the task, however, standing me up at his first job interview. He overslept, he explained later. When he managed to drag himself to the next meeting a half-hour late, I suspected he might not be the perfect man to hang the whole company on, but he might complement the 30,000-foot thinking of Desai.

All the while Drake functioned as publisher, getting our site hosted in the interim by a young upstart firm in New York named Reach that promised total reliability. He explained to me that we needed a host because we had learned that if many people go to the site at once it would crash unless we had sophisticated hosting capabilities with lots of expensive servers and computer connections to the phone lines. What we needed, he said, was money, and lots of it, to get our name around and "get the eyeballs"— people viewing our site, or "visiting" in the parlance of the Web. I remember the first night that Drake mentioned "the eyeballs" and I almost died laughing. Why eyeballs? I wanted to know. Didn't we want readers, *paid* readers, so we could make money? Drake assured me that while that was important, the game was an eyeball game and the only way to get them was through a massive, expensive direct mail campaign. I told him that I thought that Ravi Desai had the lowest cost and most effective way to get exposure, through grand strategic alliances with giants like ABC, Schwab, Fidelity, and AOL. I said that I could also help brand us much more efficiently by my TV appearances. No, he said, direct mail, hundreds of thousands of dollars in direct mail is what would make everyone hear about *TheStreet.com.* He said it was his call, he was the CEO, direct mail would be our method.

On November 16, 1996, we went "live" with Reach, our hosting company, producing about a half-dozen stories for our inaugural "issue." Reach assured us that we would be "up 24-7" but the most notable thing about our first week wasn't that we broke any stories—we didn't—but that we were often down more than we were up. That got me nervous. We had, in the span of five months, already spent roughly $1 million each on staffing and equipment and leases, and the spending had accelerated with the launch in sight. The only thing we had to show for it was a site that looked like a faded copy of the Declaration of Independence with a picture of me and, instead of photos of the other writers, pictures of typewriters—

not computers, typewriters. When you typed in the URL, you got "DNS," the Web term for a site that doesn't work. We were really DOA. Dead on arrival.

After a week of breakdown after breakdown, I stopped complaining to Drake, who seemed completely beleaguered by the setbacks and began calling the people at Reach to scream at them that the site wasn't up. I warned them that we could not do business that way and they assured me they would do everything they could.

Not long after we launched, Bill Griffeth, the incredibly gracious host of CNBC's *Power Lunch,* started a segment called "Cool Web Site of the Week" and he featured us. We gave Reach full warning and they told us they would be ready. Of course, the moment Griffeth flashed the URL on the screen, the site went down, instantly crashed by the numbers of those looking to see it. Ravi told me not to worry, that he would be going on television to demonstrate the site himself, and we could clear up any reliability problems.

After again notifying Reach of the coming good publicity, Ravi went on another business show on another network. As a password-protected site, it was vital that Ravi demonstrate how easy it was to get in and use the site. But when the TV studio red light went on, everything that could go wrong, went wrong. Ravi could barely speak about the site, he was just too excited and stuttered too badly. He tried to demonstrate the ease of use of the site. He quickly punched in his password, but got it wrong. Then he forgot it! So he failed to demonstrate how it worked, which was devastating, especially given that we were a paid site when everything else on the Web was free. Didn't matter much, though, because as soon as the site was shown on television, the viewers crashed it with traffic. This time it stayed down for most of the day.

Immediately, while Ravi was still on the tube, I set up a meeting with Desai and Drake and Reach, one of those meetings where I could not restrain myself and threatened to rain havoc on the whole operation and the people at Reach personally. When the meeting ended, steam must have been pouring out of my ears. I could tell that Drake was embarrassed to hear my profanity and my anger vented against these hapless providers. He wanted to know, when we got out on the street, why I had to be so, so, well, mean. Wasn't there some other way to get the point across, he said, besides being a tough guy? I looked at him like he was nuts. Here's some outfit that had virtually destroyed us during millions of dollars of potential publicity, and he was worried about *their* feelings? I explained to him that if *he* didn't start being tough, *he* wouldn't last much longer at the job. All this must have been some sort of a rude awakening for someone with such blessed credentials.

For several weeks, our site worked without incident. And without visitors. In those days we had maybe 100 folks looking at us an hour, mostly because I called people I knew and demanded that they look at us. In our first two weeks, I tried to get by writing three pieces a week. Rapidly, however, I could see that there was no "traction" coming from that level of submission. As the direct mail campaign beckoned, I switched to writing about the market as often as three times a day.

In the last week of November I asked Drake what we were doing to drum up some readers besides direct mail. He had no ideas. He had pinned all his hopes on a direct mail campaign that would allow us to trace users by giving them all the same temporary password. He said the direct mail piece would go out any day. However, as the days in December ticked by, it was clear that we would soon be competing with the holidays, a truly crummy time for such offerings. Finally, the week before Christmas our direct mail hit 500,000 homes across the country using lists specially culled by Drake. I also had my fourteen-year-old nephew, Cliff Mason, stuff a couple of hundred flyers into mailboxes in the Mt. Kisco area for good measure. We waited. And waited.

And waited. Each day I called Drake to get the results. Each day he said he was tabulating them. Each day I wanted numbers. Each day he said they weren't ready yet. Finally, at wit's end, at the beginning of January, I told Drake I was coming over personally, in my first visit to the office, to look at the responses to the costly direct mail campaign.

The result? Five people took us up on the direct mail. Five people! And of those five, four were from my nephew's mailbox stuffing. We had just paid $100,000 per subscriber. I turned to Drake and, without discussing the "findings" any further, I fired him. I turned to Ravi and said I would check with Marty, but from now on he was editor and CEO, because we were in big trouble and I needed someone I could trust.

Desai thanked me, told me he would never let me down, and proceeded to sketch out plans to fire our service provider, jump-start our circulation, and get our site around by having marquee names like Fidelity's Peter Lynch and the *New York Times*'s prestigious business writer Floyd Norris on our site.

What did he need from me to make this happen? I asked. He said he needed to hire a couple of terrific people whom I had recommended to Drake to hire but which Drake had not acted on, and he needed something that he felt awkward telling me about. He said he would e-mail me because he didn't want anyone to know about it.

That night I got home and on my screen was the plan for "Operation Rockbreak," a top secret plan to keep Marty Peretz away from the newsroom. Desai said that Marty was coming around regularly and distracting Desai. Marty took up valuable time and didn't help, he said. Desai wanted the okay to create immediate diversionary tactics to make it so he could do his job without the intense scrutiny of Marty.

My first reaction should have been to fire Desai too. Marty had a much better chance of keeping track of the venture than I did. We needed him as involved as possible. More important, he had been my friend for years. Here was a memo openly asking for a betrayal of my best friend on behalf of a virtual unknown, this Ravi Desai, so as to further my friend's and my company.

Feeling like this project was beginning to cost a fortune, and worried that I had to do far more than Marty to keep the thing afloat, chafing that Marty apparently didn't see that, I checked off on Ravi's nefarious project. I agreed to help him work without Marty's supervision. It was the single most cruel thing I have ever done to a friend and I know that I will regret it for the rest of my life. I did it thoughtlessly. My God, I still can't believe I sent that e-mail and conspired with someone I didn't know at all—I still hadn't spent more than a few hours with Ravi since he was hired—against my best man, someone who had given me my start in stock picking. I had sold out Marty to Ravi in order to get *TheStreet.com* off the ground, the ultimate in stupid, unnecessary, and mean compromises.

After four months we only had about a thousand subscriptions. That should have been a huge red flag for the investors. After all, our projections said that if we didn't have 25,000 subscribers paying $100 annually by year two we would never make it. But we continued to get just enough publicity to make us feel like staying in the game and we had already sunk so much money into the venture nobody wanted to pull the plug. Amazingly, given that I would never trust a businessman with those kinds of projections at the hedge fund, I continued to believe in Desai. He had been hiring some hungry folks from the *Journal* and some good recruits right out of college, and they were beginning to break some news on the site that I actually heard people talk about. I suspended judgment on the guy because he seemed to have so many contacts, so many things going on that could be home runs for us.

So, I followed through with my end of the bargain, vowing to be ubiquitous on television, beginning to appear on both *Good Morning America* in a two-minute-and-forty-seven-second market update a couple of times a week and as a regular on a bunch of business shows on CNBC, including *Squawk Box,* the electric morning show, and *Taking Stock* and *Bull Session.* I admit, however, to be willing to be on any show that would take me. The market had gotten exciting in 1996, as individuals began to embrace the Net and trade at the same time when traditional stock market players recognized that the Net wasn't going away. People needed someone exciting to talk about the market, a real live player, and I filled the bill. All I asked in return was that the Chyron, those printed identifiers under my name, say *www.TheStreet.com*

Ravi kept doing me one better, though. Every day he would e-mail me about a new triumph he had been having with Fidelity and Disney and Schwab. He told me how the big portfolio managers at Fidelity all read us, and that we were on Michael Eisner's radar screen at Disney as a possible acquisition once we demonstrated our staying power. Every time I would mention that I was interested in meeting with some of these folks, though, he would protest that it was still too early. Meanwhile, his contacts at Microsoft, he said, also were taking a keen interest in our fledgling site. I expressed some shock, given that I was friendly with Michael Kinsley, the editor of *Slate,* which was owned by Microsoft, and they didn't seem to have any desire at all to link with us. He told me not to worry, it would all gel the moment that a cover story about us in the works at *Red Herring* came out.

Red Herring? We were to be in *Red Herring,* at that time the single most influential publication for young start-up enterprises? Maybe this Ravi really was a miracle worker. Here we had poured a couple of million dollars into thin air, had no more than a couple of thousand readers, almost all of whom were comped or bought as gifts by me, and Desai had finagled a cover story in the magazine that was defining what was hot in the wired world.

Sure enough, a few days after I asked Desai for more details, a photo crew called and said they wanted me and Ravi to jump up and down on top of scaffolding in front of the New York Stock Exchange holding up red umbrellas.

The timing couldn't have been better. We were on the verge, Desai said, of signing monster deals with Schwab for massive distribution of our fund and news feeds as well as my column, as well as just a few weeks away from receiving Peter Lynch's and Floyd Norris's first articles. Even though our circulation was tiny, our buzz was deafening. For the first time it occurred to me that maybe, just maybe, my hobby could be bigger than my real job as a hedge fund manager. Had I made enough already? Could this *TheStreet.com* be something that just might challenge the establishment of journalism? We seemed to have an awful lot going in our favor.

It was hard to keep up with the whirlwind that was Ravi. About the only time he had to tell me about all of the exciting projects were those two hours it took to shoot the *Red Herring* cover. As anxious as ever about the details, I wanted to know what else I could do, who else I could call. Did Eisner want to speak to me? How about Paul Allen? Is that Starwave deal to host us coming along? Did Schwab want to spend any time with me or the staff? Should we be visiting Fidelity?

Desai told me that I was worrying too much, that ever since Drake was fired things had been going so well that he just needed me to keep appearing on television and keep writing as much as possible.

He did, however, warn me that there were a couple of disgruntled employees, real flakes he had to crack down on, and that some of them would probably come to me and complain. I should ignore them, he said, as they were standing in the way of our greatness. He also thanked me profusely for helping him keep Marty busy, as Marty no longer bothered to drop in anymore at *TheStreet.com* office at 2 Rector Street, allowing Desai more time to think and work.

At the end of February 1997, as predicted, a couple of employees quit without any sort of explanation, including someone we had considered for the chief operating officer job. She had worked there for less than two weeks. Another employee, an ad salesperson, also vanished without much of a trace. My wife, who knew the candidate, urged me to find out what was going on. I said not to worry, Ravi had everything under control. She remembered that when *TheStreet.com* first moved to 2 Rector, they would occasionally invite me for tutorials for the young staff. She said I should try to set up one of those again, perhaps just to be sure that something wasn't awry. I mentioned it the next day to Desai, but he said the staff was just too busy. When I called his assistant to ask if I could drop in, I was told that I couldn't come over unless the compliance officer checked off on it, and that she wouldn't because they were working on big stories that could impact the market and they were afraid that I would see them. No contact with editorial, she said. Desai had insisted that all e-mail be cc'd him to keep track of what people said, and editors and reporters informed me, off the record, that they were no longer allowed to communicate with me. I knew editorial never wanted me involved, as the compliance officer seemed to regard me as Darth Vader. But Desai had clamped down on the business side too. Gone were even the meetings at the Regency to explain where our $250,000-a-month checks were going.

Then, at about the same time, one of the employees, a woman I had helped hire from my contacts at *SmartMoney,* threatened to sue me for stock in the company when she wanted to quit, claiming that I had been negligent in overseeing what was going on. I grew nervous. I told Desai that he had to spend some time with me. He got angry and when he got angry his stutter made conversation unbearable. He made it clear that the only thing that was standing in the way of our greatness was my meddling and worrying about disgruntled people in the organization.

Karen suggested that we try to find out, in a nice way, what was really going on. She had no operational role at all, other than to see the checks going out the door from our joint bank account. She was amazed at how much trust I put in Desai. I told her he made you a believer, he was just that smart, that clever, and that good at what he did. I suggested that I invite Ravi and his girlfriend, whom he had told me in a recent e-mail that he was thinking of marrying, to our house in Summit for dinner. Karen loved the idea and Ravi accepted. But when the day came for him and his fiancée to come out, he suddenly canceled, saying he wasn't feeling well.

Karen persisted and invited them again. He canceled again, same excuse. She persisted a third weekend, and this time Ravi came sans fiancée, who, Ravi said, was under the weather. At the dinner, every time we tried to talk business Ravi would turn the conversation to my wife's nascent art gallery in SoHo, something she had decided to take up after Cece started school. Ravi had a terrific command of the arts, as always. He refused to talk specifics about what was going on, not willing to give away any surprises, other than that everything would come together in March, including a couple of potential surprise investors who wanted a stake in *TheStreet.com.*

When I tried one last time, he said there was something that was more important that he had to get off his chest. That I had become like a father to him, that I had recognized how intelligent he was and how caring he was and he wanted to know if I would be his best man when he got married in May. He said it would mean a lot and that he would only ask someone he had tremendous respect for. I was stunned and flattered. Sure, I said, delighted.

I came away from the dinner excited as all get-out, but Karen was extremely skeptical. She had become increasingly confused and angered by *TheStreet.com,* which she said was taking up a huge amount of my time, my energy, and my interest, without any tangible results. She urged me to press Ravi to have some deal, any deal, of the dozens he claimed to be working on, closed within the next ten days. I told her that Ravi was probably just under a lot of pressure because he was about to get married and that the best man offer warmed me toward him even more. She said that he didn't even bring his fiancée, that she doubted he was even going to get married, and that I better be sure he came up with some deal that we all could see, because as far as she could tell the guy was just another Harvard-trained buffoon.

The next day I thanked Ravi again for the best man offer but added that

Karen wanted to see something positive that made us believe we were about to break out. Given that she and I had kicked in more than a million and a half dollars at that time, with commitments to write $500,000 more in checks come the beginning of the second quarter, I said I thought she had a point.

He told me that he was working on something big and immediate, that he had a deal to put *TheStreet.com,* fax version, in every Ritz-Carlton hotel room in the country. It would top the *New York Times* fax as a way to get business news and, he said, the hotel chain was willing to pay us substantially. He just needed to spend a couple of days in Boston to close the deal. And while he was in Boston he would also solidify the Fidelity distribution deal. Furthermore, his contacts at Scudder Stevens, a large mutual fund distribution company, were eager to promote us to all of their fundholders in order to make them better informed about the markets. He would get that deal done too.

Busy man, lots of opportunities. Don't let me keep you, I urged. "Good hunting."

The next day, Jeannie Cullen, my assistant, told me that with Ravi out of town, two people from *TheStreet.com,* Dave Kansas, the fellow we had hired from the *Journal,* and Brendan Amyot, a young circulation exec we had picked up from *Vibe,* a music publication owned by Time Warner, wanted to come over and talk to me.

No one from *TheStreet.com* had ever talked to me. I asked what it was about, and she said they couldn't tell me. Shortly after the close of the market, two ashen-faced twenty-somethings came into my trading room. I whisked them into my forbidding office, the one I never used unless I had to fire somebody, and I closed the door.

It would be difficult to talk, they both said. Brendan mentioned that he needed my vow of secrecy. Dave explained that what he was doing could cost him his job.

Go on, I said, not used to waiting to hear obviously bad news.

Desai, Dave said, hadn't been doing any work at all for *TheStreet.com.* He would arrive in the morning, pull the shades down in his office, stay for about an hour, and then vanish, to who knows where, saying he wasn't feeling well. Brendan said that he never saw Desai either, even though he reported directly to the man. Brendan said when he went into Desai's office the day before, all he saw were a bunch of empty Stolichnaya vodka bottles.

I looked at them with total contempt. Ravi, I said, had warned me that some of you would come over here when he wasn't around and say negative things about him, and here you are, bad-mouthing the key to the project behind his back.

No, Dave said. The staff all knew the truth. Whenever he left, they would send out reporters to watch where he went. It was always the bar across the street, McAnn's, and he would stay there until long after the workday was done.

Nonsense, I said, the man was doing deals, big deals. I told them that he had taken some incredibly productive trips out West to cement our Silicon Valley contacts and our deal to let Starwave host us.

None of these trips had happened, they said. They were drinking binges, needed, perhaps, because he could only speak without a stutter when he was drunk. Brendan insisted that the only reason we were going to get Starwave was because he personally had been going out to see Starwave to get it done. Desai, he said, had nothing substantive to do with that deal.

But, I said, right now, as they were bad-mouthing him, he was signing a big deal with Ritz-Carlton for us to deliver a fax product. Brendan laughed. There is no fax product, there is no deal. And the Fidelity deal? There were no meetings at Fidelity. Peter Lynch wasn't about to write for us. He didn't even know who we were. *Worth* just wanted to get me to write for them.

But then there was Schwab, I said. Ravi had terrific, high-up contacts at Schwab. They were about to embrace us, big-time, I said. Well, Brendan said, they had commissioned a study with active traders and many of them said they wouldn't use us even if we were free. Only 8 percent of the active traders said they would use us if they had to pay. Ravi's best friends with the chief strategist, I said, halfheartedly, knowing now that even that might not have been true. "They don't care for us at Schwab," Brendan said.

I told them that I had heard enough, and that they could go. "How about the company?" Brendan wanted to know.

"What company?" I said. "What company?" I asked again rhetorically as I showed them the office door.

I went home that night and told Karen. She said it all made sense now, the bouts with illness, the desire to conceal, the inability to tell the truth, the deceptively grand stories. Ravi was an alcoholic and he had to be fired immediately.

I told her that I had to check some things out first, that it couldn't be that simple. One by one, I called the people I knew at *TheStreet.com* and asked them point-blank whether Ravi was drinking on the job. All said yes. They all knew his brand. Everyone commented about the discarded vodka bottles in the office and how he had simply stopped doing any work months ago.

Calling up to the Ritz-Carlton in Boston, I asked to speak to the man in charge, telling him that I had to find out for an important reference about someone we were thinking of hiring. When I got through I asked whether the manager had heard of Ravi Desai or *TheStreet.com*. He wanted to know if this was a solicitation because he had never heard of either. When I explained the situation to him to make sure that I was speaking with the right person, he said that any such product would have to go through him and no one named Desai had been by to see him or anyone in his organization.

I then called Schwab and asked to speak to the man who was in charge of *TheStreet.com*'s trial, a man who Ravi had sworn loved us much more than the *Wall Street Journal*. He faxed me the results of the study of active traders, which indeed were extremely negative, and he could only say that he was sorry that we wasted so much of each other's time. He said he had been trying to track down Ravi to give him the bad news for weeks but couldn't find him.

I couldn't either. A day went by with my assistant calling and e-mailing him virtually every hour, leaving messages that he had to come in to see me.

Finally, twenty-four hours later, he popped into my office. I confronted him immediately. He stammered that it was a pack of lies, that everyone knew he had a bad stutter and that occasionally he had a drink or two to make the stutter less pronounced, but that he had been working hard, very hard to make everything work out.

Now, he said, he had to get on a plane to go out to Starwave to sign a deal that would make Starwave our partner, eliminate our spotty technology, and get things rolling to take us to the next level. I told him that I didn't know what to do but that perhaps someone else from the company should go. He said that he had kept everyone else in the company in the dark about it because they were all such incompetents.

What could we do? I told him to go, but that when he came back we would have to talk about changing some things, getting some help for him and sending him for some treatment. All he needed, he said, was a vacation, and some money. He had gone through all the money we had paid him but if he could borrow $100,000 he would be sure to complete the negotiations with Starwave, then take a vacation and get treatment, see a psychiatrist about his heavy drinking (which he finally acknowledged) and perhaps even check into a rehab clinic. Otherwise, he said, if he didn't go, he would have to quit, and couldn't be responsible for anything that happened. Desai made it clear that without the $100,000 loan he might have to call Starwave and tell them that the deal was off. Brendan had just told me that *he* was the moving force behind the Starwave talks, but what if Ravi was just under a lot of pressure? He hadn't taken a minute of vacation, I thought, and he could really screw things up if he wanted to. He was still the CEO and the editor in chief. I saw no choice but to give him the loan. I was, in effect, being blackmailed until I could remove him as CEO and replace him. Having been shut out of the company for so long I didn't even know which deals were real and which were fake. I gave him the hundred thousand. Ravi did confirm that there were problems with Schwab and Fidelity and Scudder, but that they could be worked out after his vacation.

Three days of negotiations later he reported that he had signed the Starwave deal and that he was now going on vacation. I had insisted that he take Brendan with him on the Starwave trip because, given Ravi's state, it was doubtful he could stay with us in his current capacity. Brendan confirmed independently that we had a letter of understanding with Starwave pending some due diligence that he thought we would have no problem with.

In the next week, Ravi flew to Jumby Bay on Antigua for a week—I

know he did it because I called him there—and I lined up a local alco-
holics program for him. I also began the task of taking back control of the
business side of the venture. I was going to have to become a more active
co-chairman if I was going to sort through where we really were. I brought
Marty in on the negative turn of events, and he too took an active hand in
trying to find Ravi counseling and developing a transition to another executive staff. In the meantime we brought legal counsel in to see what we
could and couldn't do about Desai in case he decided he would not coop-
erate with us. As soon as Ravi came back I told him that he had to get help.
He said he would but that I better lay off him because he could do quite a
bit of damage to me if I pressed him. He said he could still scuttle the Starwave deal and he could make a lot of trouble for me personally because he
had plenty of dirt on me.

The whole time the guy had played me for a total patsy I had eaten it up,
but the moment he threatened me personally, everything that had been
conciliatory changed immediately. I told him that he wouldn't be the first
person to threaten me and he wouldn't be the last, but that I would see to it
that he was fired for misconduct.

That night he called me at home. He never called me at home. He said
he wanted a reconciliation with me, that he had acted rashly, that the wedding plans were proceeding apace, and that it would really hurt his fiancée's feelings if I didn't serve as his best man. But if I didn't and if I
tried to remove him, he would do something that would ignite World War
III in my life.

I told him he had nothing. He asked me if I remembered the memos sent
under the name "Operation Rockbreak." He said that he had printed out all
of the correspondence between us conspiring against Marty. It was damning. He said he had made up a FedEx envelope to Marty's home address
and if I didn't want to play ball I could consider it sent. He told me that it
was probably worth it for me to make up with him, but that the
cost for such a makeup and the destruction of the Operation Rockbreak
e-mails would be somewhere in the mid-six figures, perhaps something
like $600,000.

I told him that my friendship with Marty was stronger than that, that he
was out of his mind, and that I would never bend to such blackmail. He
said I had better rethink that because the documents made great reading.

He also said that he would call Starwave and tell them that my hedge fund had gone bust in the last few weeks and I had no more money and that I had also taken down Peretz. He said he would tell them that they would be reading in the papers how neither my company nor *TheStreet.com* could make payroll.

I hung up on him. I called Marty and told him about the conversation. I then said that he should expect to get a Fedex'd series of e-mails that were written during the heat of the battle and that they would read poorly. Marty was confused. Read poorly about what? I stumbled. This wasn't going well. I had known Marty for almost twenty years; he had been my best man. I didn't remember, I said, what was in the e-mails, but Ravi had asked me to help him make it so that he, Marty, would be too busy with other *TheStreet.com* projects to check on Ravi.

Silence.

I thought, for a second, Hey, how bad could the memos be. I told Marty that I was embarrassed and I apologized, that I should never have done such a thing. I said it in my kitchen, in front of my wife, who was aghast.

Marty wanted me to explain more but I said that it was imperative that I reach Brendan and find out the names of the key Starwave people Ravi might be calling to say that I had gone bust. And I rang off.

Two hours later I got through to a couple of the Starwave people. Ravi *had* called them. They no longer were interested in working with us and the deal would have to be renegotiated or scuttled.

What could I do? I asked. The next day I would send them sworn statements from my accountants as well as my performance letters, tax returns, and bank accounts. But the damage was done. They kept the deal in place, but the trust had been broken.

Defeated, I went upstairs to talk over the unwinding of the project with my wife. As she lay in bed, reading, I came in, sweat pouring from my brow in the middle of winter, face flushed with embarrassment. I told her all. And I said it was time to throw in the towel on *TheStreet.com*.

"Nonsense," she said.

I told her she had been right about everything, that it had become a rogue operation, and that there was no way to fix it, that I could never have control over it. She didn't disagree. But what she said made sense to me: "If you close it now, you let Ravi win and I would think that you would spend the rest of your life regretting it. Now stop moping around about it and figure out how you can make more money in the stock market to bail the thing out."

She was right. I opened my personal computer and typed out one last e-mail to Ravi Desai saying that he had done a lot in the last twenty-four hours to destroy my reputation and the firm he had helped create but that I would not be deterred. I vowed that I would finish the project and see it succeed if only because it would be the ultimate revenge against his slander and blackmail. The next day the *Red Herring*'s "Hits" issue came out, with Ravi and me looking like we were descending on Wall Street from the heavens above. I had some explaining to do.

Ravi would disappear for a few years and then turn up at the University of Washington, where he donated a chair in poetry. When he later failed to pay for that donation, his checkered history, including what turned out to be bigamy, surfaced in a lengthy article in *Time* magazine and he no longer could fool employers again. At least so far.

CHAPTER 9

The Man with Two Careers

When you think of branding on the Internet, you think about all of those multimillion-dollar deals where a dotcom pays America Online or NBC or Disney or some newspaper or magazine a wad of stock in return for some high-profile ads. That was the essence of Net capitalism from November of 1999 to March of 2000, the formula for what was supposed to be instant success as the old-line firms rallied to the new companies and the new companies offered ownership stakes in return.

We saw so many of these deals in such a short time that we tended to forget that there was a time when you could stealth promote, when you could get people to go to your Web site without giving away any equity, seats on the board, or cash after you came public.

You could brand by simply being everywhere and insisting that, within a few inches of your name, your URL appeared. For me, getting *TheStreet.com* mentioned, written about, or heard of became the all-encompassing strategy now that I realized that almost all of our potential partnerships, the ones I had banked on with Desai, had come up snake-eyes.

We know there are people who seem to be everywhere at times on the news, usually because their knowledge or insight allows them to be deemed an expert for a particular issue.

In 1997, the second year of a remarkable run in technology stocks that had caught America's fancy, I became that media expert for hire. I had run my firm for ten years by then, compiling a 22 percent return—7 percent better than the S&P 500, the benchmark we all try to beat. That performance gave me legitimacy. I ran a hedge fund, which was this super-secret entity that meant something swashbuckling, something dangerous, a pro, trying from a standing start to beat the market every day, and succeeding. That plus my solid numbers gave me cachet. I was funny and passionate about stocks, and I believed that the market should be the national pastime. I loved to talk about the market, and everyone wanted to listen, especially if I mentioned stocks that everybody liked.

Right at that time, courtesy of Amazon, people began to perceive that the hottest stocks were those connected with the Web. Whenever I got the chance to talk about it, I said that the best use of the Net was to trade online and that if you wanted honest information and opinions about stocks on the Web you had to turn to *TheStreet.com.* We had caught the wave. It was a simple formula, one that the media got. The public could find out more about stocks online than it could ever find out before. The stocks that were beginning to do the best in the market involved the Net. If you had Jim Cramer on your show, this wild excitable guy with Bozo-like tufts of brown curly hair who had a big mouth and lots of passion talking authoritatively about how you could make money by getting on the Net, you were capturing the moment as best you could.

For me, it was a grueling routine. I would set the alarm for 3:45, jump out of bed, shave and shower and be online at 4:15, reading the news. I would then file a piece about what I would expect to happen in the morning's markets. Then I was in the car, with the driver, Kyle, by five to beat the Holland Tunnel traffic, beating out another piece, an instructional one about stocks or options, while on the way to the city. I made sure I was at my trading turret at 100 Wall Street by 5:30, where I would trade American stocks overseas, and trade the stocks of Finland, Sweden, Germany, and at times, Russia and Turkey. Then, I would hop back in the car to take the trip uptown to *Good Morning America,* where they had begun using me as a special commentator on the stock markets. After a brief chat about the markets with either Charlie Gibson or hostess Lisa McRee, I would take the trip downtown in Kyle's 1995 stretch Cadillac, furiously typing another diary entry for *TheStreet.com.* By 8:30 I would be back in the office, ready to meet with Jeff Berkowitz to strategize about the day, and by

9:15 I would have that strategy, complete with suggested stock sectors—not stocks at that point because we hadn't bought anything—in my morning column.

At 9:30, the opening bell, I would intone "There goes Swifty," from the days when I bet the dogs at Wonderland in Boston. The announcer began every race with "There goes Swifty," the fast-moving mechanical rabbit that the dogs chased, and I liked the analogy so much I couldn't start the trading day without saying it. As traders are extremely superstitious, I had come to believe that if I didn't say "There goes Swifty," I would lose money that day, as if the key to the day's performance lay in the ritual itself. (For me I wish it were just "There goes Swifty." I also began to believe that if I went in the middle revolving door, I would produce bigger trading profits than through the left or right doors. And when I had a fantastic day, making more than $5 million in one session, I attributed the gain in part to a brand-new green Gap polo shirt. Henceforth, anytime I had a streak of bad luck, I brought out the green shirt to break the skein, wearing it repeatedly until the magic came back no matter how bedraggled and spotted it became. Fortunately my wife, never a superstitious trader but well aware of the power of both superstition and hygiene, kept it washed and fresh for me, until the day I retired, when it promptly disappeared and hasn't surfaced again.)

Throughout the day I would trade and write about what I saw, filing with increasing frequency depending upon the excitement of the session. Throughout the day, Jeannie Cullen, my assistant, would screen my calls, deciding which reporters to put through depending upon whether they were rude or kind. I gave sound bite after sound bite in return for the URL's mention, and by the close she would have booked me on another show to discuss the market's action that evening. If I could get on Charlie Rose, I took it, to the point where anytime the markets were up or down big I could anticipate her saying that Charlie wanted to see me. If Charlie didn't call, I would find my way once or twice a week on *Bull Session,* the CNBC evening show hosted by David Faber that recapped that day's events. If CNBC didn't want me, Jeannie would get me on CNN or PBS, or, if all else failed, Canadian Broadcasting or some non–English-speaking European network, where my gestures would suffice as a metaphor for that day's action.

I would use the incessant traffic jams that my driver couldn't avoid to pen pieces for *Time, GQ,* or *Worth,* as I had contracts with all three going at once. For *Time* I would do a simple synopsis of the action, with a couple of stock picks. *GQ* was for explanation, in sports metaphor, of the overall craziness of the market at the time, elucidating why Coke and Pepsi, which both traded in the 40s, were not equal because the "points," or the multiple, favored Coke. I saved my praise or anger at injustice for *Worth.* The latter, which was then owned by Fidelity, proved, however, to be a strained affair, because the first piece that *Worth* asked me to write was a critique of the poorly performing funds at Fidelity. Meant to be a cover story, the billing changed to a simple cover line, "Fixing Fidelity," when the powers at Fidelity went ballistic that in their own magazine I criticized the organization.

In it I depicted how some wayward Fidelity manager had blown up my mother-in-law's retirement nest egg with Latin American bonds. I recommended that Fidelity hire some of my old and now retired bosses at Goldman Sachs, including Bill Gruver, the exacting soldier who ran the training department, as a way to clean up the managerial stables.

"If there was a more dumb thing you could do than that, I don't know what it would be," Karen said when the article came out. "You've embarrassed yourself, me, Grandma, and Fidelity, right in their own magazine," she lectured. When I told her that this was the stuff nobody else would say anywhere, she said that the piece was the crudest mixture of "integrity and stupidity" she had ever seen about the financial world. Not my smartest move, in retrospect.

On days when I wasn't on *Good Morning America* I would appear on CNBC's *Squawk Box,* the freewheeling show hosted by Mark Haines, which then appeared from 8:00 until 10:00 (it has since expanded an hour). I became part of the stable of money manager co-hosts that would give opinions and ask questions of chief executive officers and analysts. I had gotten to CNBC through Maria Bartiromo, the downtown correspondent who was always looking for a money manager to get on camera to grill about the market, and had worked my way into the lineup not long after Maria profiled *TheStreet.com* for CNBC as an up-and-coming site to get information.

On the mornings I wasn't on *Squawk* or *GMA,* I demanded that the senior team of *TheStreet.com* come across town to my office to review the week's expenditures, as my regular $250,000 check per month seemed barely to keep up with the company's spending habits. We were now spending money that my wife had earned as a trader, so she demanded the meetings, just to have some accountability for the process after Ravi's departure.

She insisted on the meetings because shortly after Ravi left, we had paid a surprise visit to *TheStreet.com.* It was a surprise, because we hadn't asked for permission to come over, something that editorial always insisted on. Karen, who had no formal or informal role with *TheStreet .com* and didn't want one, thought these visitation rules were just plain absurd. "They either trust you or they don't and with all you have been through already for this ridiculous thing, they better start trusting you," she said as we walked over to 2 Rector Street. I hadn't seen the place lately either. Her jaw dropped when she entered for her first and only trip to the venture. As someone who had negotiated the real estate for our hedge fund, and had never bought a single piece of new furniture, as someone who insisted that we not even bother painting our names on the door for fear of the expense, she was shocked to see the luxury of the place.

"These desks are pure walnut, how much did they cost?" she demanded of the fumbling business manager, who came out to meet us in the lobby before I could even introduce her to the man. He was dumbstruck as she insisted on inspecting every piece of furniture, reporting to me that each large piece probably cost $50,000.

"Nah," I said, "that's way too high." But the business manager winced and nodded, saying that Karen was right, that Desai had spent mightily on these accoutrements and that $50,000 per desk was in the ballpark. Enraged, she took off down the elevator, not even bothering to look at the newsroom. For me it was a relief, because while the business folk were naive and honest, the newsroom people would have had a fit if we had come in unannounced. At times it would seem that the newsroom's most important mission was to hide its operation from me, something that Desai started but that was religiously continued by his replacements.

And on the afternoons when I wasn't on television explaining the market, I was shooting commercials for *TheStreet.com* or appearing in advertisements or photo shoots involving the stock market. Those days the tape was so hot, pretty much everything could revolve around the stock market, including shoes, as Rockport asked me to be part of its campaign for untraditional users of its new line of business shoes. One day, on the way to *Good Morning America,* I looked up at the shoe store across the street and saw a six-foot picture of me wearing the shoes, with *TheStreet.com*'s name mentioned right next to my feet. "I'm comfortable being wrong sometimes," said the ad line an inch above my waist, a mocking reference to my column, titled "Wrong," and to my willingness to admit, in print or live, when I had blown a market call. It was killer publicity for the site and the ad appeared in all of the national magazines. A year later I probably would have had to give Rockport 10 percent of my company to get that kind of branding. At that stage, though, they were donating money to charity as payment to get me to pose.

Sometimes I could astound myself with how callous and calculating I became in the pursuit of *TheStreet.com*'s success and how oblivious I was to everything else. Just days before Ravi Desai was imploding, on March 20, 1997, I had to shoot a commercial. It was a simple knock-off of the old John Houseman advertisement for Smith Barney, where I would begin as if I were going to talk about stocks the old-fashioned way, and then I changed, rapidly, into a dotcom guy, reading a few of the more outrageous lines from one of my pieces. It was a pretty typical day for the period, a run over to *Squawk,* and then back to the office and then to the Spy Bar downtown to film the commercial. At 2:00 P.M. I needed to be in three places at once, so I juggled my Motorola and a Qualcomm, one programmed for Cramer and the other for *TheStreet.com,* while I dashed off a piece on my laptop as a woman put makeup on my face and a man wrapped a tie around my neck.

My office cell phone rings as I am about to get ready to shoot the thirty-second spot. It's Jeff. He says call your wife at home, there's a problem. I call, and sure enough, our younger daughter, Emma, two years old at the time, is sick and has to be rushed to the local hospital. Dehydration, Karen says as she bundles up little Emma. Hey, I'd love to help out, I tell her, but

I have thirty people waiting on me at the Spy Bar, none of whom can do a thing without me, and two companies begging for me to help them deal with a bunch of assorted crises. She says, okay, do what you have to do, and I hang up.

One of the makeup people sees that I am troubled and asks, "What's the matter?" I had been pretty jovial up until the call. "Oh nothing, just something about my daughter being rushed to the hospital." The makeup people said nothing. And then it hit me. What was I doing? How far gone was I that I didn't even realize that our daughter was so sick that she had to go to the hospital? There would always be another promotional opportunity, but family stuff is strictly onetime only. I picked up my Motorola and punched in my home number. My wife grabbed the line and I said, "Oh man, what a piece of shit I've become. I'm stopping this shoot right now, no matter how much it costs, jumping in the car, and I will be there immediately." Twenty minutes later I walked into Overlook Hospital in Summit and I could hear my daughter crying for her daddy all the way down the hall.

I galloped to the room and when she saw me she said, "Daddy, these people put this thing in my arm and Daddy, why didn't you stop them?"

I explained to her that it was an IV and she needed the energy from it.

But, Daddy, she said, "Why didn't you get here sooner?"

I took a deep breath and said, "You know, I got here as soon as I could." For a moment I didn't feel like the totally driven reckless win-at-all-costs jerk that I had become. I hadn't lied. I did get there as fast as I could.

She got better the next day—it was a case of *E. coli* poisoning—and was released from the hospital. I ate the hundred-thousand-dollar loss for the missed shoot, one of the few times I actually felt good about spending money on the darned project.

The ad campaign was a critical success, mentioned positively in the *New York Times,* but I couldn't tell you that subscriptions were going gangbusters. We were signing up a hundred people a day on a trial basis for the service, and converting about 5 percent of them to paid subscribers, hardly a business, but not something worth giving up on. By that time we had finally completed negotiating a deal with Starwave—the Ravi incident behind us—to host our site in return for 4 percent of the company, but no sooner had we finished doing this deal than Disney purchased Starwave and wanted to know what the heck they were doing with us as a client, as they planned to make Starwave their in-house generator of Web sites. Fortunately, the stock market remained so hot that ABC needed our feed for its site, so, for the moment, the relationship had just enough synergy for Disney not to pull the plug.

After a grueling summer of appearance after appearance after appearance and article after article after article, we still had very little to show for our efforts. Our pace of sign-ups remained consistent, but our spending continued to exceed any semblance of our revenue. The toll of the round-the-clock appearances, while not damaging our fund's performances, was causing immense strain at home, as I rarely got back to Summit before eight at night.

I knew things were getting out of hand when the kids next door told me that they were seeing more of me than my own kids were, because by that fall Karen no longer bothered to change the stations to watch me.

All through the summer and late fall of 1997, the market continued relentlessly higher, and the media kept calling for me to explain the levitation act. Increasingly, though, at the office, I found the constant rallying, particularly of technology, unnerving. I compared it in my writings to the griddle at the Holland Tunnel Diner, where Karen and I liked to stop off to get egg sandwiches on the way to the 'burbs after a tough night in the city. The diner, the 3-In-One oil of greasy spoons, featured without a doubt the hottest range in the universe, one that could fry up an egg perfectly in less than twenty seconds—but would burn it to a crisp ten seconds later. At the very moment that the market, particularly tech stocks, was exploding upward, Asia, the principal demand center for so much of the technology, was cratering. Markets in faraway countries that didn't matter much to most American stock players, Taiwan, Thailand, Malaysia, Korea, and, of course, Japan, were crashing nightly. As someone who took the nightly Asian call from brokers before he went to sleep and then the recap before the traders left for home in Asia when I got to work, I found the confluence of our optimism and their catastrophic declines too difficult to reconcile.

Each day in September and October, Jeff and I pulled more money out of the market. Each day in my writings I would describe the griddle as getting so hot that it would fry up various inorganic objects. I would come on television and warn people that our market couldn't escape the Asian tsunami and that they should be selling into it, with the recognition that one day we would wake up and our markets would be crushed by the tidal wave. In September, I couldn't have looked more foolish, but I could only report exactly what I was doing, which was selling the heck out of Intel and Cisco and Microsoft and EMC and IBM and many other of my favorite tech names. Each day I would portray the incessant rallies as more and more dangerous, and by the middle of October, we owned next to nothing, having locked in an okay year, with a 24 percent return. (I could never advertise my returns because the government forbids hedge funds from garnering publicity lest they attract unsuspecting unsophisticated investors with their hype. By this point, I had closed my fund to new accounts, lest the government deem me a walking prospectus for Cramer & Co.!) My jeremiad rap was growing thin on just about everybody, when one day, October 27, 1997, the market did what it should have done for months, as the Asian turmoil spread: it crashed. In one nightmarish session the market cratered 500 points, only the second time it had ever given up so many points in a session, the first being ten years before. Of course, this time the market fell from a much higher level, some 5,000 points higher, but the devastation was palpable, particularly for so many of the new people who had just gotten into the market and were doing it themselves.

As we were almost entirely in cash, I had time to give a blow-by-blow account of the destruction of the market virtually in real time for *TheStreet.com*. When Barton Biggs, the immensely cantankerous and often wrong senior statesman from Morgan Stanley, came on CNBC with the Dow down 250 points warning that this was just the beginning of a much bigger crash, I immediately compared him online to someone throwing lighter fluid on a raging fire. Within an hour the market had ratcheted down another 250 points as the Biggs-led stampede jammed the small exits with the cry of fire that to me felt like arson.

As each century mark was taken out, I wrote that the griddle was getting cooler and cooler and that soon would come an exquisite moment where the Asian morass was now "priced in" to equities, and it was safe to get back in. At 3:30, with the market down 508 points, the same amount it had declined in 1987, I wrote that it was time to start buying. I said that in 1987, I had failed to act when it was down 508, and that I wasn't going to be so stupid this time. While Asia was a problem, it wasn't something we couldn't surmount because Europe and the United States remained strong and the Internet's emergence would stop any tech decline in its tracks. I grew increasingly optimistic as the market failed to stabilize in the last half hour, invoking the words of my wife, the Trading Goddess, that you "had to buy stocks when you can, not when you had to."

We had so much cash on the sidelines, more than $300 million, that it wasn't easy to buy all that we needed. Not to worry, I informed our desk, shouting out buy orders while I typed pieces, "Tomorrow will be even worse and we can get even better prices at the opening."

As the phone rang off the hook from media outlets, I told Jeannie to put no one through. If they wanted me, they had to quote the site, *www.the street.com.* If they wanted to know what I was doing, and I wasn't going to tell them, they had to read the site.

CNBC, CNN, and CBS wanted me for the next morning, but I was contractually bound to appear on ABC first. The network producers at ABC talked to me about coming in to film me in action, but superstition forbade such a foray. A few months before, *Frontline* had come in to do a special about the market, and under the glare of about 8,000 megawatts of lights, I had panicked and unloaded about $70 million in stock into a selling maelstrom only to have to buy that stock back and another $30 million more at much higher prices. The camera had caught me dumping 200,000 Dayton Hudson at $27 and then sheepishly buying it back at $31 about an hour later. That ignominious trade and a give-up of 500,000 American Stores at what amounted to fire-sale prices only to see it get a takeover bid literally the next week for 9 points more than I had sold it for, put the permanent kibosh on cameras filming me live. Of course, the producers had no idea why I wouldn't let them in, but Berkowitz said that he was out of there if *GMA* filmed the opening.

Just as well, overnight the markets continued to fall apart, with lower prices for virtually every bourse. I had to start buying literally from the moment I got out of bed and had no time for the endless setups of the camera, where they would ask you to repeat buys of Merck and Boeing simply because they weren't audible. You can't commit hundreds of millions of dollars twice just to please a sound guy.

The next morning, Charlie Gibson decided to move the whole *GMA* show to the steps of Federal Hall, the classical-style eighteenth-century relic catty-corner to the Exchange. Easy for me, I was just down the block. He had to nose out a bunch of foreign crews who had tried to set up there, and I found myself tripping over them on the way from my office three streets below the makeshift set. That morning was the first cold day of the year, with the thermometer in the 30s, but I was dripping with sweat from the excitement and I wasn't even wearing an overcoat. I recall how cold it was because several of the outlets demanded that I at least let them film me walking up the Street, even if for a sound bite, and I found myself walking those three blocks a dozen times before I got to the set.

As was typical of the media, *GMA* had dredged up one of the perma-bears, as I liked to call them in my columns, Jim Grant, a studious sort, who penned *Grant's Interest Rate Observer,* one of those high-priced leaflets that prophesized doom on a biweekly basis. There he was shoulder to shoulder with Gibson when I arrived. I felt a chill just looking at this man who had recently sold his apartment in Brooklyn Heights to rent one nearby because he felt that real estate had become so inflated in New York. He hadn't liked anything but gold for as long as I had been reading him. I knew the media would seize on Grant, as he lived in the same spotlight I did, getting instant attention for his professorial gloom anytime that a market dip made it to the front page of the *New York Times.* I had seen or read quotes from this erudite Cassandra so many times that I thought he had become comical in his ability each time to say that this or that decline would be the knockout punch for U.S. equities.

Sure enough, Charlie went to him first, and he said this was the beginning of the end for the most overvalued market in the world, the U.S. stock market, and technology stocks had just begun their tailspin. You had to get out now, he said. When Charlie asked him where to put the money, he said Korea was the cheapest market on earth, and that Americans should pull their money out at the opening and place it in that dramatically underval-ued market.

Holy cow, I thought to myself, this has to be the greatest single buying opportunity I have ever heard, with wrong-way Grant telling the American public to panic and place their money in one of the least stable markets between here and Alpha Centauri. I couldn't waste any more time, and as soon as we cut for a commercial, I grabbed the cell phone, punched in the office number, and shouted out to whoever picked up, "Right now I want you to buy 100,000 Intel, 100,000 Microsoft, and 200,000 Cisco before the market even opens. Go into every desk and flush out every seller. Go, go, go. Stop wasting your time talking to me. Go buy everything in sight."

I then called home, and even as the directors signaled that I only had fifteen seconds left, I called Karen and told her that we had to make our one-time uniform-gift-to-minors contributions that day, and that I didn't care how long it took to get through to Fidelity, where we had our account, we had to be sure that we got the opening prices.

As I clicked off my phone, we went live and Charlie asked me what I was doing. I told him that I was buying everything in sight and that I had to be sure I got through to my wife so that we could also get our kids' college money invested that morning. How could I be so sure? Charlie asked. I told him when I heard people advocating panic, as Biggs did the night before, or Grant did moments ago, I had to buy the panic because no one ever made a dime panicking. I told him that I had to excuse myself because I had so much more buying to do. He said that first he wanted me to take some questions from a remote camera in a diner somewhere in America where they were worried about the coming carnage on Wall Street.

One after another, men and women talked about how they were going to pull out because of the Asian problems. To each one, I pleaded that the decline was buyable, that the dip had to be purchased. As we cut away to a commercial I did more buying, and I encouraged Gibson to do the same.

At the conclusion of my segment I tore back down the street to my office to be sure my orders were executed.

GMA needed me back later in the show and I agreed, but only for a minute because I didn't want to lose my best moment to buy, which was the first half hour. By then, the media had moved on to the next big story and I handled the questions by remote from the Exchange. I reiterated that I expected the market to decline precipitously in the first half hour, as the doomsayers were everywhere that day, but that if you had been reading

TheStreet.com you knew that we were applying all the cash we had on hand in order to play what I thought would be a classic rebound into the end of the year.

Sure enough, the Dow opened hideously that morning and traded through 7,000—it had been at 9,000 a few days earlier, before coming to rest in the 6,700s. Chaos abounded as stocks couldn't open or would open only to be besieged with sell orders.

We put $200 million to work in that first half hour, buying 25,000 shares every half-point down of all our favorite tech names right into the weakness. At ten o'clock, when it started lifting, I jumped up on top of my desk and screamed at everyone in the office to pick up a phone and start buying something: "Jeannie, grab 50,000 General Motors, Clarke, you take some oils, Mark double down on Dell, Microsoft, and Cisco. This is it, you can't buy too much. Anything anybody has in size, I want. Don't worry about cash. Don't worry about margin. I want stock, I want it now. Anything anyone has of any great American company is just fine with me.

I took 200,000 IBM up a point and a half and grabbed as much Compaq as I could find without having to pay more than three quarters of a point above the last sale. I snared a couple of hundred thousand shares of Fizzy (Pfizer) and GE and tried but failed to take some General Motors and Alcoa before the Dow took off. By 10:15 we were borrowing roughly $100 million from Goldman Sachs, as we had well exceeded our cash in the frenzy. As we took stock after stock, I fired off "Dispatches from the Front" on *TheStreet.com* detailing the buys and noting that if the Dow didn't lift much beyond here I was a dead man because I had borrowed so much money (or gone heavily on margin, as it is called).

But lift it did, first slowly in the morning, and then by midday the market was in full-blast uplift, with many of the stocks recovering as much as 10 and 15 percent in just a few hours of trading. By 2:00 P.M. I was able to trim back our holdings to where I was comfortable that we weren't borrowing too much money, and by 3:00 P.M. I was off margin altogether. I gleefully shared the sales with the Web site, noting that I wouldn't sell anything if I didn't have to, but that I was extremely uncomfortable using margin once the big move off the bottom had been made. I hastily convened a couple of online chats with various portals to talk about that day's trading and to plug *TheStreet.com* some more before the moment was lost for good.

We pulled in about 6 percent that day—a good $16 million, putting us well above 30 percent and setting our sights for a plus 45 percent year. The market kept roaring for the rest of the year too, as our markets forgot about Asia, despite the fact that some of their markets, particularly Grant's recommendation, Korea, were to be cut in half and half again before the year was over. (Don't worry, he still gets quoted every time our markets get kicked in the head. Must be that natural erudition.)

Those performance numbers were dwarfed, though, in my mind, by the printouts I received the next morning from Starwave detailing *TheStreet .com*'s readership during the market break. Given the precision of the Net, I could immediately figure out how many readers we had, how many people had tuned in during the day and how many people had signed up for our service. In one day we had virtually doubled our readership.

All those articles and features and television performances had finally paid off. While many other sites didn't even bother to update during the day, we had updated constantly. Circulation doubled that week.

Advertisers, which everyone told me weren't the least bit interested in being on the Web, were calling me, asking me how they could place ads. We didn't even have an advertising department yet, as analyst after analyst, from Forester to Jupiter, the reigning champs of forecasting, told me there would be no advertising on the Web.

October 26 and 27 were, for *TheStreet.com,* our Gulf War. The staff, led by Dave Kansas, the ex-*Journal* reporter, had put out dozens of articles, I had filed eighteen times those days, eight more than I did normally, and we became *the* site to watch for many stock-market-obsessed Americans because we had been clear, gotten it right, and stuck our necks out to say that the market could be bought.

In those heady days, it was enough to propel us to the venture capital stage, and as the year wound down we began to get the knocks on the door by the same backers who had so recently laughed in my face. After that break, we were on the radar screen of a stock-market-craving public and the venture capitalists who were beginning to wake up to the fact that neither Yahoo! nor Amazon nor America Online seemed to blink during the October sell-off and, if anything, emerged as the new market leaders going into 1998.

The end of 1997 was a golden time, with Cramer & Co. finishing up 45 percent, well ahead of most hedge and mutual funds, and *TheStreet.com* finally recognized as a destination site for stock-hungry investors. At *TheStreet .com,* we were pleased to rope in Herb Greenberg, the finest investigative business journalist in the country, from the *San Francisco Chronicle,* a hire that further boosted our traffic immediately. We finished the year with 10,000 subscribers, well below the 25,000 we wanted, but still the second highest number of paid subscribers on the Web after the *Wall Street Journal.* And at Cramer & Co., I decided to make the transition of the company clear, by putting the name of my research director, Jeff Berkowitz, on the door of my company. Jeff had become an outstanding stock picker and his savvy selections after the October bottom had produced a huge share of the gains. It was time he was recognized as the man who, when I ever retired, would take over the firm. We were now Cramer Berkowitz.

The money was heady too. I had always paid out huge bonuses to everyone who worked with me, giving as much as 40 percent of the money the firm earned to the employees. That year I upped it to 60 percent. Several people made several million dollars, and every employee, no matter how low on the totem pole, got at least a $200,000 bonus. It was a great time to be affiliated with Cramer Berkowitz, and a great time to be affiliated with *TheStreet.com.*

There was only one big-time regret: what I had done to my relationship with Marty Peretz. While I thought that things could improve once Ravi was out of the picture, I was a hopeless optimist. I had hurt Marty and he couldn't hide his feelings at *TheStreet.com*'s Christmas party. I gave a toast, wine cup in hand, saying that sometimes I felt like Henry Luce must have felt when he started the *Time Life* empire. I said I didn't know if we would ultimately make it, but that we had done something new and different and good and we should be very proud.

As soon as I was finished it was Marty's turn. He had said little to me that night and I wasn't sure what to expect from him, but I had a feeling there might be fireworks. He didn't disappoint. "I know Jim compares himself to Henry Luce," he said, pausing. "In one respect he was right. Henry Luce was a real bastard."

Everyone in the room was stunned. Now the whole staff knew there was tension at the top. We both went home without saying good night to each other, for the first time in the sixteen years that Marty and I had been close friends.

CHAPTER 10

Media Man

Flush with press clippings like "Wall Street's Pied Piper of Capitalism," a feature story that appeared on the front page of *USA Today*'s "Money" section right after the October '97 minicrash, which also called me "the media's most electrifying market pundit," I tried to capitalize on the publicity and move *TheStreet.com* from its narrow market niche to a broader, more sportslike place in the media firmament.

At least that's what I told myself. Karen thought it was all either a foolish attempt at boosting a site that would now have to swim on its own, or a massive self-aggrandizement experiment by an egomaniac. Whereas I called the strategy the "ubiquity" plan, she would call it the "omnipotent" plan. Yeah, she said, she knew that ubiquity cost *TheStreet.com* nothing, and got it massive publicity. But it could only work if I genuinely believed that I was "omnipotent," and, of course, nobody human was omnipotent. I dismissed her complaints as those of someone who wished I were home more, but I secretly had to admit she had me nailed. I didn't know whether I was doing it out of the sheer will to make *TheStreet.com* succeed or out of the momentum that came from being in demand, or just my desire to want my fame when I had a chance to grab it. How base was it to do what the people behind the camera wanted?

Especially if I believed I could help people make money? How wrong was it to want to venture out of the obscure world of money management, managing for the super-rich, to do something that seemed ultimately much bigger?

Nonsense, Karen would say. My power came from the hedge fund's performance and I should never forget that. My "I would walk a mile for a camera" attitude was going to lead to a year I would regret.

I couldn't figure out how she could possibly spout such negative clap-trap. It was harder for me to be on television and be writing more as I did in 1997 and didn't we finish up 45 percent, topping almost every fund out there? Hadn't I made my greatest call in the October 26–27 period, in front of a national audience live on *Good Morning America*?

Karen patiently explained that it was the fund that paid all of the bills, bought all the nice vacations and the country house, not to mention the chauffeur and the rest of the perks that come from running an extremely profitable company. My hobby, she said, kept me away from home, an-gered the partners, who would vent their wrath the moment the numbers turned down, created a whole roomful of folks who took my money and treated me with a contempt reserved for Satan, and ran the risk of getting me in trouble with the journalism police, if not the real regulators, every time I mentioned a stock. Not to mention the angst and worry that it caused my mind and body to be in overdrive for nineteen hours a day.

I wouldn't hear it. My latest gambit was *RealMoney,* a half-hour tele-vision show that I was trying to sell to ABC as part of my work with *Good Morning America.* I wanted to have a *Wall Street Week* for the new gener-ation of investors, one that talked about today's market in terms that the baby boomers would find more compelling than the world that Lou Rukeyser exposed them to on Friday nights.

During a break after the public unveiling of the new *ABCNews.com* site in mid-1997, I had approached Roone Arledge, who was still revered by many of the people at ABC. I broached the notion of a *Wide World of Money,* something that captured the spirit of the stock market with all the excitement of sports.

Arledge looked at me with that big red face of his and nodded his head, saying that he thought I might have something. I don't know if he had ever seen me on *GMA,* but somehow the idea stuck in his head that I could be like John Madden, a colorful coach who explained it all in the booth. I know it stuck in his head because not long after, at a party for *Time*'s seventy-fifth anniversary, he spotted me talking to Barbara Walters and said that while he didn't remember my name, he knew that I was the John Madden of business news. I pressed for a lunch with him and got on his calendar the next day. I had some internal champions at the network who saw the potential for a mainstream show and joined the lunch.

Not everyone was on board, though. David Westin, the head of ABC News, seemed lukewarm to my *Wide World of Money* idea every time I had bounced it off him when he hung around the set of *Good Morning America*. As that show's ratings plummeted, the last thing he seemed to want was a spinoff of an ailing show. But ABC was a big outfit. It had room for pilots that might take off, and others in the organization were determined to make it happen.

I thought my Roone lunch might be the opportunity to get everyone behind the show, but as Westin and I waited for more than an hour for Roone to arrive, we spent more time talking about the legal ramifications of a trader talking stocks on television than about the prospects for the show. He was worried about it. And bored by it.

Worse, when Roone arrived, he could only remember me as John Madden. He seemed to like the idea, especially when I told him anecdotes about how poorly managed some of the greatest American companies were, but from the chemistry at the meeting I realized that it would be Westin, not the affable Arledge, who was going to make the decision. I left discouraged, thinking that if I didn't get that show, I would rather be exclusively on cable, because I couldn't help *TheStreet.com* much more than I was doing with my two-minute hits every other day for *GMA,* which was dropping in the ratings while CNBC's numbers were beginning to soar with the stock market.

We did, however, get a go-ahead for a pilot, known as *RealMoney,* a suggestion from my friend Kurt Andersen, who, along with his wife, Anne Kreamer, were huge believers in the concept. Anne had come along to help out but she found the ABC bureaucracy eager to shut her out from any credit.

The show opened with some true cinema verité, a filmed opening of my getting up and dressing to go to work. They crew came to my house in Summit at 2:30 A.M., and I feigned getting out of bed and slinking off to the bathroom and then doing my own version of Roy Scheider's showtime, from *All That Jazz,* replete with buy and sell cuff links and some well-timed splashes of aftershave. We took three hours to film the sequence, none of which was ever used save a shot of the cuff links and even then you could barely see them. I figure the scene alone wasted a couple of hundred thousand dollars. It shouldn't have had to cost a dime because I was willing to work for free and just wanted a couple of graphs to show where the action was and an audience to talk to.

Between that filming and the studio taping of the core of the show, I got the chance I needed to break out into the mainstream with an appearance on Bill Maher's *Politically Incorrect.* I had never done any programming outside of stocks, but the producer thought I would be perfect for the show, given how everyone was talking about the stock market and the bounce back from the '97 crash.

On virtually no sleep I flew out for a taping after the close of the stock market, unwilling to miss a trading day. I arrived, totally unrefreshed, and got whisked to the green room for the show, where I met up with the other guests, Bobcat Goldthwaite and Gloria Allred.

They had never heard of me, nor I them, except I remembered that I once tried to call some liberal lawyer in L.A. for comment for a *Herald Examiner* story, and sure enough she was the same Allred. No one introduced me to Maher and I spent about forty-five seconds with the producer, explaining to him that I was there to help *GMA* and to get some press for *RealMoney* and *TheStreet.com.*

He told me Bill knew all about the promotion and that he would do his best to help me out.

Next thing I knew, we were in front of a live audience and Maher was asking me what the heck I was doing there. I told him I'm the markets guy for *GMA* and he said, So what? I told him I run a hedge fund, and he assumed that I was a broker or something and wanted to know again why I was on his show. He didn't let me answer.

I said nothing. A few minutes went by and he brought up Monica Lewinsky and turned to the other two guests, like I wasn't even there, for a discussion about that breaking story. He talked about how guilty President Clinton obviously was, and I interrupted to say that one of the most disturbing elements of the Lewinsky case was her obvious deficiencies outside of her sexual strengths. How so? Maher asked. I said that when trouble brewed the first thing that Clinton tried to do was get her a job in public relations in New York, one of the easiest tasks imaginable, and she couldn't get hired. No one laughed. What should he have done? Maher retorted. I figured that if they really wanted to have a successful cover-up they should have put her into something like a Rand think tank, where at least they could claim she was intelligent. He stared at me and said that she was an idiot and she couldn't get a job at Rand. I know, I said, that was the joke. He pointedly then referred to me as an idiot for suggesting the idea.

Before I could explain again that it was simply a joke, we cut away to a commercial. Maher turned to me once the camera was off and said that he made the jokes, not me, that I was on because someone made a booking mistake, and would I kindly keep my thoughts to myself and not interrupt.

I didn't say another thing. I think my crimson face spoke louder than anything I could possibly say, anyway, and I had to do my best not to cry from the embarrassment.

When the show ended he took me aside and apologized for being an asshole—his own description of himself—but he said the show wasn't going that well so it played best to attack the Wall Street dummy. Next thing I knew I was being driven back to the airport, frantically calling my wife, my father, my sister, and anybody else I knew, telling them they were *not to watch Politically Incorrect,* no matter what.

Red-eye back and then straight to the set to film *RealMoney.* I was in no mood to help ABC, having been mortified nationally. I quarreled with the graphics people, cursed at the prompter, and made a point of expressing displeasure every second the camera wasn't on. That just compounded the nightmare and by the time the special appeared, as a half hour tacked onto *Good Morning America Sunday,* I could tell I had done some really bad television. Unless you were in my living room watching that half hour, you didn't know *RealMoney* ever appeared. No one I know watched it, including any of the executives running ABC or Disney. If they did, they sure didn't tell me about it. Worst of all, the director made me wear a sweater vest! Geek trader!

At the same time that I was starting to flame out nationally on ABC, my fund was having its first rough quarter in years, the first quarter of 1998, as I couldn't seem to get a grasp on which stocks to play. Going into the beginning of the year I had made huge bets on technology, notably Ascend and Cascade, and in the financials, Citicorp and Merrill. I had bought these stocks all the way down, only to panic out right before they turned up, as I neared the 4 percent down threshold that I had always used informally as the level to go into cash since my early days when I almost wiped out my fund at the Steinhardt Partners office. It was a more refined version of the "down 9 percent clear your head" strategy that John Lattanzio had advised me to use a decade earlier. But this time my stop-out sales created a disappointing first quarter that ended right at the time of the Maher and *RealMoney* bombs.

To make matters even worse, *Fortune* called to say it was doing an article about how my fifteen minutes of fame were used up. Roone Arledge also "stepped down" at ABC at that time, leaving me to deal with David Westin, who was now telling people at the network that "Jim Cramer is no John Madden." As the big shots at ABC stopped returning my phone calls about *RealMoney* and the production team disbanded, I knew that we had reached the outer limits of how far I was going on network television. Shortly thereafter I declined to renew my contract and moved over to cable exclusively.

It was time, I realized, that I had to stop trying to do both *TheStreet.com* and Cramer Berkowitz. Focusing on *TheStreet.com* too much was finally beginning to cost me money. It was time to turn the hobby over to the venture capitalists, who, as I've mentioned, had gotten interested in us because the stock market's darlings at that time were the online brokers. We were perceived to be in that red-hot cohort. While I had sworn after the humiliating first-round attempts in 1996 that I would never surrender control to these arrogant masters of the universe, I began to take their calls and have meetings with their minions. Most meetings happened during market hours, which meant that there was no time for anything but gruff small talk, with me supplying the gruff.

I burned through a bunch of folks from both coasts, including some we had seen in that ill-fated trip out West in 1996, before I found someone who could handle my trader's temper and not be put off, the people at Flat-iron Partners, a venture firm in New York City that was affiliated with Chase Capital Partners. I met with Jerry Colonna and Fred Wilson in the back office of 100 Wall Street. Like every other venture capitalist, they questioned what would happen in a bear market to *TheStreet.com*. I told them in a prolonged bear market we would be wiped out along with every-one else, but I didn't see one happening for a couple of years. They persisted. I walked out of the meeting, telling them that they knew how to get out of the office. They didn't seem to mind the high-handedness. Rather, they apologized for doing their due diligence. And Jeannie Cullen, who sat in on these meetings, told me that unlike the others who came in, these people were actually nice to someone else besides me at the firm, and that they treated the back-office people with respect, not as a bunch of waiters and waitresses to be asked for the occasional Perrier.

I went back to work, composed, and said that I thought we could do some business. Within a few weeks we received a contract for $10 million in exchange for a huge chunk of equity. If everything checked out, we would get $10 million and, with it, a promise that professional management would be brought in. I willingly agreed to step aside to become talent, and let the people Flatiron picked take over the business end of the operation. The venture capitalists would take it from there and I could go back to running my hedge fund.

Or so I thought.

CHAPTER 11

Cendant

Once the professionals came in I thought I would no longer have to pony up another dime to keep *TheStreet.com* afloat. I had put in almost $4 million now, in what I thought was going to be a $400,000 investment, and, if the Flatiron deal closed at the end of the first quarter of 1998, Marty and I would be through with the onerous contributions. Though I now thought we had a chance to hit it big at *TheStreet.com,* I still hated that I had to take so much money out of my hedge fund when we were making so much. But, at the beginning of 1998 we had run into a cold streak of unbelievable proportions at Cramer Berkowitz, with a down January followed by a down February, something that had never happened to us before, back-to-back bad months.

At the beginning of February we chartered a couple of buses and took everyone who helped us make money down to Atlantic City for a tenth anniversary party, a Harrah's weekend, where I offered to match whatever anyone won at the tables with a check to St. Jude's Children's Hospital in Memphis, a favorite charity of my wife's from her days of trading with John Lattanzio, the head trader of Steinhardt Partners.

Lattanzio, a magnanimous gentleman, ran the Wall Street division of the hospital's annual gift-giving drive. Predictably, a bunch of brokers connected big at the craps tables and in blackjack, which I was more than happy to make good on, but felt, because of the poor year I was having, that it was a bad omen, one born of a level of hubris that comes with having ten good years in a row. In our seventh week of losing money, I took little solace from the great year that we had just had. One of my biggest weaknesses, one of all traders' biggest weaknesses, is an inability to value myself beyond my last trade, and all of our last trades at Cramer Berkowitz were stinking up the joint. I made a toast that evening and said we'd pull out of this tailspin, somehow, some way, because, well, we always had. I think most of the one hundred twenty people we lugged down to Atlantic City—our dozen employees plus brokers we did business with—had no idea what the heck I was talking about. They only knew us as winners, and on our tenth anniversary celebration, they didn't want anybody to be morose, least of all me.

When you fall behind, and you are not used to falling behind, you press. I had a whole series of maneuvers I always used to break any sort of spiral. I had already tried circling the wagons around a few good positions and day-trading back into the black, meaning not letting any position stay on the sheets overnight, so-called trading flat so there was no overnight exposure. And I have thrown maiden after maiden in the volcano. That's trader talk for taking favorite positions and throwing them away to appease the gods. In 1995 I had broken a horrendous trading streak by taking Altera, then my biggest position, and throwing her into the volcano as an ultimate sacrifice. It worked and we traded positive to the market for pretty much the next two months. In 1997, I took Cascade, long a favorite, and sacrificed it to the gods, breaking a four-week tailspin.

But in 1998, not even the maiden in the volcano worked. I had thrown a half-dozen maidens in the volcano, everything from Xilinx to good old Altera, to no avail whatsoever. We decided to redouble our efforts around a few stocks that we knew were loved, just loved by institutions, betting that near the end of the quarter they would come and embrace their favorites and "walk them up," or take them higher in order to magnify performance. Pretty much everyone in the business knows that there are some funds that live for the end of the quarter. They know they can "juice" their performance by taking up big slugs of stock in the last few days of a quarter. So, if you owned a million shares of National Gift Wrap at $30 you might buy an additional half-million shares with a level of aggression that was sure to move the market, maybe taking the stock up to $34 to boost your performance by $4 million. All stocks, even big stocks, can't handle a buying blitz without some move upward, as demand can momentarily artificially exceed supply because of an aggressive buyer. I know, it seems like a profligate act, but in order to get marketing money to promote your fund, you have to have top performance within your mutual fund company. That competitive edge justifies such chicanery in the final days of a quarter. The worst that can happen is that: you have to buy some when the next quarter begins, just to cover your tracks so no one from the federal government can say you deliberately "marked up" or inflated your performance, which is a charge that can get you kicked out of the business.

Going into 1998 no stock was loved as much by institutions as Cendant, the merged entity of CUC International, a direct mail company, and HFS, the hospitality franchise company, that also had the same initials as its founder, Henry F. Silverman.

This entity, which represented everything from Century 21 to giant buying clubs to software for kids' computers, sported what was known as a "giant" multiple, meaning that institutions were paying a huge amount for the consistency of double-digit earnings. In 1998, institutions would be willing to pay 40, 50, even 60 times earnings if they knew those earnings would continue to grow. Nobody raised the bar more times, nobody inspired the confidence of buyers more than Henry Silverman, with the possible exception of Walter Forbes, the patrician builder of CUC International. When the two companies announced their merger at the end of 1997 you had to get in line to buy the stock. The queue drove the stock higher.

Jeff was smitten with Henry Silverman, who was the consummate stock magician of his era, always giving conservative expectations and then trumping those expectations with dramatically higher earnings. He played the Street like a synthesizer; he could make his stock sound like a value play, an asset play, or an earnings play depending upon who he was in front of at the time.

I liked CUC International because of the steadiness of the earnings and because I thought that CU had a chance to win the Web. CU wasn't a maker of anything, it was more like a giant Price Club or Costco, which allowed members to buy all sorts of things at reduced prices. It had purchased, though, some state-of-the-art game companies and had invited a bunch of us up to Greenwich, Connecticut, to unveil its Web strategy in the late fall of 1997. By designing beautiful, useful sites that allowed its members to make purchases at reduced prices, CU had a revenue stream that was the envy of just about everyone on Wall Street.

For me, I was smitten also by the Davidson CD rom products. My eldest daughter's class had recently been part of a pilot program to sell Davidson software diskettes, and my wife, as class mom, had data which showed that with CUC's Davidson products we had run the most successful fund drive in the history of class programs. I figured if this division rolled the fund drive out nationally, CU would be coining money, as the margins for the product were huge, off the charts, and, most important, weren't "in the numbers," meaning that no analyst was looking for anything from the Davidson software, which would enhance earnings.

After a day of razzle-dazzle about Web initiatives, all of us were pretty stoked about the stock, and we had enough firepower on that bus to Greenwich to propel the stock to the moon. Whenever I made these forays to see companies, I always tried to pull up with the execs in private to be sure that they felt as bullish as they did in public. On the way out, I told Forbes that I was extremely excited about this Davidson initiative. He told me that Cosmo Corigliano would be thrilled to hear that because he was in charge of the initiative. He gestured me to go speak with Corigliano, the CFO, to see what his reaction would be when I told him about the results of the pilot program in Summit's elementary schools. I walked over to where Cosmo was standing, on the side of the conference room where Forbes had made his presentation.

"Cosmo," I said, "looks like this Davidson elementary school program's a winner." He looked at me as if I were speaking an unknown language. "You know," I said, "the pilot program in Summit, where we are selling Davidson software. My wife's in charge of the program and they are selling like hotcakes. And I understand that it is not even in the numbers."

He asked me what the heck I was talking about. I repeated what I had said about the school gift program that his company was running.

He said, "Oh yeah, so what?"

"My wife says the program's going great."

"So?" he asked.

"I just thought you would like to know," I said.

"Thanks," he snapped and stalked off. I chalked it up to a bad day for Cosmo, whom I didn't know from Adam. Maybe he didn't like my false intimacy. Maybe he just didn't like me. Whatever. It wasn't exactly reassuring, though.

No matter, I told myself, when the merger between the two occurred, all it did was make it more likely that the combined Cendant would dominate the Web. You merge the Web-savvy folks at CU with the man who hired Bob Pittman from MTV, one of Silverman's great claims to fame, and you had a huge home run.

Now here we were, at the end of the quarter from Hades, and we owned 600,000 shares of Cendant, our largest position, with the stock hovering around the 37 level, near its high for the year. In a never-ending quest to break the spell of bad days, my wife had booked us into Room 417 at the St. James Club in Antigua. From that room a few years before we had owned a position limit in Intel calls, meaning we weren't legally allowed to own more than we did, because of SEC regulations. Out of nowhere, a man in a tuxedo came up to us on the beach in front of 417 and deposited a bottle of Cristal where I had been building a massive tunnel under the sand with the help of my two kids. He handed me a card: "Intel's up 15 on a huge court victory over AMD, relax and enjoy." It had been one of our biggest hits ever. Now my wife was hoping to inject some confidence back into me, by re-creating the same conditions.

I told Jeff that if Cendant came in as projected, this was a great chance to bulk up the position. The very next day the stock got hammered. After the close the company announced that Cosmo Corigliano had committed some accounting irregularities, nothing big, but certainly noteworthy. I was making my way to the airport when the news hit. Jeff told me that while it sounded bad, it might be the buying opportunity we were waiting for, pending the conference call at the end of the day.

After listening to the conference call, Jeff contacted me on the cell and indicated that, indeed, all was well at Cendant, that the company said that the irregularities were immaterial and dated back to some revenue recognition issues that were several years old. The stock had lost a billion in value over a couple-hundred-million-dollar irregularity from pre-Cendant days. I reiterated that this was the opportunity, and Jeff took down about 200,000 Cendant, bringing our position to 800,000. I told him to round it up to a million if the stock didn't rally, and he did so the next day. We were no strangers to big positions, having taken down a million shares of Dow Jones the year before. Here was the number-one growth story of all time and it was coming in for totally bogus reasons! What a fantastic moment. We figured that momentum-oriented managers, trying to beat their benchmarks, would walk the stock back up to the fifty-two-week high at the end of the quarter.

Instead, though, the stock didn't rebound. I told Jeff that I didn't need to hear it, though, that I was burned out, having not had a vacation in months, and I told him that he was going to have to man the ship, I didn't want any calls. This was to be the vacation I had not taken, one where I didn't want to hear about stocks or *TheStreet.com.* Not since 1986 had I been out of touch with the market for a *single day,* and that was only because my partner at Goldman had booked me on a Club Med trip after my mother passed away to get my mind off just about everything. With Jeff fully emancipated as a name partner, and with the venture capitalists imminently making their closing moves on *TheStreet.com,* I figured this was the honeymoon my trader wife and I never took, even though we had the girls with us.

The next day, I basked in the sun, playing, not a care on my hunched shoulders, oblivious to all but the piña colada in my left hand and my sand shovel in my right. I stayed up late to play blackjack, one of my favorite games, and had way too much to drink for the first time in three years. That's why I was almost shocked out of my boxer shorts when the phone rang at what looked to be 7:30 New York time.

It was Jeff. "We've got a couple of problems we have to go over."

I laughed and said, "Well aren't you being a little serious." He said nothing for a moment and then asked which problem I wanted to address first, the little one or the big one. "Hobson's choice," I said aloud.

Jeff said nothing. Jeff didn't even joke. He always joked. He was always supremely confident. He was never anything but calm. Okay, I said, let's knock off the easy one first.

"You can't make payroll at *TheStreet.com,*" he blurted.

I screamed, "That can't be, that just can't be." We had hired this crackerjack accountant type from Reuters and the day before I left he assured me that we had much more in the bank than was necessary to close the deal with Flatiron, which was meant to happen that very week. Unfortunately there was one more payroll to make before that closing and the controller had misjudged our cash flow. "What are we doing about it?" I said.

"I can cover you, for a week, to get you by," he said.

"Oh man, I said, that's just horrible. That's just unbelievable, once again we have no #!@%#& financial accountability over there at *TheStreet*," I screamed, loud enough that my now awakened wife closed the door from the outside so as not to scare the kids.

"I thought," I said, "you were to give me the easier problem first."

More silence. "We just have a problem position."

"Okay, if it's just a problem position let's address it." I wanted to make a vacation out of this vacation, not turn it into a work vacation, as the last four vacations had become.

"It's Cendant, and it's bad," he said, stalling.

"How bad?" I wanted to know.

"Real bad," he said.

Enough already. "Spell it out, Jeff, how bad is bad, how bad can bad possibly be?"

Silence.

"Give me the number, then," I said. "How much it is going to cost us?" adding that it probably couldn't be as expensive as this phone call.

"Seventeen million."

My turn to be silent.

"Did you hear me? Seventeen million."

I still couldn't talk.

"Seventeen million and the stock isn't open yet, but it looks like it will be cut in half, maybe more."

I still couldn't talk. I quickly calculated that we were now down more than 11 percent for the year. I had never been down more than single digits in my whole life. My head was spinning. I felt dizzy and faint and I had soaked my T-shirt as if I had been caught in the shower.

"Seventeen million?" I asked plaintively.

"Seventeen million, I hope. I mean I think we can contain it to seventeen million."

That's when I really exploded. "You think we can %#&@#! *contain* it

to @!#%* seventeen million, do you? And what kind of %#@ contain-
ment policy is that?"

Jeff said he had been able to unload 200,000 on some unsuspecting
third market broker down 10—

I interrupted him, furious. "You sold stock down 10 points, down 10
&!%&# points?"

For the first time, he felt hurt. "Hey, man, the stock's at $15 now, I can
buy it back 10 points lower."

Go do it, I said, we gotta trade this sucker to the long side now, just to
make some back. I heard Jeff scream, "Buy 200,000 Cendant."

Before he could take a breath he said, "We bought 200,000 at 13." How,
I asked, could we have bought it back so fast? "The stock's still in free
fall," he said.

"Buy another 300,000," I said.

"But, but, you don't even know what's wrong," he said.

"Is it going out of business?" I asked.

"No, I don't think so," Jeff said.

"Then buy it and we will flip it back at the open," meaning that we
would sell it at the opening of trading. "Now, get off the phone and go convince some of these clowns on the sell side that this company is going to
stay in business. Then call me back before the opening and we will trade
this one back and forth all day until we contain the damage to something
less than $17 million."

Sure enough, the stock opened 3 points higher and proceeded to trade a
point higher still. We dumped all 500,000 shares that we had bought, for a
nice gain, but not enough to trim the loss to less than $15 million. I worked
the order personally from Antigua, getting the position down to 400,000
by midday. By that time I had gotten the full story, that CUC had covered
up a massive accounting fraud and that everything that was said on that reassuring conference call that made us take the position to a million shares
was simply a lie. Cosmo Corigliano had orchestrated the whole deal. The
numbers were off by billions, not millions.

Silverman had merged with a totally bogus company, one that had no
profits whatsoever. The stock deserved the whacking and anything else
that could be done to it.

By the end of the day, we had made about $5 million of the $17 million back. But that hit left us down 10 percent, the worst I had ever been down. I proceeded to keep an open line for the rest of the week, taking a break only once, when I rented a helicopter with my daughter Cece to fly over Montserrat.

My Vietnam vet pilot seemed to understand my angst, but he balked at my desire to physically throw effigies of Silverman and Forbes into the volcano, so I had to resort to dropping dozens of pieces of paper with Cendant's symbol into the molten core of the volcano, asking that the pilot get as close as possible so there could be no doubt that they went into the core. I even took pictures of the ceremonial dumping and showed them on *Squawk Box* a week later.

Cendant subsequently traded higher in the next few months, where we sold the balance, and then it cratered to well below where it opened that fateful day, and stayed there. It still languishes below that opening price. The damage to our fund was done, though. Every momentum player, every casual player, every dotcom player was having a field day in 1998, except for me, and unlike everyone else, you could read about my woes, every day, in my own column in *TheStreet.com*.

CHAPTER 12

Berkowitz

When Jeff Berkowitz came to my rescue with the payroll of *TheStreet.com* in April of 1998 it wasn't the first time he bailed me out, and it certainly wouldn't be the last. You see, Berkowitz is the anti-Cramer, no emotion when emotion seemed to take me over the way the devil took over Regan in *The Exorcist*.

He could be coolly analytical when I screamed for revenge. He survived trial after trial of my emotions. He didn't flinch on his first assignment, which was to stake out the chief executive officer of Scotts, the lawn care company, because he wouldn't return my calls. Berko nailed him in the elevator on the way home from work and got the all-clear to buy. He didn't mind when I introduced him as my capital equipment and trucking specialist, when I fobbed him off on an analyst who was wasting my time in the office. Nor did he flinch when he told me to buy Compaq in his first months and I threw a full Poland Spring bottle at him when I found out through skullduggery (no one gives up names in our business) that Fidelity was selling it to us. "Why the %$!# are we buying this &#%@ when FIDO is selling it?" I demanded. "Because they are wrong," he said, just like that. When I said I was going to reload with something heavier than a bottle of water if he was wrong, Berko just smiled and said, "Be my guest. I am not."

Confidence was something you rarely found in this business. People always wilted the moment you challenged them on a stock. I've been behind the scenes with managers who have been bulling stocks on television and I have told them, "Did you know that so-and-so from that company might be leaving?" or, "The semi equipment line to Korea isn't selling well," and seen the faces drop, the confidence ooze out like pancake syrup from a bottle with a bullet hole. Most people just fold when challenged.

Not Berko. He liked to buy more. That's why I didn't flinch in firing my research director back in 1991 when Berko's summer internship was over. That's why I paid him $400,000 as a summer associate when he asked for $50,000.

Yet it never went to his head. When Karen and I presented him with the $400,000 check, she turned to me and said, "Now let this nice boy from Wharton go call his mother and tell her the good news."

"Damned straight," he said.

I don't know whether it was the year he spent working with Dan Benton, the world's best money manager, who was an analyst and Jeff's boss in the tech department at Goldman. I don't know whether it was Wharton, or the fact that he was a great team player—All Long Island in football in high school. Whatever. The man stayed all day that first day, after a two-hour interview, and is still there since I left the firm. As he should be, because Jeff can pick stocks better than anyone I ever met.

I think I first realized he had the talent to replace me that first summer when I told him we were in trouble on Rubbermaid, a position I liked since my days at Goldman because with innovative products Rubbermaid was slowly taking shelf space away from others. I told Jeff that the stock had been acting doggie and that he ought to go attend a management road show meeting, something that happens periodically, when a company's top guns come to New York to tell the story. I told him to try to go a little earlier and see if something was really wrong with the darned thing, or if it was just a bunch of sloppy sellers, meaning a group of funds that were selling the stock badly, knocking it down, because they didn't know how to trade well.

As a summer associate, Jeff went early to the "21" club, where the Rubbermaid meeting was being held, pulled up at the bar and had a Diet Coke with the man in charge of the company. He schmoozed the guy for a half hour and then called me on the cell and said, "Dump the whole thing." I told him I couldn't because I'd owned it for ages and that it always came back. He told me I didn't know what I was talking about, the company was falling apart, the wheels were coming off, the engine was on fire, and was I stupid?

I unloaded the whole position while I put Jeff on hold and then told him to come back in. How did he know? I said.

"The guy couldn't help it, he had to unburden himself to me about how bad the fundies [fundamentals] were," Berko said. I doubt if that stock had an up day in the next month and Jeff saved us a fortune.

It was always like that with Jeff, from the get-go. People liked to talk to him. One night when he and I were at 56 Beaver, our office above Delmonico's, some guy buzzed to be let up (the building was a converted apartment house).

I asked who was there and he said, "John, John Cunningham, to see Jeff." I asked Jeff who the heck John Cunningham was because I wasn't letting anybody up. This was an office next to a homeless shelter and we were always getting winos hassling us after hours.

"Let him up," Jeff said. "He's a friend."

Next thing I knew he was introducing me to John Cunningham, the chief financial officer of Whirlpool, whom Jeff had befriended because I told him that if Whirlpool, another core position, ever slipped up, I would fire Jeff just to teach him a lesson.

If you are as boisterous and emotional about stocks and people as I am, you need a Jeff just to keep yourself out of trouble. Like the time in 1997 when I tried to strangle a young analyst because he had cost me so much money buying Parametric, a failing software company. "Look, just fire him, don't kill him," Jeff said later, after pulling me off the poor fellow. "It's cheaper, and you will stay out of the papers that way." The guy was always looking out for me.

We had a constant stream of analysts coming in to pitch us stocks, to tell us that Iomega was the greatest thing since sliced bread—it wasn't— or that ANET could be the next Cisco—it never was—and Jeff always kept the analyst from getting me so excited that I might even buy something. At times, when he knew there was a particularly persuasive analyst in from the West Coast pushing some obscure technology dog that would surely implode the moment we touched it, he would deliberately not inform me of the analyst's presence. One time, enraged that he had kept me from a meeting with a young gunner from Goldman, I walked in with a Goldman Sachs squeeze ball jammed into my mouth. I sat and listened in for a few moments quietly nodding, and then, when I thought the analyst was too cocky, I opened my mouth and sent the saliva-soaked squeeze ball in the analyst's general direction and then excused myself. I knew Jeff wouldn't be shocked, and could explain away pretty much everything, although he later admitted that the squeeze-ball eruption taxed even his suasive skills.

Or how about the time when I told a two-year veteran (whom I'd hired from a job as a waiter on Nantucket at the behest of Marty, who knew him) to go home after he had failed to exercise a call, leaving us short Philip Morris, a $40,000 error because when you are short a stock you owe the dividend.

When the guy didn't show the next day, I asked Jeff if I had to call him and invite him back. "No, that was as bloodless a firing as you'll ever have." I didn't know I had fired him, but Jeff explained that when the boss says, "Get the fuck out of here and go home," in other parts of the world that means "you're fired!" He urged me to leave him alone because he was a friend of a partner and he didn't want to have to explain why I thought that torturing the analyst until he died or made back the money was justifiable homicide.

Jeff was always using common sense to keep my brainstorms from blowing us up. But he could never keep me totally out of trouble. Like in 1996, when after a fantastic run at the end of the year, I appeared on Charlie Rose's show to talk about how the market wasn't done yet. I had, offhandedly, hired the booker, Tim, as an analyst for Cramer Berkowitz.

"Does he know anything?" Jeff asked me.

"Seemed like a smart guy. Told me he knew stocks," I said.

"Yeah, but does he know anything?" I said we'd find out.

Jeff just shook his head. Nevertheless, I told Jeff, I couldn't just call Tim up and uninvite him into the firm. He was all excited to come work with us. Jeff then traced out what would happen in the cycle of Tim. "First," he said, "Tim will come in and do some trade that works, he will be very lucky, or someone will owe him something, and he will get it right. Then, you will walk around with Tim at your side introducing him as your best friend and your New Jeff. Then you will give him a ton of capital to play with in some market you know nothing about. Then he will proceed to blow us to kingdom come. Then you will embarrass him every day and point him out to everyone as a freak and a loser and you will try to make him cry, because you can't stand to lose money. And then you will ask me to fire him, because if you do it you will try to mutilate him and mortify him beyond what the Eighth Amendment allows."

That Jeff knew this would happen after only four years with me earned him high marks. The only thing that happened differently from his description was that Tim made *two* lucky trades in the beginning, enabling him to lose even more money on Grupos like Grupo Tribasa, the bankrupt road construction company, or Grupo Posadas, the bankrupt hotel chain. Things unfolded so much the way that Jeff predicted that one time, shortly after I had shown Tim around as the New Jeff and he began to lose money repeatedly, Jeff had to ask me to stop picking on Tim because Tim's crying was disrupting Jeff's ability to pick stocks. Within the week that Jeff predicted that he would have to fire Tim, he did. And with that episode over, I agreed that I would never hire anyone again without Jeff first signing off on it.

I liked to pick stocks from looking at the tape, deciding what was wrong, or oversold, or way too high, and then doing the research to make the quick decision to buy or short. Jeff, however, was all Rolodex. He liked to befriend execs so when their stock was down he could call them and say, "Hey, Jeff here, there's a seller of 400,000 Newbridge, and he is killing your stock. Is the guy right or wrong?"

Enough execs would call him back and thank him for the info that we could make good money just from clueing them in on their own stock's dislocations. It became a regular annex to our business, as Jeff would call an exec when an analyst downgraded his stock, give him the lowdown on the downgrade, and get ammo to give to other analysts who were thinking about downgrading, to keep them in the stock. As long as he accurately reported what the execs said, we could be a conduit from Wall Street to Main Street and pick up some quick profits on stocks in the translation.

It augmented my tape reading perfectly, and led to some very big hits. Jeff also stood by me during my periodic blowups with the press. I don't know of anyone who could run a war room the way Jeff had to when Dow Jones was investigating me back in 1995. As I described earlier, he had developed histories of all 120 stocks I had written about that showed, conclusively, that I had never intentionally tried to capitalize off my writings. He grilled me endlessly so when Dow Jones picked twenty stocks and asked me to explain what I did, I could do so without any paperwork, and remember every date, every trade, every eighth that I paid in the buy or the sell. He also flacked for me with particularly worried partners. I had little patience for those who doubted my judgment. Jeff could explain that I was busy and not being rude and he could fill in the explanations, if necessary, to those who were not appeased by our monthly, daily, or even hourly performance. More important, Jeff's quiet judgment of my stock picking led to our avoiding some bad buys, which is often the best way to make money on Wall Street.

And as part of my endless TV gig, I became friendly with a bunch of chief executives who came on various television shows because, thanks to Jeff, I had done enough homework to actually ask them questions that made sense, affording them an opportunity to explain things.

The problem with this, of course, is that the fundamentals weren't always as great as these chief executives made them out to be, and my exuberance for them personally got in the way at times. That's why I always insisted that the top guns swing by our office so they could get the "Jeff Test" and see if they measured up in reality. You can't believe how well something like this good-cop, bad-cop routine could be used to smoke out chicanery. Like the time at the beginning of 1997, when Chainsaw Al Dunlap had taken over Sunbeam, the appliance company. Everyone loved Chainsaw. He had stripped Scott Paper of everything it was worth and then sold it for top dollar to the hicks at Kimberly-Clark (too bad, they are very nice guys) and then he had gone on to resuscitate Sunbeam.

When he came in, wearing his trademark sunglasses indoors, we bearhugged and high-fived and would have smacked knuckles if Chainsaw had known what I was doing with my clenched fist. Jeff was already rolling his eyes. He had seen this level of enthusiasm before, notably when a Hambrecht & Quist analyst had been high-fiving me at the peak of the small cap craziness of 1996. Jeff knew exactly what to do then—sell everything that nobody had ever heard of that was going up. And he knew what to do now with Chainsaw.

We drew up, Al's team and mine, in the back conference room, and Al immediately started regaling us with his new products and how much they were going to put on the board for Sunbeam. I loved all the new gadgets and kept asking my assistant to tell me where the stock was—at $45 and change—just in case we wanted to add to our 600,000-share position of this great momentum name.

After each new product spiel, Jeff would say, "Hey, Al, terrific, but how is the first quarter going?" Al would ignore him, turn to me, and then tell me about his new thermometer that glowed in the dark, measured heat in turkeys, or told you when popcorn was done popping, or something ridiculous like that.

"But how about that first quarter, Al, how are the gross margins, how about inventory?"

After the third interruption, Al turned his back to Jeff and said to me, "Hey, what is it with this guy?" I told him not to worry. I told Jeff that he could leave, and "do what he had to do."

By this time, Jeff and I knew our signals better than Navajo code talkers in World War II. "Do what he had to do" meant sell every share, because if Al didn't want to talk about numbers, then the numbers were bad.

We sold every share into Al's worldwide tour of Sunbeam and when we were through we shorted it. As the stock got cut in half after the first quarter—of course, extremely disappointing—was reported, we coined cash and made a fortune.

We did it again in 1999 when I had the effervescent Rich McGinn in from Lucent. With the stock in the 70s, down from the 80s, we called McGinn in to figure out whether his last quarter, a seeming disappointment to us, was as bad as we thought. I schmoozed McGinn, telling him he was my favorite guest because he had such command of the situation, such presence. Jeff, on the other hand, pressed McGinn about the particulars of the quarter. McGinn said the quarter could have been better but when he was vacationing with his mother he discovered that some multigazillion-dollar Latin America contract hadn't been signed in time to make the quarter.

Talk about red flags. One contract didn't make it? That's all that missed? A multimillion-dollar uncheckable Latino contract? Give me a break. I kept schmoozing, while Jeff slipped out to "do what he had to do," which of course was sell every share of Lucent. That's how we avoided the debacle that so many others were victimized by, face-to-face discussion. Nobody ever lies to you face-to-face, and if they do, it is awfully easy to tell.

Jeff also performed emergency surgery on the portfolio whenever he deemed it necessary. When Naveen Jain of InfoSpace, another favorite exec of mine, high-fived me and hugged me the moment he came in to see us with his stock at $250, I overhead Jeff saying to Todd Harrison, our fantastic head trader, "Oh boy, this meeting's going to cost us five million. Don't let Cramer buy any stock, he's way too pumped."

By the time the lovefest was over, Jeff had sold us out of our entire position—while the exec thought we were buying—because neither of us heard a single reason why the stock should be where it was. The triggering event? When Jain boasted that he expected InfoSpace, his wireless dot-com, to pass Microsoft in market cap. "A trillion dollars, just you wait," said Naveen. With that Jeff got up and told me he knew what he had to do. In less than a year this $250 stock traded at $3. It never traded higher than the day we were high-fiving and Jeff was doing what he had to do.

At times Jeff could be moody and deviate from his even nature. By our last years together I had corrupted him enough that he began to dent his desk with the phone, toss a plastic letter holder into a wall, or fire people with the level of emotion that I frequently exhibited. And he could be "A and C," as he called me, for arbitrary and capricious, if it came to losing money for our firm. And I loved him for it. Even though I (and Karen) owned 100 percent of the firm, when it came time to move, I wanted him to have the biggest office and I wanted his name first on the door. Yes to the first, but no way to the second, he said. He hadn't done enough to earn it, but one day he would.

His unflappability would come in handy during the trials that we were about to experience in the fall of 1998, when our cozy, secure world of Cramer Berkowitz began to fall apart, right before our mercurial and injudicious eyes.

CHAPTER 13

The Hiring of Kevin English

You can make only so many mistakes when you are selecting a chief executive officer. In baseball, they let you have two free strikes but then you are out of there. Now we were about to see how forgiving the umpires of business were going to be toward *TheStreet.com.* The dapper Mr. Drake had lasted only six months, and the delirious Mr. Desai had logged four months before being canned. But like home run hitters in a shortened season, these fellows were now mere asterisks in the history of the business.

With the pros coming into *TheStreet.com* in late spring 1998, notably Flatiron and its tag-along investors, a series of venture capitalist firms that moved in on our financing once Flatiron checked off on us, we were about to experience the wonders of a search firm picking a CEO. I had lots of contempt for these firms, having been solicited dozens of times by cold callers during my stretch at Goldman.

I figured these people were just paid a lot because so many people hung up on them. I always thought that if the phone could somehow convey the true feeling behind the slam, executive recruiters would be a rapidly endangered species.

Our headhunter recognized the daunting task of finding a CEO for a dotcom in the middle of 1998. While some of the dotcoms that had come public had been stalled, in mid-1998 the initial public offering window had been slammed shut because of problems around the globe, problems that had manifested themselves after Long-Term Capital Management, a giant hedge fund, lost billions and caused many other firms to get hurt, domino style.

For us at *TheStreet.com* that meant uncertainty, and in that vacuum I doubted we could get the ideal helmsman. I had no idea how these searches worked other than somebody coming up with thirty names and then calling them regardless of whether those people were interested in the job or not.

Which was why I was so surprised to see Jonathan Fram's name on the candidate search list with a check box in the "interested" column. I had met Fram a year before while visiting Michael Bloomberg during one of those periodic visits everybody in the business had with Mike at one time or another. I had dropped by to say hello to Mike, who had pitched his Bloomberg terminal to us in the 1980s—we were an early customer—on the way out of a Charlie Rose show. Charlie borrowed space from Bloomberg to make the program.

Bloomberg had put together the single greatest information source known to man and kept improving the darned thing every day. I had thought that once we had gotten Starwave engaged, we could begin to do some of the high-end analytics that Bloomberg had, but no sooner had we signed our contract than Disney had taken over Starwave. Disney wasn't the least bit interested in doing an at-home Bloomberg knock-off. You paid huge money for a Bloomberg terminal, but it was worth every penny, and I know many traders who would prefer to go on vacation with their Bloomberg than with their wife and kids.

Mike had told me to make an appointment to see him; he wanted to talk business. He had been a big fan of my *New York Observer* column, a column that was simply a rehash of a week's worth of my own columns that appeared online. I said sure and I booked the meeting the next day.

Jonathan Fram, Bloomberg's Web master, or whatever, because no one has titles at Bloomberg—everyone was a private except for Mike, who acted more like a tough one-of-the-guys sergeant than the general that he had every right to be, given the billion-dollar empire he had built out of outflanking Dow Jones and Reuters—set up the meeting. (Mike's secret? He thought like us and knew what we needed, as did his salespeople, all of whom I would have hired in an instant if they ever left him, which they never did.)

I had met Fram a few months before; he had set up a breakfast with me and Mike, one that didn't go well because he neglected to get the whitefish salad from Kaplan's at the Delmonico that I like so much and Bloomberg chewed him out about it right in front of me. It was pretty embarrassing. At that meeting Bloomberg said my site seemed worthless away from me. I told him that he would do better to pay me $50 million to shut it down, because we could become a fearsome competitor once we became public. He agreed that if we got money we could put up a bit of a scrape instead of folding on our own volition, but that he didn't think we were worth much one way or the other. However, unlike just about everyone else, he said that the market was just wacky enough that we would get money, and that we would become an overvalued dotcom before we went under. At least he caught the irony that one day my site could be worthless and the next worth a fortune, at least on paper. Most people couldn't be as insightful as Mike was.

There, on that list of possibles for our CEO, was Fram, the man who screwed up the whitefish order. I knew that if we could get him, we would be made, because Bloomberg taught people more about the business of financial services in one day than anyone else could in multiple lifetimes.

Fram, it seemed, could be the ideal candidate to get behind too, because Marty Peretz was helping to run the search, and Marty liked him. Relations between us had never recovered from the Rockbreak and Luce twin kiboshes. In fact, they had been deteriorating steadily to where I had begun to hear that Marty was bad-mouthing my fund. As my numbers coming into the second half of 1998 were not respectable, although well into the black, I sensed that Fram represented the compromise fellow that we could both get behind to patch things up.

Right before the selection process began, in a fit of petulance, I had resigned from some of Peretz's trusts I had been doing work for in the last decade. It was a totally gratuitous move. The trusts didn't require a lot of work and the people on them were good people. I was just trying to register my unhappiness at having to work so hard at *TheStreet.com*. My resignation killed any hope of rapprochement, though, until Fram came up. When Marty told me he liked Fram, I, although not on the search committee, said, "If you like him, Marty, I want him." We had one more chance now to patch up the feud I had created.

Fram had radical ideas I loved about how to reform *TheStreet.com*. He wanted to make it more television-like, more sexy, and to bang out a great mixture of commodity news cheaply and proprietary analysis more expensively. He also wanted to stop the burn; he thought that without my day-to-day focus at *TheStreet.com,* the site was wasting a lot of money. His vision and professionalism shined through during both our meetings.

Marty too recognized that maybe with Fram we could right the ship so that if the stock market recovered from the hedge fund drubbing that late summer of 1998, we might actually make some money from a venture that everyone had considered, by now, to be a terrible folly. Fram did massive due diligence. He came by repeatedly. He pored over every book, every scrap of paper. He got to know our organization cold. There wasn't anything we didn't show him. After Fram's tenth call to me for information about how we worked as a Web site, I joked with Jeff that either he was making the single most informed decision ever, or he was serving as a fifth column for Mike Bloomberg.

So when Fram said yes a day after we made him an offer, Marty and I were both thrilled. With a real CEO, I knew I could get back to focusing on the fund and wrap up another good year. With Fram as CEO I knew Marty and I would stop being at loggerheads about everything, because I would no longer resent how hard I had to work. (I was still holding regular meetings with the business side and getting all sign-up and page view numbers, and they were holding up during the tumbling of the market that summer.)

That's why when Karen told me that Sunday that a Jon Fram was on the phone, my heart belly-flopped and landed on the body's equivalent of the pavement, not the pool. What did he want? I asked. He wouldn't say, she told me.

"What could he want?" I said.

"I'm not a mind reader," she said. "Pick up the phone."

"Jim," he said, and I cut him off.

"What's the matter, Jonathan?"

There was a pause, then: "I can't take the job."

"You already took the job," I said.

"Okay, well I can't tell Mike. I can't quit, I just can't. Nobody quits Mike Bloomberg."

"It would have been better if you had thought about this before you accepted the job. What can I do to make you stay?"

He said there was nothing. I replayed in my mind the awful thought that Fram was nothing but a spy for Bloomberg. I would have accused him of that, but what would it mean to have committed high crimes and misdemeanors against a fledgling dotcom?

I hung the phone up disgusted. Fram called Marty and Marty called me soon after he had gotten the call, to ask me what we should do. I said we had to go to the second person on the list, Kevin English, our backup.

At the time there were hundreds of dotcom companies being created that were all out there trying to get chief executive officers. We had interviewed six candidates and when we knew Fram was going to take the job, we had, as a courtesy, told all but one, Kevin English, that we had made our selection and wished them the best. They all quickly took jobs elsewhere. We couldn't run another search. By September we had burned through Flatiron's investment from back in April. We could not "do another round," meaning get more financing, until we had a chief executive officer. Nobody would give us money without one; you just can't have a full-time hedge fund manager holding things together in his spare time and expect to get the $25 million we needed to go to the next level. But there was a big problem; neither Marty nor I had spent much time with our runner-up. I barely knew him, having spent no more than twenty-five minutes with him. I was all the way with Fram. Marty had dismissed English out of hand and had focused entirely on Fram. But we were in a real jam. We didn't have time to do anything but turn to the only person we had held back as a number two.

Our ad campaigns, including "Cramer, you bad, bad boy," which featured a beautiful married woman who hopped out of bed at midnight to read me, had pretty much wiped out all of the cash we had raised and we needed another round of financing badly. Flatiron Partners, our lead investor, told us that we had to take English. In fact, Jerry Colonna, one of the lead partners, told us he thought English would be terrific. With Colonna pressuring us, with the money running out, the nod went to a man that neither of the two founders liked at all but the venture capitalists liked very much. English negotiated a fantastic contract with the venture capitalists that compensated him hugely regardless of whether he succeeded or failed. It was a travesty but it was done with no due diligence by either me or Marty, as the VCs assured us the contract was standard. They assured us that lots of things were standard, but, boy, were the standards awful.

So in September the job went to English, and simultaneously Marty and I stopped talking to each other. The warm relationship, so great for so many years, had turned ice cold, and it was my fingers on the thermostat. The timing couldn't have been more miserable for me and for Cramer Berkowitz.

CHAPTER 14

Crisis in 1998:
Part One

You don't ever get tenure in this hedge fund game, no matter how many years you beat the market. There's no job security, no real sense of anything permanent. No First National Bank of Cramer's Hedge Fund. You can be up 60, 70, 80 percent one year, shoot the lights out, and then disappoint the year after and be put right out of business, have to go back to the firm you were at before you started—if they will take you. In good years, making $10 to $20 million personally is almost a given if you are handling more than $300 million as I was going into 1998 and if you know what you are doing. The recipe is simple; at the end of the year you take 20 percent of the gains you made, both realized and unrealized. You simply journal the profits from the limited partners' accounts to the general partners' account, "the good guys," as I always called us around the office. (Karen and I owned 100 percent of the general partnership at our firm even though I had made Jeff a name partner. He was an employee of the general partnership.)

If, in a given year, you turn $300 million into $400 million, a respectable 33 percent gain that your partners might expect you to achieve to stay competitive, you took home 20 percent of that profit, or $20 million, at year end. After I paid my staff bonuses—and I liked to pay out 40 to 60 percent of our profit, much higher than anyone else I knew—I would have $10 million in personal compensation. Add that to your 1 percent management fee—again, used to pay your staff, but you can take a nice cut of it if you owned 100 percent of the general partnership that controls the fund, as Karen and I did—and if you are a large partner (that is, investor) in your own fund—I was the second largest in 1998—and you can see how lucrative a proposition hedge fund management can be. Going into 1998 I had been generating 23 percent a year profit since 1987, so I had many multimillion-dollar years, and no down ones. Which was pretty darned good, because a losing year carried huge baggage with it.

Remember, you only get paid a percentage of the gain *if* you make people money—the 1 percent management fee isn't enough to live on if you have to split it with your employees—and you have to pay your people no matter what. If you have talented people on the payroll, they needed to make big money or they would be out of there, recruited to a hotter hedge fund in a flash. And you have to get back to even the next year—the year doesn't start at zero if you are down the previous year, it starts where you ended—before you can start getting paid a percentage of the winnings again. A bad year could put you in the hole so badly you could never work out of it, so most hedge fund managers just give up and close down after one year of horrendous losses. We all accepted that one-strike-and-you-are-out rule when we started.

I figured that, going into 1998, with ten good years under my belt, ten years where I had beaten the averages every single year, most of the time pretty handily, I might be due for a poor year. I had made millions for so many people, and hundreds of millions for the partnership itself. Most of my eighty-nine partners (known as partners because they are "limited partners," with losses limited to what they invested in the fund and no more) had been with me for at least a decade. Some of them had been with me at Goldman Sachs. Several had more than $25 million with me and another ten had $10 million or more, most of which I had made for them with my investing acumen.

Many of them had let the capital accumulate year after year, even paying the taxes I generated with my trading out of other money away from the fund so their capital accounts could accrue. They had grown accustomed to my style of consistent, grind-out gains, without interruption, whether the market had rallied hard or sold off hugely. They knew my work ethic; they understood that I put them and their money in my own personal and worshipful pantheon, even though I didn't go out to dinner with them when they were in town, schmooze with them much on the phone, or consider myself their buddy, good for fifty-yard-line seats at Giants games or eighth-row tickets for the hottest play on Broadway. They understood that I felt the losses as no one else did, that I carried them with me on my back wherever I went, and that I couldn't bear to be down even for a day, let alone a month or a quarter. A down year would be the stuff of true personal catastrophe. Unlike many other hedge fund managers, I treated the money they gave me as their money. Hedge fund managers tend to regard the money given to them as their own until it is withdrawn. I had set up my partnership differently. Your money was yours. Yes, I had given my partners what was known as "limited liquidity," in that I only opened the fund a couple of times a year, typically at the beginning of the year and in April for payment of taxes. Those were your only scheduled opportunities to come in and go out. Mutual funds inherently underperform hedge funds because they are kept open for contributions and withdrawals constantly. That "money-in, money-out" requirement can crush performance at the worst possible times.

You need to invest money to make a killing just when fear is highest. But, left to their own devices, that's exactly when clients pull out if they can because of the pain of potential loss. That's why limited liquidity works to the benefit of all partners. But if you requested that I open because of a personal emergency, because you really needed the money, I would always comply. However, because it would be unfair to let one partner have preferred treatment over another, I would let anyone in or out on the rare occasions when I did open on request. Again, it was the partners' money, not mine. I would send out a notice that I was open for contributions or withdrawals for five business days when I did let people in and out, and I would send cash or take in cash—not stock, never stock, because you could hurt an investor by sending him stock in a losing position rather than returning the cash, and I never received stock because I could get hurt while I liquidated it—the day after the window closed. Of course, there was no real window at my firm, only a proverbial one.

We had an office manager, Pat Shevlin, who looked after the partners' day-to-day needs, and she would, by hand, take care of additions and redemptions, making sure that when you wired your money in you got a receipt and when you wired your money out, you got your money. (People wire money when there are large sums, because they don't want the "float," the interest that accrues in transition, to go to the bank as happens with a check. With a wire, they get to keep earning interest until the exchange is completed. If you are talking about sending around chunks of $10 million at a clip, it is irresponsible to use a check; that float is too big to give to the bank. A wire is a simultaneous transaction; it, and the interest it accrues, is yours until the last second.)

We didn't keep any of the partners' money in the office. We kept it at Goldman Sachs, which was known as our clearing broker. In other words, Goldman was the real bank for us. If we needed to, we could borrow money from Goldman against the assets we had—up to 50 percent of the equity we kept there. Goldman would calculate our performance daily, generate trading document runs that showed how we were doing, and issue reports each morning, known as margin runs, that told us precisely what we owned and how much it was worth. We needed these documents because even as Goldman cleared our money, we used dozens of brokers at other firms besides Goldman to execute trades. On a given day we might do 200 trades, maybe as many as twenty or thirty each with seven or eight brokers, and they would have to report those trades to Goldman's back office, which would then reconcile them with our instructions. I might put in an order to buy 10,000 shares of IBM with Merrill Lynch. Merrill would then buy the stock for me, send it to my Goldman clearing account, and get paid by Goldman after I authorized the trade. So even though we used dozens of brokers to trade, including Goldman's own, in the end Goldman was the repository of the master account and all of its money. Nonetheless, if a partner needed his money, he requested it of us. We took care of the additions and redemptions and reported them to Goldman. Fortunately redemptions were rare because—take my conceit for what it was worth—no one was doing more to make your money grow responsibly than I was, so what was the point of taking it back?

I thought I was something special to the partners, someone who had been their trusted advisor for so many years. I never regarded myself as their bank, a place to come and go as you please. I was better than that.

In other words, going into 1998, I had hubris. I could recite the litany of my greatness in my sleep: Never had a down year. In cash for the crash of '87. Made money in the minicrash of '89. Weathered 1990 and 1994 better than most; two years that closed lots of funds for awful performance. Coined money on national TV in the Asian contagion. By 1998 I figured I had the moneymaking process down pat. I knew that if I came to work every day with just my wits, made my calls, looked at my stocks, looked at the tape, the procession of stocks crossing the ticker, checked in with my sources and my analysts, I could make $400,000 in twelve hours. I could beat my trend line. Everybody would love me no matter what, even if I had an off period, because I had been so darned good.

What a dope I was. This is money we are talking about, not love and not a home sports team. Money's fungible and molten. It flows to wherever the hottest hand might be and it departs cold hands as quickly as someone might change the channel on a boring television show. There's no loyalty with money, even after years of outperformance. Which is why 1998 leaves the most bitter of tastes in my mouth even now, four years after the debacle.

I thought I had pretty much seen everything in my previous years of picking stocks for others, but 1998 just wasn't like any other year. In most years there were patterns, tradable patterns that worked a huge percentage of the time. When interest rates were going down, you bought the financials. When the economy was strong, you stuck with the cyclicals such as the aluminums, capital goods, or steels. These patterns had made me a huge amount of money for so long that I thought they were more than just patterns, they were movies others were watching for the first time even as I knew how they ended; when interest rates went down, the movies ended happily, not sadly, with huge returns for those who stayed long.

Not in 1998.

For Cramer Berkowitz nothing went right in 1998, and from the get-go. We just couldn't get the rhythm of the market. We came into 1998 all in cash, frolicking in the last few weeks of 1997 because we were so far ahead of the market. We had also taken in a nice chunk of new money, bringing our total assets to $325 million, because our performance in 1997 was so strong that we had many requests to come into the partnership. During that bountiful fourth quarter of 1997 I had bought the office a Ping-Pong table and an electric knock-hockey game that played "The

Star-Spangled Banner" before you squared off with your opponent, just so we would have diversions and not trade at all. I didn't want us giving back any of the gains, something that so many hedge funds are prone to, after they should have locked in a great year. We spent hours in Ping-Pong and knock-hockey tournaments, with the always competitive Jeff the reigning king in both games. In the last five days of 1997, we turned off CNBC and watched action movies on the office VCR: mostly *Crimson Tide,* over and over, a favorite of the office because of Gene Hackman, by far the trading desk's most popular actor. So when 1998's trading began we were both rusty and itching to get started.

We put our hundreds of millions to work almost immediately, in the first hours of the first trading day of the new year. We bought gigantic positions in the financials, scooping up hundreds of thousands of shares of Merrill Lynch, Citigroup, and Morgan Stanley, among others. We just piled right in at one level, rather than buying, say, 10,000 shares every half point, on the way down, and legging into the positions over many days, as we would have when we were less certain of ourselves. That was more hubris: we'd been so right for so long that we thought we knew the right levels instinctively. We thought we were bigger than the market and knew more than it. We rebuilt our positions in telecom stocks and we restored our classic longs in favorite growth manager security blanket names: Microsoft, Cisco, Dell, Intel. We did it by rote, like piano players who didn't even need to read the music.

And we got every note wrong. Very wrong. We were down 4 percent on day four of the new year, our worst start ever, a truly bad omen for someone as superstitious as I was. No matter, we were still oblivious, still celebrating our previous up 65 percent year. Soon we were down 8 percent for the year as our positions just kept cascading all January and we took no evasive action to avoid the losses. The declines were too swift; we couldn't adjust. By February, that fantastic 1997 was just another old season.

We pulled out of the tailspin in March, fighting back into the black with some aggressive trading and a market that turned benign and easy to figure. When we got the firm's bottom line back to slightly more than even, others were already having a huge year, and for this competitive manager, that was just as insulting as losing money. Then, just when it looked like we could catch up to the leaders, we were decked right to the canvas with that devastating Cendant loss, caused by the chicanery of top-level management.

The stock market kept roaring, though, all through June and July, giving us a chance, once again, to catch up. If you have to, and the market is a hot one, you can simply tag along in the most visibly explosive stocks, and that's what we did. We caught up to the averages midsummer, a heroic but short-lived comeback, using high-risk call options to play the momentum in the most volatile names. It is not a good way to make money and I knew it. (It was the way that a lot of the hedge funds made money in the mid- to late 1990s only to give it all back and then some when tech turned down in March of 2001.)

But we were sloppy about our comeback. That was the summer a clerk on the trading desk made the $40,000-in-a-nanosecond error, my worst ever, because he didn't listen to a simple instruction I had given to cover a short in Philip Morris, forcing me to pay the dividend that normally the company owes. (The short seller is just borrowing the stock from someone else to sell it short, and the short seller has to pay that dividend to that someone else unless he covers his position first, that is, buys back the stock, which you should always do, and which I had explicitly said to do.)

Then September arrived and Cramer Berkowitz, known as one of the most solid franchises on the Street, began a quiet descent into near collapse, as close as I have ever come to giving up the ghost.

Of course, irony played havoc with my decline. Right as we were about to begin our tailspin into double-digit declines—our first ever—*Money* magazine called and said it was doing a cover story on market whizzes and it wanted me to be one of the gurus pictured and written about. (Frank Lalli, my old nemesis, had been dismissed for a variety of reasons, including circulation staleness, the year before.) Vanity—and revenge from the knock *Money* had put on me three years before—kept me from saying, "You don't want me, I don't know what I'm doing, I'm lost here." So there I was, staring out from the newsstand, telling you what to do with stocks and the market, just when I was the most confused I had ever been.

It wasn't all my fault. It wasn't all my conceit. Bizarre things were happening in the markets, things no one had ever seen before.

Starting in the summer of 1998, bonds and stocks began acting in a way they had never done in all the years I had been managing money. Typically, when bonds went up (because interest rates went down) stocks started climbing almost automatically. It was the easy money trade to game and I had gamed it a gazillion times, always right.

This time, however, the money trade wasn't working because there were other forces at work, more difficult to grasp. Every few years there would be a market that attracted the hedge fund cognoscenti, some market that seemed impenetrable to all but a few funds that always thought they knew better. One year it might be Mexico. You would dine with other hedge fund managers or brokers who handled their accounts, and you would hear that the Mexican telcos were hot, or the Mexican banks had to be owned. Typically, you would rush in, just when the Mexican banks were ready with inflated stock and bond offerings that raised large sums at the top and paid out hefty fees for the brokers who had recommended the stuff. The Mexican "blue chips" would then peak and crash, leaving the last in to justify to their bosses and clients how they could have stupidly bought into some fly-by-night situation that any person with common sense would have known to avoid. I had seen the Brazilian markets be the "only place to be" during one spring, and the Argentine markets be "the next big thing" a few months after Brazil had been annihilated. Occasionally, the rush would be on to banks in Singapore or construction companies in Bangkok or casino and hotel concerns in Malaysia. They would shoot up and those who got in early would make a fortune, but those who came in late would simply be taken to the cleaners. One hour Martinizing, as I always called this process to the brokers who tried to suck me into its sexy vortex.

Somehow, in 1998, the "smart money" that spring had convinced itself to congregate in one place that was so ridiculous, so outlandish at that moment given the chaos involving the country, that you couldn't believe anyone with a fiduciary duty would accept it: Russia. That summer Russia had drawn everyone from academics to gunslingers, all of whom believed that the nation had been transformed into a capitalist wonder, second only to the United States as a place to coin money. You would go out with your fellow hedgies and they would talk up some Russian phone company or a Russian bank, as if they were talking about Verizon or Bank of America.

My Turkish foray years before, where I had been crushed by the Turkish Whirlpools and Turkish Citigroups, had inoculated me against such foolishness. I often thought that the $3 million I lost virtually overnight in Istanbul was the cheapest lesson I had ever been given in trying to find the market that would outdo the United States without as much risk. It doesn't exist. And I wasn't the least bit interested in Russia. But in the hedge funds business, one market's catastrophe can travel faster than smallpox and infect a perfectly healthy market in weeks if not days or, that year, hours.

It wouldn't have mattered if everyone under the sun had embraced Russia that summer, as long as one firm chose to avoid it: Long-Term Capital Management, in Greenwich, Connecticut. But the opposite was true. Long-Term, by virtue of its fantastic salesmanship, had managed to become the largest hedge fund in the world by 1998. I say salesmanship because the firm's record was never that good. But the people who ran it knew how to sell. They were trained by the best salespeople on the Street: Salomon Brothers, a firm that, in my experience, could always get you to do the wrong thing for your partners. They knew something that I could never know: certainty. When Long-Term Capital pitched you, it did so in a way, with a tone, that made you feel that the moneymaking was automatic and riskless. I had learned how to make these pitches myself when I was at Goldman. I had learned how to do it, but I wouldn't. I knew too much, and, because of some quirk that marked me as a terrible hedge fund salesman, I couldn't play the risk-free game, where you pretended that no matter what happened, you had no risk and massive reward.

In fact, if you had to find a fund that was more diametrically opposed in principle to the way Long-Term pitched itself, it would be Cramer Berkowitz. Long-Term would tell you that given their "models" they were going to generate whatever return they chose to get. They could earn a solid return by just following their models, but if they turned on the juice, used leverage, borrowed money, they could make phenomenal returns. I always figured that in private these guys knew the truth: who the heck knows what your return is going to be in this game? Luck trumped skill so often that unless you were humble about it and realized that things could go wrong, you were simply dissembling to get the money, making a sales pitch for a vacuum cleaner that never broke down.

The mystique of hedge funds, and the sheer lack of transparency—believe me, nobody, including the manager, ever really knows what the strategy and thinking behind every move are—make them difficult to grasp and hard to describe. You are never going to see the inside of one. In fact the goal is to be secretive and quiet about what you do for fear that someone will steal your ideas. And you don't want anyone to see how naked you really are, how much you are at the whim of uncontrolled forces. Many pretend they are like insurance companies that are always adequately reinsured, until that 100-year storm breaks out and they lose everything.

When I went in to see institutional accounts to solicit funds, something I did rarely and only when pursued aggressively by the fund plan trustees themselves through some positive word of mouth—typically college or corporate endowment funds—I didn't speak of quadrants (high-risk, high-reward; high-risk, low-reward; low-risk, high-reward; low-risk, low-reward—that type of gibberish where, of course, everyone claimed to be in the low-risk, high-reward quadrant, as massively bogus as that is), or rates of returns, or levels of performance that you could expect. I didn't use terms like market-neutral, a convenient bit of agitprop implying that a manager won't get hurt if the market goes up or down. Talk about nonsense, these market-neutral managers blow up all the time. Funds always correlate with some aspect of the market, and they become unglued when that portion of the market inevitably comes unglued. What I talked about was how I would work hard and with a little bit of good luck beat the market.

Managers pitch themselves as having strict stops on the downside, hard and fast rules about selling "overvalued" stocks—whatever the heck those are—or ironclad strictures about stocks with high price-to-earnings multiples. The more certain and insistent and self-assured a manager comes across, the more warning lights should flash in the client's head. The humbling nature of stocks and bonds is the only true precept, and those who have no humility are the first to get their bells rung. The great ones never admit that their principal attribute is luck, but they know it and confide it to others when they are in the hedge fund clubhouse, safe from the clients' ears.

I knew that all the hedge fund sales presentations glossed over the true risks and dangers that existed in the market. When I "pitched," I talked about living at the office until I got it right, doing massive amounts of homework and still being derailed by chance. I described the shocking imperfection of the markets and the fallibility of my judgment. Sometimes, when I was giving a presentation during market hours, and I saw on a stock screen in the room that one of my equities had fallen, I would just break off the sales pitch and return to my trading turret immediately. I owed my existing partners too much to be out trying to raise new money as my own stocks went against me.

Funny, but institutions loved the phony rigor of the professorial types at Long-Term. In retrospect these experts were simply a group of gambler salesmen who hired academics to gloss up the joint and give it a look of certainty. We accepted the markets for what they were, totally unpredictable, chaotic, and incapable of being gamed by large amounts of money without distorting the process. Or, in our parlance, you couldn't be the house and beat the house at the same time.

Long-Term didn't agree. That summer, by dint of terrific selling, this firm was running so much money and had so many positions all over the world that its losses could impact everyone from quiet pension funds that owned bonds, to my own, unleveraged firm. That wouldn't have mattered if their "genius" had been contained to their own positions, but as was so often the case, when one firm commanded the respect of Wall Street, the brokers who entered its orders would tag along for the ride. Brokers can't help themselves. They all talk about what the big money is doing, and when the big money doubles down, by borrowing money from the brokers, and then doubles down again and again, using many times its capital with still other brokers on the sly, the traders at the brokerage houses do the trades themselves and tell every other client to do the trades too. I can't believe how many times I was told to do a trade because the boys at Long-Term deemed it a winner. I also couldn't believe how many responsible people at major firms would piggyback *with no homework,* because they heard that a Nobel laureate at LTCM had liked the trade. Nobel laureate? What's that got to do with real life? (I never fathomed why Long-Term Capital didn't understand this piggybacking. John Merriwether, who ran the firm, came out of Salomon Brothers and knew that everyone talked about everyone else's trades. But the academics have no knowledge of how Wall Street really works and they might have believed they were doing trades without anyone tagging along.) So, whether LTCM knew it or not, at least a half-dozen major firms were mimicking whatever it did.

Long-Term Capital had big positions in Russia. When the trades back-fired, everybody got hurt, some for as much as hundreds of millions of dollars. I never thought my little firm could ever fall prey to another firm's woes, just another domino in the line of managers and brokers who fell when Russia's capital evaporated. We shouldn't have. We had no foreign exposure whatsoever. We didn't use leverage, borrowing money from the casinos (that is, the brokerage houses that made margin loans or IOUs to hedge funds so they could be more aggressive, something that mutual funds never did). We had used margin only two or three times in eleven years. We shunned leverage as too risky. It could wipe us out if the market went against us.

However, we did run two kinds of portfolios, one a trading portfolio that generated trading gains—the one that many people were familiar with from my writing and television appearances—the other, a long-term small capitalization value portfolio that was meant to generate long-term capital gains. I never talked publicly about that part of the fund after the *Smart-Money* imbroglio. For a decade I had used that part of my portfolio to buy out-of-favor stocks that I thought, over time, would come to be in favor again. That way we would have the perfect mixture of short- and long-term capital gains to have consistent quarterly growth, just like we wanted to see in the publicly traded companies we owned.

My favorite area for undervalued stocks, historically, was the finan-cials, particularly savings and loans, small savings and loans from out-of-the-way places like Westerfed, the second largest bank in Montana (where the Unabomber kept his account), Klamath First Federal, the third largest S&L in Oregon, Cape Cod Bank and Trust, the remaining independent fi-nancial concern on the Cape, or Third Federal Savings of Doylestown, Pennsylvania, where I banked personally.

We would take down huge chunks of these boring institutions and sit with them, sometimes for years, until they either increased in value via improved earnings or got takeover bids. They were illiquid stocks, that is, stocks that traded "by appointment," so to speak, so that you couldn't get in or out of them in a hurry without creating severe dislocations either way. (Federal law forbade you from taking down more than 10 percent of any one savings and loan.) We had bought a bunch in 1994 and bought a little more every time we got new money in. By 1998 these positions were all giant-sized and dwarfed anything else we owned simply because every time we took in new money we bought more of them to maintain the level of ownership in the hedge fund.

The stocks of savings and loans do best when the yield curve on bonds is sloped positively, meaning that short interest rates are as low as possible and long rates are much higher. (Picture a curve sloping gently upward, the further out you go.) If that was the optimum, the bane of savings and loans was an inverted yield curve, where short rates were higher than long-term rates, a hill that went sharply lower as it went out in time.

This inverted situation hardly ever exists, as is to be expected—lenders should almost always be able to get a higher return if they are going to take the risk of lending money over thirty years as opposed to thirty days. After all, there is a lot more danger, including inflation, that can occur during the period that the lenders are waiting to be repaid.

Nineteen ninety-eight was no ordinary year, though. We got that inverted yield curve that summer because of the ongoing destruction of Long-Term Capital, not because of any Fed policy or economic hardship or inflation spike. LTCM had gone long on every piece of paper in the universe, from Mexican day put bonds to Russian government bonds, and against them they had shorted, or bet against, the U.S. government bonds as a hedge. They wanted to capture the higher interest rates of other countries, and yet hedge out the risk. Once Russia went belly-up when its treasury ran out of rubles, actually walking away from its sovereign debts right after it had borrowed billions, brokers who were playing tagalong to LTCM recognized that LTCM was too leveraged and could actually be wrong. That meant LTCM could go bust. If it were to go bust, it would have to sell its exotic bonds and buy back the plain vanilla U.S. bonds it shorted against those exotics, or unwind the trade, as it's known. Then it would have to return whatever remaining capital there might be to its limited partners after hideous losses.

In fact, the way Wall Street works is that high-level traders at sell-side firms like Merrill or CSFB take down any positions they want for their own firm's accounts, mimicking good clients whom they regard as smart money—*until they go awry.* Then as soon as these sell-side position traders, as they are known, start losing in the tens of millions, the bosses get wind of it and they demand that the trades be unwound, or literally taken off the books. If you owned Mexican bonds and were short U.S. Treasuries as a hedge, the firms would make you buy back the latter and sell the former until you were "flat." So, all of the LTCM tagalong brokers unwound their positions at the same time because the potential for out-sized losses was recognized simultaneously.

Of course, since LTCM had constructed its massive portfolios using these brokers, these firms also knew the positions Long-Term had, knew how much the firm had borrowed, and knew that it was losing money every day.

There are no loyalties on Wall Street. When you smell blood in the water, you become a shark. There's simply too much free booty to be had. So, those who had revered Long-Term, and would do whatever LTCM did, now turned against LTCM and began to take the exact opposite positions. Large traders knew that they could take the other side, bet against Long-Term and then leak to the media that Long-Term was in trouble, to ratchet up the pressure and break Long-Term's bank. That late summer I didn't know of a hedge fund that wasn't shooting against Long-Term, pressing every position to the max to get LTCM to capitulate.

"Shooting against" is strictly a hedge fund term and until you have been shot against you have no idea what it means nor how debilitating it can be. Put simply, when you know that one of your number is in trouble, you don't lend him a hand, you try to figure out what he owns and you start shorting those stocks to drive them down. Or, if he is short an instrument, whether a currency swap, a bond swap, a derivative, any piece of paper that's other than a solid instrument, such as an equity (hence this is a strange misnomer), you begin to buy up that instrument in large quantities until the shot-against institution goes belly-up. Once an institution—any entity that manages large pools of capital—gets into the collective crosshairs of rival hedge funds, it becomes almost impossible to get out alive.

Everyone plays this game. A mutual fund's in trouble? Find out what the fund owns and bet against it until the target can't take it anymore and capitulates. A hedge fund's in trouble? Gang-tackle them and make them go bust. When the biggest Kahuna is in trouble, everyone gets involved, from the biggest brokers to the smallest hedge funds because the profits are so easily gamed. You know that, ultimately, that fund is going to have to unwind its positions and give the money back, so you can pretty much predict that everything in that fund will be sold, with that selling knocking down whatever the fund owns. If you owned two million shares of thinly traded National Gift Wrap and Box Company, currently valued at $28, and I knew you were getting massive redemptions because of poor performance, I would sell National Gift short. Then when you went to cash out, your big slug of stock might knock National Gift down to $25 where I could buy the stock back (cover my short) and make good money. I knew that you returned cash, not stock, so you would have to sell that National Gift and I would get my opportunity to cover. Similarly, if you were short two million shares of National Gift, betting it would fall, and I knew that you were folding up shop because your partners had lost faith in you, you couldn't distribute that short to your investing partners, you would have to buy it back and take the loss. I could run ahead of you and buy National Gift and then flip it to you when you inevitably came in to cover. That's child's play on the Street. If I buy 50,000 National Gift, anticipating you have to cover, I might make $100,000 without a lot of risk when you go in to buy it up 2 points. Your frantic buying will move the market.

You could feel the whole Street collectively buying long-term U.S. bonds to squeeze Long-Term Capital into buying back those bonds at the highest possible price. Long-Term had to buy the bonds back in order to tally losses, meet the partner redemptions, and close down in an orderly fashion. Because Long-Term Capital had shopped its firm to others (by September it needed to be bought in order to survive), allowing many to know what positions it had that needed to be liquidated, shooting at it was like shooting fish in a barrel—with no limits!

So many funds were betting against Long-Term, anticipating that LT would have to cover its massive short position, that they actually moved up the prices of long-term bonds with their anticipatory buying—

and hence lowered the rates on long-term paper (and the home mortgages benchmarked off them) to absurd lows that were, in fact, lower than the short-term rates. The sharks had created an inverted yield curve, long-term rates lower than short-term rates, to pressure LTCM into capitulating.

I didn't care about what was happening to Long-Term Capital in August and September of 1998. I had my own problems and I didn't want to pile into the thirty-year Treasury without some fundamental reason other than the Squeeze, as we all called it. And there wasn't one.

But I did care about what the bond squeeze was doing to the balance sheets of all of those little savings and loans that made up almost half of our equity positions at Cramer Berkowitz. With the thirty-year U.S. bond ramping up continually as funds shot against LT by buying up the bond, the savings and loans were losing money every day they turned the lights on. These S&Ls borrow from depositors at the short rates, which now were *higher* than long rates. The thirty-year bond moved up in price and down in yield with a rapid pace never before seen. The savings and loans, part of the real world, not the hedge fund world, were caught flatfooted by this move. Suddenly they were loaning out at much lower rates than they were borrowing because their loan benchmark is the thirty-year Treasury. That inversion meant losses for all of the savings and loans in my portfolio.

Anyone who knew how to read the yield curve could predict that these savings and loans would lose big money. So naturally everyone dumped these stocks before those losses would be reported.

Everyone, that is, who could. My positions were too big to maneuver. I couldn't cut them back. I owned too much of them. My selling would destroy the stocks. I had to watch helplessly, hoping that the inversion would cure itself and the yield curve would revert to a more normal pattern. To make matters worse, other hedge funds shared my philosophy toward these undervalued stocks. Unlike us, though, they often used leverage to magnify their gains. As the long bond rose day after day after day in late August and early September, other hedge funds with a game plan similar to mine capitulated because they needed cash. Their selling drove the stocks of S&Ls to levels that further impacted our own portfolio. Put simply, we were getting nickel-and-dimed down on our Westerfeds and our Cape Cods and our BayViews every day we came to work. When you own millions of shares of stocks that are being nickel-and-dimed, you start running into real multimillion-dollar losses.

Normally I would have salivated at the prospect of buying these big blocks of stock of companies I knew and loved that hedge funds were dumping. But it was August. When fall earnings season started—when these savings and loans reported their earnings—the stocks would be hammered again when they revealed how they had been hurt by the shenanigans used to bust Long-Term Capital. That's when I figured I would make my move and average down, as I would have to, as I was now underwater on every one of these banks. As a rule, I always kept spare capital, spare cash, around for just this kind of occasion, when stocks had gotten so out of whack with the fundamentals that I could make big money. So in August, despite the markdowns, and the losses in our untraded portion of our portfolio—unrealized of course—I wasn't unduly concerned about these positions; I regarded the declines as a short-term buying opportunity and I vowed to take all of these savings and loans up to the 10 percent legal limit once the coast was clear.

Still, though, the stocks getting marked down every day meant that our performance, which was subpar to begin with, having never caught the averages when things were good, was headed deep into the red for the second time that year. We owned just enough positions that were related to Long-Term Capital, that correlated with that monster now in its death rattle phase, such as stocks in brokers that were losing millions of dollars because they hadn't been able to swing from Long-Term Capital friend to foe fast enough to save their quarters, that we were getting killed. Because of our poor trading, our lagging S&L stocks, and some other small capitalization disasters, we dropped deep into the red at the end of August, the latest we had ever been down during a year. We were flirting with being down almost 20 percent some days that miserable summer, depending upon how our small cap portfolio positions were "marked," or how they closed at the end of the day.

This was shaping up to be a catastrophic third quarter, and yet there was no one bad trade or trades to key on and lament. It was just an overall succession of loser days.

This was new ground, bad ground, quicksand, and I didn't like it. By this point in almost every other year we were already breaking out the big vacation schedules, taking lots of time off, even going to the movies, play-ing Ping-Pong or knock-hockey because we didn't want to give up our lead with unlucky trades.

The tendency to overtrade when you are on top is great, and you have to take extreme measures to avoid doing so. This time, I told the desk in the waning days of the third quarter, we had to hunker down, get tough, stem the erosion. All vacations were canceled. Nobody was going anywhere. We will ride it out, I said. We always did. And since we ran a closed fund we had no opening scheduled, so even if our performance was negative, we weren't capital-constrained. If partners were unhappy with my perfor-mance, they couldn't do anything until the end of the year, by which time I was confident we could make the money back and then some. It was em-barrassing, I told people at the office, but not catastrophic, as many hedge funds were being roughed up by Long-Term Capital and a market that couldn't get out of its own way.

Then, one day in early September, I got a call from one of my biggest investors, Eliot Spitzer, who was making his second bid for New York State attorney general. When Eliot studied with me at Harvard Law he had seen how driven I was and how much I loved the stock market. When I set up the fund he had come in as a partner early on and I had made the man a ton of money. Now the papers were saying that Eliot might be violating campaign finance disclosure laws by getting hidden money from his fam-ily. That was a total crock and I knew it, as I had made a boatload for Eliot. But there was only one way to refute this charge and it was pretty simple: Eliot needed money from the fund. He needed me to open up the fund. It was an emergency. My rules were clear: in an emergency, I had to notify all the partners that I was opening for contributions and withdrawals.

Until that request from Eliot I had *never* had anyone ask me to open the fund; everyone was willing to wait until the designated openings. In fact, I had never lost an investor other than through my own neglect or temper, as when I kicked out a certain movie mogul because he tracked me down during a trip to the Negev to berate me for owning Intel during a momen-tary market glitch. People always tried to get into the fund and I often turned them down because I didn't know them or like them. But leaving the fund? It just wasn't done. Eliot's request, given our double-digit de-clines and the chaos of Long-Term Capital, which was giving all hedge funds, even ones that didn't use leverage, a bad name, couldn't have come at a worse time for me.

When I told Karen about Eliot's request that night, she said I had to honor it and open the fund for everyone. But she told me that I had better brace myself for massive redemptions, given that I was down for the year and that many of our investors might have been in Long-Term Capital or other hedge funds that had been hurt. I might be their only source of liquidity. Nonsense, I told her. After year upon year of beating just about everyone, I had nothing to worry about. Most people wouldn't pull, I said. They would just toss the opening notice, which would allow them to pull their money out during the first five business days in October, into the waste pile.

Karen said that she was surprised that after all the hardball she thought she had taught me that I could be so naive about my performance and its impact, especially after the general tide against hedge funds that summer.

"People are scared," she said. "They might be losing lots of money away from you. Your performance sucks this year anyway"—as half of my stake in the fund she never minced words about how I was doing—"and don't forget Operation Rockbreak and the Marty factor."

I told Karen not to worry. *TheStreet.com* was my hobby, not my business, and when it came to making money, Marty knew I was good even if my performance lately had been shaky. Our relationship at the fund was sacrosanct. Whatever disagreements we had, he'd never leave, I assured her.

Karen just said, "You'd better brace yourself for a run."

I didn't want to believe her, but the most annoying thing about my wife is that, when it comes to business, she's never wrong.

As September drew to a close and the October opening of the fund beckoned, our performance didn't get any better. I kept hearing Karen's warning to brace for a run. I couldn't imagine what it would be like, after years of success, to brace for a run on my fund.

But I was about to find out.

With the final collapse of Long-Term Capital in September, I figured the worst was over for the market, and I started committing a lot of sidelined capital—we had $100 million in cash out of a total of about $325 million in assets going into September. I put much of it to work betting on a rebound. Indeed, the market got a little bump-up in September, some 400 Dow points, but Cramer Berk made only a little bit of money, and we came into October way too long on stocks given that a snapback rally had already occurred and we would soon have to face the partnership redemptions from the Spitzer opening.

The first day of October the Dow shed 200 points, the brunt of it borne by the financials, our own most exposed position. We dropped $30 million in one day. It was our largest loss ever in one session, a drop of almost 10 percent. It happened like lightning. Suddenly, after this brutal session, we were down 25 percent for the year, way behind the averages, which were only down a handful of points. Positions large and small killed us that miserable first day of the toughest trading month of the year. Tech, small cap, large cap, didn't matter. Our largest position, Hayes Modem—we owned millions of shares and had been buying all the way down—had been cut in half, diminishing from $4 to $2 a share on rumors of bankruptcy, a massive unrealized loss.

A million-share position we had in Fairchild, a ne'er-do-well maker of airplane screws, got knocked down for a point; we had been riding that stock down from $26 to the low teens all summer, but it suddenly ticked down to single digits! We also got clocked by BayView, our San Francisco–based savings and loan we owned 9 percent of, for another multimillion-dollar unrealized loss. We weren't making it back in trading either. We owned trading positions in financials and tech, both of which were being killed, and we were shorting high-multiple health care, like Cardinal Health and United Health, a drug distributor and an HMO, and they were rallying. They were perceived as safety and had people running toward them. Not a single one of our more than 100 positions went with us; every single one lost money. It was a terrible day, just horrible, the worst I had ever had, and all the work we had done to try to catch up to the averages all summer was wiped out in one session. At the end of the day I didn't want to leave my desk. I didn't want to talk to the partners who called to ask whether we had been hurt badly or not. I was just dazed and crushed by the array of losses; I really did suck at this job.

It was in that atmosphere that my investors were debating whether to take advantage of the opening, or to stick with a Cramer who seemed to have lost his touch for making money. If anyone was on the fence going into October, that first day moved them solidly into the redemption camp. Pat Shevlin, my no-nonsense office manager, whom I had hired away from my lawyer at Paul Weiss, didn't want to tell me about the pile of faxes that had started building up from the partners who wanted their money back as part of the Spitzer opening. She didn't want to hurt my feelings; she worried that it would shake my confidence. She was hoping that I would make so much money in the first few days of October—you could pull out up until the 7th of the month, a Wednesday, and you would receive your cash on Thursday the 8th—that the redemptions wouldn't even matter. She believed in me so.

In particular, she didn't want to tell me about one of them, which was different from all the others because of the name on top of the letter and the amount to be redeemed. She had received a curt redemption note from Marty Peretz, with an instruction to wire every penny out of the firm that he had helped create and build. He chose to do it in the same bloodless fashion as my withdrawal from his trust, no call, no sit-down face-to-face meeting, just a piece of stationery that signaled the end of the relationship that had launched my hedge fund and my career on Wall Street.

Because of my partners' trust in me, I had never had to sell into a down market to raise cash for redemptions. I certainly didn't think I would have to do that this time, either. I had always had cash around to play the bottom. It had been my hallmark: lots of cash ready to deploy just when everyone else was panicking. It would be the same, this time, when this market was done washing out, I told myself. I couldn't have been more confident as I sat there and graded the day. I gave myself As, Bs, Cs, Ds, and Es for each of the 200 trades we had done that day, as I did every day, and I was struck by how many failing trades I had done.

There had been no As or Bs and only a handful of Cs. Everything else was a failing grade. I had bought into the downturn and there had been no snap. By the end of the day, I had committed a ton of our cash—I calculated we only had $18 million left on the sidelines—without any lift whatsoever. We had always bought weakness, but we had bought weakness with abandon that day. We would need a huge up day to rid ourselves of all of the inventory I put on that didn't rally at the bell, all of the Ciscos and Telebrases and Telmexes and Caterpillars and dozens of other stocks I had bought 50,000 shares of over the course of the day expecting the lift that never came.

Pat had been keeping Jeff informed of the redemption notices, though, and as I sat at my turret going over the $30 million in losses, trying to understand how they could have happened, trying to make sense of the day, Jeff pulled up next to my Bloomberg machine, the one with my "You can kill more flies with napalm than honey" Post-it affixed to its base, and said he had to talk to me about something important. I hated to be bothered when I was recapping and grading; it was a solemn act and I liked doing it alone. But I had a sixth sense of what his dour face and hushed tone was going to tell me.

"Let me guess," I said out loud. "What could be worse than this day? How about a withdrawal notice from Marty?"

He nodded, saying nothing in front of the others on the trading desk. He didn't seem surprised that I guessed it; in fact he seemed perturbed about how cavalier I was about the implications of Marty's retreat. He seemed exasperated when I said, "Look, it will be no problem," because we still had some cash left even after I had put so much of it to work. The $18 million should have been enough, and I knew, if worse came to worst, we could borrow money from Goldman to repay partners, even as I hated that prospect. I was aware that everyone in the trading room was listening to this dialogue. Having been obviously rattled all day by the losses, I did my best to appear as confident as I could in front of the troops.

No, Jeff said, there was something else he had to tell me. I said let's go into your office, the big one with the twenty-four-by-twelve-foot glass window to the trading room. You could pretty much see and hear everything at our place, all the better to enter orders shouted by Jeff. Nope, Jeff said, he wanted me to come into the back room, the conference room, where *TheStreet.com*'s nascent staff had once clustered. We never went there except to discuss marital or health problems, the real deals. You went back there when you thought you might cry and didn't want to be seen. So you never went back there.

I figured there was something wrong at home with Jeff. He always had the same calm expression on his face, just the opposite of me, so the office geography spoke loudly. He wouldn't say a thing until we were out of employee earshot, eighty feet back in the hall with the door closed.

"It's looking like $60 million," he said.

"Sixty million?" I scrunched my eyes, disbelieving. "Sixty million what? What's looking like sixty million?" I had just calculated that we had lost $30 million, what was this $60 million all about? I needed to be left alone to game-plan the next day, I didn't need to hear that we had lost $60 million when I knew to the nearest million that we had lost $30 million.

That's when he dropped the atomic bomb: Pat, he said, had faxes that added up to $60 million in withdrawals and it was only the first business day that we were open. There were plenty more that could still come in. We had agreed to honor any withdrawal requests that came in during the first five business days of October, and it was only day one!

"Sixty million?" I asked. Had to be some mistake. "We are having a bad year, but not *that* bad a year."

He nodded and said, "It's a bad year."

I then had to ask, "Is it really that bad?"

To which he said he knew many worse but we had to admit that we were down double digits and that defined bad.

"We only have $18 million in cash," I said to him.

"I know."

"We have to raise cash in this environment?" I asked rhetorically. "In this screwy market we have to sell to meet redemptions?"

Who the heck was pulling out? I wanted to know. He said he couldn't be sure, but it seemed to be everyone that had ever been referred by Marty Peretz during our eighteen-year association. It then dawned on me; Karen was right: we had a run on our hands.

"The franchise," I whispered. "The franchise is in doubt."

He acknowledged: "The franchise," his voice trailing off.

In tough times you always have to protect the franchise. We were never worried about the franchise, the living, breathing organism that was Cramer Berkowitz, the money machine that had made $300 million in profits in the last few years alone. We had been worried about our cut, our take, how much we would make, how much we would share in bonuses, who should be hired, who should be fired, but we never worried about whether we would make it. Survival had become a given. Now, after one day's trading and a pile of redemption notices, we were worried about our jobs. We were knocked down some 25 percent for the year, and we didn't have enough cash on hand to meet that $60 million that would have to be wired out. We had to sell stocks to raise capital, or we had to borrow money against our declining stock positions, take out a margin loan to pay off departing partners, something that would be the ultimate in recklessness. We had to take one of these two actions into the worst tape I could ever recall. I never had to sell stocks to raise capital. I never borrowed to cover up for losses. That's what amateurs do. Pros always have enough capital on the sidelines. I pretended that I wasn't all that worried.

"We will lighten up tomorrow. We have until the 8th to raise the additional $42 million," I said. I added that I had no intention of borrowing the money from our clearing broker. It was just too dangerous. We would sell stocks and raise cash. "We have nothing to worry about," I said even as I was obviously incredibly worried. I wear worry like a neon sign. Jeff wasn't fooled.

"If no more redemptions come in," he said.

If no more redemptions come in, I acknowledged. If they do, though, we will be back in this room again tomorrow night, planning strategy.

I went home that night and tried to act as normal as possible, as if nothing were wrong at the office. I was such a terrible actor, though, that every time I answered, "Nothing, not a thing," when Karen asked what was eating me, it only betrayed my anxiety more. As did the huge pop of Glenmorangie I had poured, before I had even taken my coat off.

Once the kids were put to bed, with my halfhearted rendition of "The Three Little Pigs" delivered to Emma, our youngest, we lay down ourselves to get ready for sleep. It was then, after I tried to read a few pages, that I couldn't resist. I had to tell Karen what was going on, even as I knew she would be brutal.

All at once, I told Karen what had happened, told her everything, from the amount of the redemptions to the departure of Marty, everything except the exact details of how poorly we were doing.

"You knew it would come to this," she said immediately. "You knew when you took Marty on it would come to this, just when you are most vulnerable."

I told her that I never really felt that I had taken Marty on. All I did was disagree with him over *TheStreet.com.* She told me to stop kidding myself at last, that I had precipitated the breach by not going along with every-thing he wanted, and never correctly apologizing, like a man, to him for my betrayal of him for an alcoholic I barely knew who couldn't be trusted. I had compounded it with quitting those trusts and just being downright unfriendly on a score of issues about money.

All true, I said, but I wasn't going to give up. I told her that I would call all those partners except Marty who were asking for money and talk them out of it.

"Don't waste your breath," she said, adding that my performance had been so subpar that they had reason enough to leave without Marty's in-fluence. "They are being killed at every hedge fund. And they are being told to get out. You will just get more frustrated. Worry about your perfor-mance, not the quitters."

I knew she couldn't resist asking, I knew I wasn't going to get out of this conversation, not with this former hedge fund trader, without the cru-cial question.

She didn't let me down. Right before we went to sleep, as she had done dozens of times in our marriage, she turned to me and said, "How *is* the fund doing? How bad is your performance?"

Not that bad, I said, not looking at her.

"How much are you down?"

I gritted my teeth, averted my eyes. The betraying beads of sweat ap-peared magically on my forehead. Will they ever not?

"Twenty-five percent," I said meekly, as if she would somehow take pity on me if she knew how much it hurt me to say that.

"And where's the Dow?"

"Oh, a little less than that."

"How much less?"

"Oh, about half of that." It was actually about a quarter of that.

"Oh man, that is terrible. What is happening there?"

Unlike with Jeff, I couldn't ask, "It's not that bad really, is it?" The wife never played those games. Terrible meant terrible, as in "You really blew it, you idiot." "Look," I said, now boiling in perspiration, "if you think you can do a better job, why don't you come in? I need the help."

She raised herself off the bed, looked right at me, and said she would. I was shocked. She hadn't been in the office in four years, hadn't traded in five. She said she couldn't come in the next day because she had no sitter. But she would be there next week, maybe as early as Tuesday the 6th, or Wednesday the 7th, to see if she couldn't make some sense of what we were doing wrong.

I was on *Squawk* Tuesday, so I said it would have to be Wednesday. Her resolve to come in was too pat; it didn't seem at all spur-of-the-moment. "Did Jeff tell you I was freaking out?" I asked. "Is that why you are ready to come in? Did he call you and tell you how bad it is?"

"No, Jim," she said. "You did. Every day, with the way you walk around the house. The way you don't even hear what anyone is saying. The way you don't care about anything. The way you keep reading the same page of your book every night." True, I seemed to be forever on page 174 of Paul Carell's *Scorched Earth: The Russian-German War, 1943–1944,* forever reading about the third battle of Kharkov, having long since forgotten about the first and second.

I might as well have made a bed of Kingsfords, soaked them with lighter fluid, lit a match, and then tried to put them out with my body, that's the kind of crummy sleep I had. It was 3:15 A.M. on the clock before I knew it, and I wasn't sure I had slept at all when I decided to get up to go to work.

CHAPTER 15

Crisis in 1998:
Part Two

Sure, I had promised Jeff that the next morning, Friday, October 2, we would raise some cash as soon as the markets opened. I knew we had to meet the redemption notices that were piling up in Pat Shevlin's crowded corner office and we couldn't wait until October 8 to sell stocks to raise that cash. You had to pass Pat's nook to get to the small rest room in the back of our offices on the eighth floor at 100 Wall. I dreaded going to the bathroom that next morning, lest I see her. I did my best to avert my eyes so she wouldn't cry.

I didn't have time, though, for the bathos. There were too many redemption faxes flying around to keep this run a secret. Everybody gossiped on Wall Street about franchises on the rocks. I knew that, given the breadth of the pullout, the sheer number of accounts that were departing, the size of the withdrawals and the number of different banks that had to be let in on the withdrawals (each partner submits instructions about where to wire the money and then notifies those banks to expect a large wire from Cramer Berkowitz's account at Goldman), and the coolness with which the partners were leaving, that word had to leak out that we might be on the ropes. I had a paranoiac's sense, finely honed by the suspicions that you need to be a skeptical manager, that people would be buzzing about how Cramer was on the verge of folding. I feared that we would be turned into a Long-Term Capital, where others would know we would have to raise cash, and they would knock our positions down ahead of us. I was a visible guy on Wall Street, and not well liked, given my penchant for carpet-bombing my enemies on television and in *TheStreet.com*.

I didn't have long to wait to find out how widespread the knowledge of our problems was. David Faber, the enterprising reporter from CNBC who often sparred with me on *Squawk Box,* rang me up that morning, an hour and a half before the opening, ostensibly to chitchat. After we had joked about how awful the market had been, how it seemed to go down every day, he said he had something to ask me about, something sensitive. I figured maybe he wanted to come to work with me, either at the hedge fund or *TheStreet.com*. We were that friendly and he knew I thought he did some of the best journalism around on or off TV. I always wanted to hire him.

"Shoot," I told him. "We have no secrets."

David drew a breath and then said, "Jimbo, I hear you are in trouble."

What a moron I am, I thought to myself, to even think that he would want to come to work for the soon-to-be-defunct Cramer Berk! He wanted to bury us! I knew we were dead if David broke a story ahead of our redemption deadline. I mused to myself about the tease: "*Squawk Box* co-host and *TheStreet.com* founder Jim Cramer may soon fold up his firm. Details in a moment." What partner would stay on if he reported that? We had just a few more days left before the window closed. I had to stall him, but I couldn't lie to him. He'd kill me. Twice! But we would never be able to sell anything if people knew we might be folding. All the bids for our stocks that we needed to liquidate would disappear. No one would let us get out. All of these years in business, all of the hard work and the headaches and the stress, and now I was going to end up like Long-Term Capital with every Tom, Dick, and Harry hedge fund leaning against me, shooting against me, trying to put me out of business. Many of my holdings were public, because of regular SEC filings on large positions. I was an open book, easily mutilated. But how much did David know? Maybe he didn't know. Maybe he was just fishing. Maybe "trouble" had a percentage attached to it. Man, was my brain spinning, stream-of-consciousness maximus.

"How badly do you think we are hurting?" I asked David after about six seconds of silence. There had been so many hedge funds going belly-up lately that I didn't even know what "trouble" was.

"I hear you are down 40 percent."

Phew, I thought to myself. We are doing terribly, horribly, miserably, but hallelujah, down 25 percent is not down 40 percent. "Nope, we have not lost that much, although we are down well into the double digits," I admitted.

"Are you going to close up shop?" he wanted to know.

"Not unless someone kills me or you run a piece saying I am," I joked, even as I was now pondering just such a fate pretty much every waking moment. "I am not going to get driven out of this business," I said. "I am not leveraged. I'm not going down like the geniuses at Long-Term Capital. I am not going to let that happen."

David said he understood that we wanted to stay in the game, but so did Long-Term Capital. I agreed, but I said I thought we could make it because we hadn't had to borrow money. I didn't tell him we would have to get a margin loan with shaky collateral for close to $70 million four days from now at this redemption pace or blow out of whatever positions the market would let us and still be able to regain some capital. I asked him if it was a story that we were hurting even though we weren't leveraged. It was the leverage that killed Long-Term. He said everyone was hurting, but if we were borrowing a lot of money and we had a capital call, that was different. And if we were folding it would be a huge story, one he wanted to go with first. Great, I thought to myself, guy wants an exclusive on my obituary. Like it will matter to me anymore once that story breaks anyway. I'd be finished on Wall Street even if David were sympathetic. Anyone with a mouth as large as mine, who stumbled as poorly as I was stumbling, would be endless fodder for even the dumbest of reporters, and Faber was certainly not one of those.

He suggested I ought to address my poor performance when I was on *Squawk* early that next week. "Clear the air," he put it. I told him that I would talk about it as best I could given that I wasn't supposed to talk about my performance, good or bad, on television. What a blessing that rule turned out to be now. When my numbers were great, I always kicked myself that I couldn't talk about it, because federal regulations forbid hedge fund managers from pushing their funds publicly to unaccredited investors, ones with less than $5 million in liquid assets—the test I used to be safe—or almost the entire audience. Now, the same nonpromotional rules worked *for* me, given my terrible performance, a bizarre unintended benefit of an obscure portion of an obscure securities act.

"Maybe I should pour some gasoline on my head and light a match too," I suggested, and thanked him for at least waiting until I failed to break the story of my failure. He rang off but not before he reminded me, "There's a lot on the line, Jimbo, between your fund and *TheStreet.com.*" There was no denying it; my fund's going belly-up would most likely be the end of *TheStreet.com* too. How ironic, I thought, that the run on my fund, begun innocently to meet a redemption of my friend Eliot Spitzer, had now snowballed into a cataclysm led by *TheStreet.com* co-founder Marty Peretz! Didn't Marty realize that if I didn't break this decline, I was finished, and *TheStreet.com* wouldn't have much credence if its star writer lost his hedge fund? He had as much to lose financially as I did at *TheStreet.com,* even though he would get his money back from Cramer Berkowitz. Of course the comeuppance I would get would be staggering. Maybe that more than made up for the financial loss in Marty's eyes? But that sort of reasoning was too tortured even for me to comprehend.

I was beside myself after Faber's call. I looked around the room. I took all my calls on the desk, the horseshoe-shaped piece of furniture Karen had designed so we all faced one another. I was surrounded by traders, two to three feet away from me. Nothing was private. Did Mark know how bad things really were? Did Clarke know? Sal? Did they hear that conversation? Could I trust them? Did they know how precarious things were? Too late, anyway, I figured.

The press now knew. Faber couldn't be more than a day or two ahead of the others who would want this one. One negative story between now and the redemption deadline that loomed so close, the following Thursday, and we would simply have to give up, no matter what the bravado. Maybe the next reporter wouldn't be as demanding of the facts. He wouldn't want them to get in the way of the great story of Cramer's demise.

I could see, though, that no one on the desk had paid much attention to the call. At least they didn't act that way. There had been so much desperation that summer that maybe this new bit of catastrophe just whizzed over on them. Jeff was off the trading desk, on the phone, in his office. I made a throat-slitting signal to get him off the phone—we always talked in hand signals—and let his door slam.

"Word's out," I said. "They know. We are in big trouble."

"Who knows?" he asked.

"Faber."

His jaw fell two inches, eyes bugging out behind his wire rims. "Oh shit," he said. "We're dead if he does a story. How much does he know?"

"Not enough," I said. "He doesn't know the extent of the damage and would only be able to say that we are hurting like everyone else."

"Did he promise not to do one?"

Jeff, I said, it doesn't work that way. If he wants to do one he does one. More important, I said, we have to change our game plan. We can no longer sell into this market. "I don't care how much money we have coming out. We can't start offering our stocks, the stocks we are known for. We can't risk knocking our stocks down to get out." That would be blood in shark-infested water. We'd be eaten alive in seconds. We have to hope that stocks go higher or we'd have to borrow all the money.

Jeff reminded me, calmly, that this was Friday and all the money that had to come out was due by next Thursday at the latest. We couldn't wait any longer to start raising cash. He said that even if we sold a lot of stock, raised a lot of cash, and then asked for a loan for the rest from Goldman Sachs, we might not have enough truly liquid collateral left to secure the loan. Goldman might not want to give us the full borrowing power against thinly traded goods like Westerfed and Cape Cod Bank and Trust. Goldman might regard that as too risky to do. We could be maxed out and not have enough borrowing power. There was a legal amount of money, regulated by the Federal Reserve, that you could borrow against your stocks, and our illiquid stocks wouldn't be regarded as acceptable collateral. It was entirely possible, he said, if we didn't raise the cash, and we borrowed against our stocks, that we wouldn't have enough borrowing power to send out the money. It would violate our partnership agreement to send out stock instead. We would be sued for the cash personally. Or Goldman would shut us down for borrowing too much. We would be liquidated! Just like Long-Term Capital. And we still had a few days to go where people could pull money out!

"We have to sell today," he emphasized again, no matter what the consequences to our performance.

I told him that I knew the way Wall Street worked and that he was dead wrong. If we were seen trying to sell any of the stocks that we are known for, any where we have filed that we own more than 5 percent of the outstanding stock, the other guys will bury us. We might as well just fold up the firm. They will just eat us alive. I explained to him that even though brokers are never supposed to "give up" clients' names, there was something about a dying client that sent these brokers to go to the untapped pay phone downstairs—all brokerage calls are recorded—and tell their buddies, "Cramer's bailing, get short Fairchild," or "Cramer's bailing, go buy some puts on BayView," our two largest positions at the time.

I told Jeff I wasn't going to let the shorts get the better of us, not after the pasting we had been taking and the massive declines the stock market had undergone, despite what amounted to relatively positive fundamentals, particularly for tech. Even though we only had a few more days to raise the cash needed to meet those redemptions or else run afoul of the margin rules and risk being shut down as a firm, we had to defend our positions, not sell them, especially the big ones. We had to buy, not sell, I said. We had to commit our remaining capital. We had to shore up our positions and chance that the market would go our way.

Before the call from Faber I had asked for preliminary levels of where our stocks might be opening with an indication that we might be big sellers. Now, knowing that people were whispering to reporters that we were about to go belly-up, I decided to buy, not sell, our stocks, borrowing from Goldman Sachs not to pay to partners but to pay for more stock in order to throw the sharks off the scent. I switched every order to the buy side. Once the opening bell rang, I took the orders into my own hands—away from my head trader—and began to bid up all of our bigger positions, every one of which had gigantic sellers weighing on them.

You know there are sellers because you can ask your broker for a "floor picture," if the stock is on the New York Stock Exchange. Every large position I had checked had "the world" for sale, to employ the slang traders use for a stock that is overwhelmed with sellers. I asked my best broker, Max Levine at Hoenig, one of the many firms I used to execute trades, check to see whether any of the sellers were selling short, betting against the stocks with the hope that the stocks would break down and they could buy them back and benefit from the declines. Max said he would make some calls. He came back just a few minutes later and told me there weren't a lot of long sellers. He told me not to worry too much. He had been my broker for ten years, and my wife's for four years before that. He was our friend, a friendly avuncular broker who knew when his clients were up a creek.

"Come on, Max," I said. "I can handle it. What's this 'not a lot of long sellers'? What's the real picture?"

"All short, Jimmy, sorry. Tens of thousands of shares offered short every eighth or quarter point up for most of your smaller names." I sighed. I didn't need to say anything. "Looks like everybody's betting against you," Max confirmed to me. I thought, at least I'm not paranoid. They really are out to destroy me. Solace on the mental illness front, trouble on the financial front. I told Max to bid wildly and aggressively to show people that I was alive and not going down. He understood immediately: we were not to surrender.

Frankly, I didn't want to buy any more of these hurtin' stocks if I could avoid it. All sectors of the stock market had been hammered mercilessly for weeks on end and I was beginning to see bargains everywhere. The Nasdaq had just fallen almost 10 percent. Big bank stocks were being creamed. I didn't want to buy some little dinky savings and loans or some stupid maker of aircraft fasteners. But we had no choice: defend what we owned or die, even if the merchandise wasn't going to bounce. We had watched our two million shares in BayView go from $38 to $15 in the last few months. Man, did I hate those clowns at BayView. Bunch of terrible loaners and managers. I had inherited it from an acquisition of a good bank we had owned that was also in California. And I had stupidly bought more all the way down. Now that it was flirting with hat sizes, we had to step up and buy, regardless of what a bunch of morons they were. We had to take advantage of the distress our own potential demise was causing.

Same with Fairchild, the down-and-out rustbelt screw maker. We had battled Fairchild for six straight years. We had started the position at $2 a share when my wife was still with us because she liked the chart. We had ridden it up to the mid-20s in the last few years, during the boom of the airline cycle as demand for aircraft fasteners went through the roof. Like fools we had sold nothing up there. Fools! Now it had lost two thirds of its value in just several months, another unintended result of the world's financing mechanisms coming unglued because of Long-Term Capital. Because of the credit crunch there wasn't any bank money for airlines to buy more planes. The last thing you wanted right now was to buy more shares in a poorly run maker of airplane screws. Boeing was going down every day. Who needed to own shares of its largest fastener supplier? Boeing catches cold, I get typhoid.

What was I to do, though? If I didn't bid for stocks like Fairchild, which everyone knew we owned, if we let these short sellers lean all over them, we would run the risk of appearing dead in the water. Then the decibel level of the rumors would only grow. I couldn't risk that.

Sure enough, I managed to battle some of the larger positions into stability by 11:00 A.M., buying call options well above the price of the stocks, just to make things more difficult for the bears who bet against us. If Cramer was buying calls, short-fused instruments that win only if there's a quick move upward, the bears might say, maybe he really does know something good, short-term.

The bluff worked. The giant sellers who had kept lids on virtually all my positions walked away after I bought the calls. They canceled their sell orders. My gambit succeeded momentarily, even as I knew that I would lose money in all those call positions. But if I had protected the franchise, this would be money well spent. However, the unseen enemies then came after some of the smaller savings and loans, mercilessly knocking them down to mouthwatering levels, levels I couldn't do anything about because I was already maxed out at the 9.9 percent legal limit on each of them. I was a sitting duck on a half-dozen large positions that I couldn't buy more of even if I wanted to! Our inability to stem the declines in those smaller thrifts knocked another $10 million off our net worth by the closing bell.

Our huge loss occurred despite the Dow's rallying 152 points. None of these stocks that got walloped were correlated with the big capitalization stocks of the Dow. The Dow's jump on a day where we lost so much money shamed me to the core. It's bad enough to lose a lot of money—and $10 million was a huge amount of money for any fund—but to lose money on a day when the averages rally that big, well, that just made our viability that much more difficult to maintain. Unless you have taken a $10 million hit to your fund's net worth in a matter of hours, *on an up day,* you can't understand the depth of self-loathing I felt. Friendly partners called that afternoon—yes, there were still a couple rooting for us—wondering if we had been able to make a little hay while the Dow sun shone. I couldn't even take their calls, fobbing them off to Jeff and Pat. I couldn't lie.

Once again, at the end of the day I methodically pored over what we did wrong. And I bumped into Pat going back to the gent's. "I don't want to tell you this," she said as soon as she saw me.

"How much?" I said, reading her mind like a 500-square-foot neon billboard.

"Another $14 million in redemptions." All one client. I looked at the name. I couldn't believe it. No, not Larry. Couldn't be. I thought I had won him over. I had made him a fortune over the years. I had to talk him out of going.

I told Pat that these folks were cashiering out at the bottom. They couldn't be more wrong. While the credit conditions in the country had deteriorated, if the Federal Reserve, which had cut interest rates once in September, just moved aggressively, the whole market could turn up. This was all due to Russia and Long-Term Capital. Our markets were sound. Tech was booming. The market had headed straight south in a line that had taken it almost 20 percent from its top, and I told her to tell partners that it was ridiculous to sell now. You don't sell in those markets, I explained, you buy. She said that's exactly what she told every partner who was pulling out. She was well rehearsed in calming; a stalwart airline stewardess with three engines out had nothing on Pat by this point. All for naught.

I urged her to give me the phone number of Larry, the guy who was yanking $14 million. I'll talk some sense into him, I said.

"His mind's made up," she said. "I wouldn't bother."

"I have to try," I said. She told me she didn't want me to call him. It would just make me more depressed. I said I had to try. I simply wasn't this bad a manager. I knew if they pulled out at the bottom, I would be pulling out at the bottom.

A few seconds into the call I realized Pat was again trying to do her motherly best to protect me from the anger people had toward me for losing their money. What a mistake I had made. I had jotted down what I

wanted to say, as I was too tired and too petulant to leave it to extempora-
neous thinking. Larry's secretary put me on hold for about four minutes
and then he picked up, brusquely and brutally, with a "Yeah?" This guy
didn't want to hear from me. I had known this guy for a decade, made him
millions upon millions of dollars, and now it was a "yeah?" like I was
some sort of cold-calling broker from nowhere.

"Larry, I want to thank you no matter what for being a terrific partner,
and to ask for another chance, a chance to make back your money."

Larry didn't mince words: "Nope. No way. Told Pat that you shouldn't
bother calling me. We want our money now. You can't make it back. Don't
kid yourself."

I had made up my mind not to use the word "but" because losers always
start with the "But, but, but" stutter that makes them sound desperate. Yet
I found myself saying, "But, but, but, I am confident I can get us back into
the black." What a loser I am, I shuddered to myself.

"No one comes back from how far you are down, no one," he said. "We
will only be left with less money at the end of the year. We don't want you
to lose any more of our money." Thanks, man!

I told him that I wasn't a quitter and that I could methodically make it
back. He told me that obviously I wasn't as good as I thought or I wouldn't
be down so much to begin with, and that it was inconceivable I could come
back. It would make more sense just to quit, because I wouldn't be able to
pay my people at the end of the year anyway because we hadn't made anything. I didn't get angry, but I said, "Man, that's a little harsh." I told him
that I thought I deserved better, that I deserved another chance.

"Not after that kind of loser performance," he said. "Anyway, everyone
else wants out, why should I stay in? You are too busy being on television
to even know what's going on anymore."

Ouch! I saw a *New York Post* headline, THE KING OF ALL FINANCIAL
MEDIA GETS CROWNED! flash in my brain.

The call only lasted a little more than a minute. I don't remember either
of us saying goodbye.

But a lifetime's worth of achievement had just been packaged, tied up,
pronounced worthless, and thrown into a stinking Dumpster. *My* lifetime's worth. I stared at my law degree hanging on the wall. Oh no, any-

thing but back to that. For a few minutes I sat there, phone in hand, repeating what Larry had said to me. "Not after that kind of loser performance. Everyone else wants out. Not after that kind of loser performance. TV! Fucking TV!" I don't even remember hanging up the phone.

For someone whose only security came from finishing first, the words stung so deeply I might as well have been told to kill myself. For a moment I thought, That's why those people jumped in '29. They jumped because they *should* have jumped. They jumped because they had just lost a lot of money and were losers delivering loser performances, and people wanted that money back. They couldn't give it to them. They jumped because it was rational. Because it was right. Because it was, yeah, the honorable thing to do. Because it was quicker than hiding or disappearing.

As I left my office Jeff greeted me with a level of optimism that, after that conversation, was totally surreal. Somehow he believed, as I did, that I could still turn on enough charm to keep partners in.

"He told me to fuck myself," I told Jeff.

"Guess he's not staying," Jeff said. I couldn't tell if he was joking or summarizing.

Jeff had been busy calculating the losses and the withdrawals, telling me that we would now be borrowing more than $80 million if we wired out all the money, now $74 million, that we needed to repay the departing partners. He was getting on my nerves with this stuff, like the Big Ben of margin, constantly telling me the clock was ticking. Right in my face.

But Jeff was just doing his job. He was worried, correctly, about the fund being shut down by our broker because we had overborrowed. I knew that, given our large, illiquid stock positions, Goldman Sachs would never let us borrow that much against the stocks. We didn't even have $200 million in true liquid equity to borrow against, now that we had lost $88 million. It was too risky for them to loan us the money. It was too risky for us to take it. We had to find a way to sell to meet the redemptions. Get cash. But if we sold anything in size, the rest of our stocks would collapse because the world would know immediately we were bailing. I couldn't see my way out of this jam. We sell, we crater. We don't sell, we crater.

We walked to the back room again, out of earshot of any of the employees. "Should we fold, Jeff?" I asked him, my face buried in my hands. "I don't see how we can get out of this box in time. And even if we do, nobody's getting paid this year. You know I can't pay you if we don't make any money."

Jeff seemed hurt I would even ask. I never showed him this level of fear, ever. He was uncomfortable with it. Uncomfortable with what it meant for the franchise. We had never had a contract with each other. We just had a handshake we'd been living off of for the last half-dozen years. He said he would be respectful if I wanted to pack it in. However, he thought it would be hasty to give everything up after a couple of bad days. He said it was time to summon the inner strength he thought I was famous for. It was time to suck it up.

He said we were great pain takers. We had three months left. We could pull it out. Me, I was getting sick of the pain. Maybe it wasn't a couple of bad days, I said. Maybe Larry was right. Maybe my time had come. I told him I wanted to take the weekend and think about what had to be done. Maybe we couldn't make it back.

He told me that I had to get my head out of the negativity and think the way I had taught him, that we could come back from anything as long as we worked harder than anyone else. "Easier said than done," I told him. But I understood what he was saying. If I didn't get my head out of the funk that said, in a virtual tape loop, "I am an idiot, I am a loser, I don't deserve people's trust," if I persisted in thinking we were going to lose, then we *would* lose.

I mentioned that earlier in the week, on still another night when I couldn't get to sleep, I had gone downstairs to the den where the kids play. There on top of a pile of coloring books was a *National Geographic* article about Ernest Shackleton, the explorer who had been set back many times while on a trek through Antarctica, but had managed to turn defeat into victory through optimism. I told him that maybe I would stop by Borders on the way home and buy the book *Endurance,* by Alfred Lansing, so I could read it over the weekend. (We were short Amazon. I didn't ever patronize something we were short, on principle, until we covered and went long.) Maybe Shackleton's diary would give me strength, I said. Shackleton's innate optimism had saved him and his crew in trying situations much worse than the one we faced.

I wish I could say Shackleton's great voyage had an immediate effect on my performance. It didn't, but it did buck up my attitude that interminable weekend when I waited to see if we would have more redemptions and more red ink at the fund.

I devoured *Endurance* twice that Saturday and Sunday and came back on Monday morning, October 5, renewed for the fight and anxious to right the proverbial ship. Karen hadn't yet lined up a sitter, but I got in at 4:00 A.M. to game the day. I loved to sit down with a pencil, still, and go over the permutations of what would happen with each position based on certain contingencies. It gave me solace. When I was finished I looked up at the huge white board where we would always write down the day's meaningful numbers as well as whatever underwritings that we might be following. I rose and grabbed the thick permanent marker we used to write down the facts of the deals. On the top of that board I wrote out in big block letters: "Optimism Is True Moral Courage," one of Shackleton's great observations. When the troops came in I talked to everyone en masse about how Shackleton led his expedition through one frozen disaster after another without a man being lost, and I would do the same now, without a person or a dollar being lost.

I said we were now down almost $90 million for the year—everyone pretty much knew that number, as many people were involved in calculating it each day for us—but that we were going to battle back and everyone would get paid even if it meant getting paid out of my own pocket instead of by the partners. I didn't know how I was going to do that, but I said it and meant it. I got everyone really pumped.

We went back out on the playing field, bolstered by some Shackleton sayings, and by my renewed determination. And we promptly dropped another $10 million by 10:00 A.M., a half hour into trading. The Nasdaq crashed another 4 percent and the Dow shed 50 points, so at least we weren't alone. But we had now lost $20 million in two days. Almost $50 million had disappeared since the month of October began, and we were only in day five! World land speed record for money loss.

It was another brutal day where our core positions dropped precipitously as short sellers pressed every one of them down. But tech nosedived too. Our core positions in Microsoft, Dell, Intel, and, most problematically, Cisco, ate whatever capital the S&Ls didn't. Cisco, long our largest technology holding, slipped 7 points, or 14 percent on a downgrade by Chris Stix, a highly respected networking analyst then at SG Cowen, a prominent broker, who had never ever had a bad word to say about Cisco before. He had cited some proprietary networking survey of business use; I think, in retrospect, he downgraded it because he didn't want to be recommending a stock that now cowered like a loser. Cisco had held up much better than our other positions, our financials, during this decline, but now it was getting killed too. Our large banks and brokers were all hit for 2- and 3-point losses. We were reeling by the end of the day. We defended BayView and Fairchild, the fastener company, but that's about it. We put very little money to work, not willing to waste the remaining few million in cash on what looked to be the beginning of another down leg in the market, this time led by tech.

Good time to go on national television and talk about what you think of the market, I said out loud at 4:00 P.M. that Monday in mock joviality about my pending *Squawk Box* appearance the next morning. Our losses had now reached close to $100 million for the year—I still carry around a tattered photocopy of the front of the margin run from that day, which tells you how much you have made or lost to date, between pictures of my wife and kids in the plastic folder portion of my wallet. I couldn't believe I had to face a national audience being down almost $100 million—whether they knew or not!

The CNBC gang had taken the show on the road and we were headed to Philadelphia, my hometown. It should have been a triumphant trip. When CNBC first told me about the trip, I couldn't have been more thrilled. Local hero. Cover of *Money* magazine. Trader king. Back at home and on top!

But now I was dreading it. We were now down 31 percent, a disastrous performance, even with the averages down big for the year, and while I had no desire to hide how badly I was doing, to come to my hometown and put on a good face seemed too much to me. Trader fraud. Pastrami king.

That morning, as I shivered in the cold across the street from the Liberty Bell waiting for *Squawk* to begin, I watched a makeshift monitor as Alan Greenspan was talking live to the crowd at some business conference. Greenspan had started cutting rates in September, with his usual caution, but the rate cut had had little impact. Still, with the Long-Term bailout (that is, a supervised, orderly liquidation) completed, Greenspan seemed sanguine and oblivious to what was happening in the capital markets in the aftermath of LTCM. As I watched Greenspan out of one eye, I was shocked to see him joking about the shape of the U.S. economy. Joking. How dare he? When I went on camera I asked, Didn't he know how badly everyone was doing? But I thought to myself, Didn't he know how badly I was doing? He may have thought the financial crisis had passed, I told the camera, but he was oblivious to the shutdown of credit in this country and how it could quickly drive us into recession. He thought there were no problems. I wanted to know what market he was looking at. The supermarket? What's he talking about? Financial crisis past? He's dreaming. The companies we talked to at my firm were reeling from losses incurred because short rates were so much higher than long rates. There was no liquidity, a true credit crunch in the system as rates got lower and lower but nobody had enough capital to lend, and if they did, they lost money on it. We cut to a commercial. My televised rant had lasted for what seemed liked ten minutes. Obviously I was taking it personally, even more personally than usual.

During the break Mark Haines could tell that I was really distraught, no acting. He didn't want to ask me how bad, but he said we had to discuss it. I agreed. When the cameras and mikes turned back on, Haines asked me how my firm was doing through this tough period. "Lousy," I said. I told him—and the national audience—that this had been my worst year ever, that I was getting killed, and that judging by what Greenspan was saying, it would only get worse. I said that Greenspan was out of touch, and that his slowness would cost investors fortunes. I needed the rate cut, I said. I needed it to make back the losses I was experiencing. I babbled virtually incoherently about my situation. Me and Greenspan. Like he cared about Cramer's fund.

Haines rescued me with a question about what people should do in this market. Hold tight, I said, and if the Fed said it might ease again, buy aggressively because it was in the Fed's power to stop this decline with rate reductions.

During another break, later in the show, my dad, who had wandered into the crowd from his apartment a few blocks away, came up to the makeshift stage next to Independence Hall. Before he could even say hi, I told him that I was down, down big. He said everyone was down. I told him I didn't care about what others were doing, I was drowning. I told him people were deserting me like rats on a sinking ship. He told me he just came over because he was proud to see me and that I had to realize that there was more to me than the last five days of trading. I told him you were only as good as your last trade, and that I sucked. You can't let people see that, he said. He urged me to think positively and to just keep fighting and that he was confident that I would make it back.

He had brought a picture of me from Springfield High in Montgomery County, nine miles from where we stood, to show to the *Squawk* boys. Either he didn't understand how much trouble I was in or he didn't care, because he loved me regardless of how much I was worth. In my agitated state this was too hard to fathom. He showed the picture of me with hair to Mark. Mark put it on the air, and we finally left the topic of my lack of performance to talk about my lack of hair. You know you are down big when you are relieved that it is your baldness they are making fun of. I felt better, and only mentioned a couple of more times how this was my worst year ever. I took off for the office in New York two minutes after ten, barely saying so long to the cast or my dad, who deserved better, of course. The market was already starting its daily spiral and I had to get back to defend my positions.

My *Squawk* show was hardly confidence-inspiring. When I got back from Philadelphia, early that afternoon, I wasn't surprised after that frantic performance that another $20 million in redemptions had been called in. It was Tuesday the 6th, the second to last day to pull money out.

I was just heartsick, cursing myself for being a showboat and a joker, just furious at myself. We kept the losing streak alive that Tuesday once again, dropping $6.3 million as the Nasdaq lost another 4 percent and our savings and loans got drubbed once again from Greenspan's rosy comments.

We still had sold little to raise cash, still trying to delay for fear we would be buried by our own sales. We were shell-shocked. We would now be borrowing over $100 million on invested liquid capital of less than $200 million, just to meet the redemptions. We would be more than maxed out. That's something the regulators would never sanction, as 50 percent was the legal limit. We needed the market to rally so we would have more equity to borrow against. If it didn't we might just have to liquidate the whole fund on October 8. It wouldn't be up to us. Goldman, our clearing broker, would close us down. You can't wire out more money than you can borrow without being flagged by the regulators, I had always been told from my days of working with margin clerks at Goldman thirteen years before.

I barely spoke to anyone at home that night other than to say how much we had lost and how big the redemptions were. I said this stuff to my kids, as they tried to tell me about their nice day at school. I didn't even attempt to hide how distraught I was. I ignored the high grades on the fridge from the just-taken geography test. Fortunately, the kids were as oblivious to me as I was to them. Now there's a relationship! I thanked God they were seven and four.

They wouldn't even understand the concept of Loser Dad. Trader pawn. I barely heard, over my own bellyaching, that Karen said she was coming in with me the next day. She had at last gotten that sitter. We would ride in together, as we did ten years before, this time in a chauffered limo, not a yellow cab, but with me feeling just as poor.

The next morning, Wednesday the 7th, Karen went in with me at the more decent hour of 6:00 A.M. after telling me that she wasn't going to start doing the 3:45 A.M. thing. She cared, but she didn't care that much! After about a minute's worth of pleasantries with people she hadn't seen in years other than at the Christmas party, she moved to the desk, claiming her old seat where she had sat for so many years when we worked together—my seat. As if she had never left the desk. She checked her levels—seeing where the S&P 500's support and resistance were, as well as the support and resistance for the Nasdaq, and the fifty- and 200-day moving averages of both, so she had her bearings. She made her calls, and buzzed her old brokers again, as if she had never left. We use screens and direct wires that link us right to trading desks, so all she had to do was hit GSCO (Goldman) or HRZG (Herzog), or LEHM (Lehman) to check in with the same people who covered us, or handled our business when she was with us. "Just here to help Jim out," she said to everyone. "He's short-handed." That was a nice, generic euphemism, and I appreciated it.

Minutes after the opening bell—no "There goes Swifty" intonation anymore; too beleaguered for laughs—she heard firsthand what I had been saying to her every night for days, that other hedge funds were tightening the noose around our necks by leaning on all our positions.

"Every one of your positions is attracting sellers," she said. No kidding, I said to myself. "Must be that stupid Web site," she rubbed it in. "Must be people you angered. Must be, well, everybody!" Succinct description of the jam I had gotten myself into.

What are we to do? I asked. She said she would defend the stocks, move them up if she had to, but we had to get on the phone to each company we were bleeding from the eyeballs with and demand that they do buybacks. "Tell them they better buy back their stocks, or we will bury their stocks with our selling. Tell them you will take their stocks to levels where they will get bids and lose their jobs. Tell them we will do it with glee because they are such bad managers." Man, I thought I played tough. She had moxie. And she was determined to commit capital we didn't have to defend stocks. She was willing to margin us up before we even got to redemption day, some twenty-eight hours from now. (You had to send money out by Fed wire and that wire would close at 1:00 P.M. on October 8.)

Come on, Jeff, let's get to work calling these jamoches, I said, just like the old days, more worried about my wife's fury than anything these execs could unleash on their hapless shareholders. At least we were taking action. It seemed like forever that we had just sat there and taken the pasting. Now we could give it out, even if it fell on the heads of people who didn't care. It felt good not to stand still.

Dutifully, I called the chief financial officer of BayView, the repulsive San Francisco S&L that had fallen some 60 percent during the last few months—I couldn't believe he was in that early given how poor his performance was—and told him what a disgrace his stock was. The fall from $30 to $12.50 since we had bought it, especially the decline in the last few weeks, from $19 to barely a teenager, was criminal, just criminal, I screamed. He had to find buyers of his stock or accept that we were going to have to puke it up all over him in the open market, something that would take it down to the mid single digits and presumably into the arms of some larger bank that would swallow them up. He told us things were going not so hot, and that he couldn't help us. He said that the yield curve was killing his firm but that he had heard rumors that we were in trouble and that others thought we were going to sell so they weren't about to step up and buy.

I told him that we would bury him with sell orders. He said he would try to find other buyers but his confidence was less than inspiring. It was a bust, but I got off the phone hungry for more lashings, anxious to instill some of the fear I had been feeling in others who were as complicit as I was in letting their stocks run down without a comment.

With the other savings and loans, we actually had some luck with Karen's suggestion, though. If we waited a couple of days, two execs said, they might buy back our stakes in the open market. They just needed some time to organize their buybacks. I said we didn't have time. They all seemed to understand. None of them particularly liked us as shareholders even though we never put pressure on them to do anything. They didn't like New York hedge funds as shareholders. They wanted locals, people who did business in their towns, people who didn't want the banks bought by other institutions with nice premiums for shareholders. We were too smart, too eager to sell out when the selling was good. In one case, Westerfed, they were thrilled to hear we were bailing and said they would do their best to buy us out. Fast.

"Just do what you can," I said, holding out the possibility, again, of taking their stocks to levels where a Zions Bank or a Bank of America would reach out and grab them. Again, I felt a ray of hope, and a sense that at least we weren't sitting back and letting others put us out of business.

Unfortunately, all these execs knew we were hurting. Fortunately, their stocks had plummeted well through book value, which meant the stocks were trading through their cash positions, making them incredibly cheap historically. If the Fed decided to lower rates aggressively, these stocks would go through the roof. I could see a situation where these stocks, which now represented the lion's share of our positions, would be the best place to be in the whole market. I hate to use this term because it is so brokerese, but these S&Ls were the proverbial coiled spring.

We couldn't scare the management of Fairchild, though, a two-million share "steaming turd" position, my wife called it, with our bluffs. Jeffrey Steiner, the CEO who ran Fairchild like a private fiefdom, and a mismanaged one at that, had created a second class of stock that he owned that made the company impervious to hostile bids no matter how cheap it got. He was an embarrassment. Nor could we tell him what a joker he was. We needed him to support the stock. They had an authorized buyback. Why weren't they using it? we wondered. Jeff and I urged Steiner to buy some stock too. He agreed.

Again, a position that could sink us stabilized almost before our eyes at my wife's suggestion. A few minutes after the phone calls, bids appeared "underneath," meaning below the market, for the stock. Fairchild had fallen to below $9 intraday from $15 a few days before—a colossal loss given the size of our position. Our two-million-share position now leaped back into the double digits.

"Is that you moving Fairchild?" I asked Karen.

"Nope," she said. "Real buyers."

Nirvana! Our first break during the whole spiral. Real buyers. Real buyers didn't need our capital. We could conserve it for other positions being hurt by the sharks who were nibbling us to death.

While we were making our calls, Karen had made about $310,000 in trading gains, the first ones we had made that month. She made her money mostly on the short side, against Internet stocks, stocks she hated, a legacy of her having to hear endless stories about the wonders of the Net from me. All old pros hated the Net. They knew it was a bubble, but they had been shooting against it for two years now and it wouldn't burst. She shorted Excite and some more Amazon. And she was also able to sell some of our big cap stocks into strength to pay for her early morning defense work of some of our smaller names. Midday, Karen pulled us off the trading desk into Jeff's office. She lay down on the couch and told me to get her a bottle of water. And some fruit. Some French fries from the Hanover Deli, her favorite place down the block. What the heck, sure, I thought. How about a foot massage? I joked. She was winning; get her what she wanted.

She said that if we had a chance to make it out of the morass we had created for ourselves, we had to circle the wagons around a few names, and give up on some others to raise cash to meet the redemptions. She said, though, "Unless the Fed signals an ease, I don't know how we are going to make the sales we need to raise $100 million." She asked me what the likelihood of that interim rate cut was, and I said, slim to none, because Greenspan had all but ruled it out on national television the day before. Could he change his mind? she asked. Anything was possible, but without that rate relief, we were history, I said. She wasn't giving up yet, although she said she wasn't happy that I had told her we weren't that far behind the averages. "You suck right now, but I believe in you the only way I know how," she said, waving a check for $154,000, her money that she had kept in a joint Schwab account with her mother from when she was single. It was all she had away from the fund, but she said it was important to show the flag. "Better than a sharp stick in the eye," she said. She was always saying that. Everything was always better than a sharp stick in the eye. It was our only contribution during this dreaded opening. I had to choke back tears; I couldn't believe she still wanted to bank with me after the mess I had made.

Karen then got back on the desk and resumed trading until the 4:00 P.M. close, going back and forth skillfully on America Online from short to long and long to short, each time buying the stock when it cracked, and selling when it spiked, taking in another couple of hundred Gs. She used our friend Max for the trade, and periodically would tell him how well we were doing, hoping that he would tell other accounts we were alive and well, not even contemplating getting out of the game. For the day, the Dow barely budged, the Nasdaq dropped another 2 percent. Because we defended our positions from any further raids at Karen's wise advice and good trading, we "only" lost $3 million in the session. It was pathetic, but it was our first day of outperformance versus the Nasdaq for the month. Take it where you can get it, I said to myself. I was actually feeling a little better; $3 million in losses after the beating we had been taking felt like a win.

At the end of that Wednesday, the 7th of October, we were now down a little more than $107 million for the year. With twenty-one hours left until the money had to be sent out, the redemption window finally closed. We had received $100 million in redemption against $154,000 in contributions. We had less than $120 million in equity to borrow against, ex the withdrawals. We would be a small fund when the next day came, a fraction of our former size, and we would have to sell at least $40 million, and maybe as much as $50 million, in order not to get closed by Goldman because of a margin rule violation, as many of the stocks we were using for margin would not be considered acceptable. No way around it.

Jeff and I were totally bewildered. The market looked horrible. We were down a staggering 35 percent. With the next day's sales, we would knock our performance down, perhaps as much as 40 percent. No one ever made it back from there. And that assumed Goldman would allow us to borrow to the max, something that seemed increasingly unlikely given the motley crew of stocks we had left to borrow against. But Karen was either totally unflappable or the Katharine Hepburn of the trading game, putting on a remarkable act. "We will be back at them tomorrow," she said. "We'll get it done." She made me go home shortly after the bell. She wanted to go to the movies, but I said I had to go over the portfolio again and catch the opening in Japan to see if there was any bottom coming from overseas.

Like the old days, we didn't talk about the market once we got home. Oddly, for once, I left it at the office as I used to when we traded together. That too felt good.

Shortly before 9:00 P.M., I checked with my brokers in Asia. I don't know why I was thinking I might catch a break. It was all bad over there. All down huge. And now the dollar had joined the rout. Karen offered me a Xanax. I took it and went to bed.

We woke up to a rainy miserable Thursday morning, redemption day. More accurately I woke up. I couldn't get Karen up. It was 2:45 A.M. I joked to Karen that at least there could be no more redemptions after today but I wasn't sure if she even heard me. In those dark days I often talked to myself, hoping she would hear and wake up to somehow comfort me from the demons of underperformance. She opened her eyes just long enough to tell me that I should go in without her. She would catch up on some ZZZs. "We'll need it," she said, rolling over and slamming a pillow over her head.

When you are a hedge fund manager, you should never care which direction the market goes. You are supposed to make money regardless of direction. You are supposed to make money no matter what happens. You can't be beholden to the market.

Not anymore, not for Cramer, I thought to myself as Kyle took me through the Holland Tunnel. "We're just completely at the mercy of this market," I mumbled to myself, slamming my head against the glass of the Mercedes. Kyle wanted to know if everything was all right. "Yeah," I said. "Kind of a big day."

"I have faith in Mr. Cramer," he said.

I sure wish I did. "Wait three hours and then pick up Miss Karen."

Kyle wanted to know if she was going shopping in the city.

"Yeah, she's doing a little buying." Karen had only come into the city in the last few years to shop. If things didn't go well today, I had a feeling that her shopping days were numbered. Every penny we had was in our fund. Virtually every penny.

"Okay," he said. "I am sure Miss Karen will have a good time." And he pulled away from 100 Wall, to the pitch black of the night.

It was 3:45 A.M. Time to see how bad things looked on a day that might be my last in the business if the stock market closed down big. Hostage. Totally hostage. Like a rank amateur. A pathetic rank amateur. Caught long when I should be maximum short. Hung on a stick, ravens picking at my eyes and entrails. Yes, this stuff actually goes through your mind when you are awake, alone, at that hour, rising in an empty elevator to a dark, foreboding eighth floor, paying attention to nothing other than your feet in front of you.

CHAPTER 16

Crisis in 1998:
The Trading Goddess Returns

October 8, judging from the closing levels of the major averages, seemed like a pretty unspectacular day. The Dow Jones Average shed 9 points, around .1 percent to close at 7731.91. The Nazzdogs took it a little worse, losing 3 percent, or 43 points. Thirty-year bonds dropped about a point and a half, bringing their yields to 5 percent on the nose. The dollar got clocked, giving up a big chunk of that year's gains.

But these numbers masked the most important day of the last decade of investing, because on October 8, the bear market of 1998, the vicious, gut-wrenching, horrid decline that had taken stocks well past their two- and three-year lows, and brought some averages down to as low as 40 percent off their highs, came to an end. On October 8, a dreary, chilly rainy Thursday in New York, a day so out-of-kilter that even the Dow Jones Averages didn't trade at the opening (that was the day that Travelers switched into Citigroup, causing a confusing delay that kept people in the dark about the true prices of the averages until a half hour into trading), the stock market bottomed.

At eighteen minutes after 12:00 P.M.

I ought to know. I caused it. At 12:18 P.M. I capitulated. I couldn't take it anymore. I gave up both literally, at my fund, and virtually, on my Web site, *TheStreet.com,* where I penned a piece entitled "Get Out Now." And the prop wash from that article marked the low point in the most vicious bear market of the last century.

I didn't set out to capitulate that day. My spirits had been buoyed by the return of my wife to my trading desk after an absence of four years, and she had generated the first trading profits we had made in weeks and weeks and weeks. The day before had been our first outperformance day versus the Nasdaq in many months. I came in that Thursday thinking we were going to be cool, despite a breathtaking combination of $100 million in losses and $100 million in pending redemptions that had reduced my $325 million hedge fund that I had run successfully for a decade to a pitiful $100 million fund that was down 35 percent and in danger of going under if it didn't raise millions upon millions in cash.

I came in that day as one of the last of the bulls. I thought the market had gone down so much that it had to be near a bottom. I thought, even though we hadn't sold much of anything, we could make it, somehow, without selling and without capitulating. I thought we would be able to ride out the once-in-a-hundred-years storm that had decked so many hedge funds, and do so without having to bolt from the stock market and sell into the abyss, into the cataclysm of the market's mean, miserable maw. I came in thinking that, like Shackleton's crew in *Endurance,* we may not get to the South Pole, but we were going to come out unscathed and looking great and that a floor on the market was truly at hand. It had to bottom. It just had to.

I was wrong. By a minute. And by a mile. This is the story of how that bottom got formed over my own panic and my own personal crescendo of pain.

The day didn't start out ugly; the ugliness from the day before never ended. When I arrived at a quarter to four in the morning, booted up my Bloomberg and my ILX and hit my European trading wires, I saw that the bottom had fallen out of the Nikkei, as the Japanese benchmark lost 799.55 points, or 5.8 percent, wiping out a promising 6 percent gain from the night before. For weeks on end our market had been gyrating lower, but the possibility that Japan, long mired in recession, might be finally getting its house in order offered hope to some funds looking to that nation to help end the international financial crisis that had started more than a year before in tiny Thailand and had since engulfed all of Asia, Latin America, Russia, and with Long-Term Capital's demise, this country too. I had begun to put money in Japan. A small position in Mitsubishi Bank of

Tokyo I had put in late last month to play the world's best acting bourse was now even smaller as of last night. I didn't even bother to get a closing quote. I knew it would be down substantially. Sayonara capital! The Japanese market was never to recover from the decline and still hovers lower than that sell-off today. If the world's other bourses were going to bail me out that day—something I desperately needed—it wasn't going to start in Japan.

Germany had given up 4.5 percent overnight, erasing the remnants of its once monumental gains for the year. I had been looking to Germany as another source of a turnaround. Nope, not today.

But the true slap in the face came from Britain, where the Footsie—the FTSE—plunged 196 points, or 4.1 percent, crashing through the seemingly impregnable 5,000 barrier, despite a rate cut by the Bank of England that very morning. Too little, too late, the market said. I had told my wife that I thought the British might cut rates, that the worries we had were spilling over there. Britain had been one of the remaining pillars in why I wanted to stay bullish. Rate cuts mean everything to me. When they happen, I want to buy, not sell, and I told her that when she came in at 8:30 she would most likely be greeted with a rally caused by the U.K. cut. We had gotten the interest rate reduction, and all that happened was an acceleration of sales overseas. That wasn't part of the plan.

The moment my machines glowed on after boot-up, on that drizzling depressing morning, the S&P 500 futures told the full story: down 24 points, a huge discount to where they were the night before. That's "down limit," a term borrowed from the commodity markets indicating that things had fallen as far as they could legally go at that moment until the index itself that the future was based on began trading. It was the most I had ever seen, a crevasse that made you tremble as you peered for a bottom. And that wasn't the worst of it. The dollar, the strongest currency in the world the week before, had started skidding suddenly with value vaporizing as if it had tripped an invisible claymore mine. Until the decline in the buck, bonds had marched seemingly inexorably toward 4 percent. Now they had whiplashed traders and were headed back full throttle to the 5 percent benchmark. As someone conditioned by sixteen years of trading that any declines in bonds and currencies were bad news for stocks, this reversal seemed outright lethal for our portfolio. Dollar, bonds, stocks, all going the wrong way at once—at *warp* speed! "Can't anybody here play this game?" I asked the empty trading room. I couldn't believe that in this environment we were going to have to redeem our departing partners' cash. I couldn't believe that I actually thought we would have an up day in which we could do our selling in tranquility, and not chaos.

The contrarian in me might have wanted to make a judgment that things were finally so ugly that you had to step up to the plate and start buying, that the market would open so low that prices would finally reach some sort of equilibrium. But just about anybody with a cast iron constitution would be shattered early on by what brokers were saying around the Street. And, after the beating I had taken, I had a more nervous stomach than just about anybody in the game that morning. I had steeled myself for days on end about why all the bears would be wrong and why this market had to bounce. I had written endlessly that we were on the verge of a bottom and those who got out now would be known as quitters, fools, and phonies when the market roared back. I was polishing the bull's horns daily. Yet when faced with bright red stimuli this gray morning, I felt myself wavering and for once I couldn't stop the feeling. Not with that redemption deadline beckoning.

As my traders and assistants filed in I learned one piece of bad news about the market after another. First, Prudential, the giant brokerage, pronounced the market inherently unstable and ready to go much much lower. Ralph Acampora, the firm's chief technician, had cemented his reputation as an astute market caller earlier that summer when he pronounced the bull dead, expecting the stock market to decline some 2,000 points. Now we were at his price target. I got all excited for a moment when Sal asked me if I wanted to hear Ralph's new comments. I figured this could be it, the first man willing to stand up to the selling onslaught. His hands were clean. He could say that the market had reached his downside target and was ready to roar right back. I half expected him to do so. It would have been a master stroke. And it might bail me out of my redemption deadline without much bloodshed.

Nope, nothing came easy that year. In the heat of battle price targets have a way of getting adjusted, and this morning, looking at the futures and the action overseas, it was time for Acampora to take that target down. Once a raging bull, Acampora was this very morning trying to stake out a role as Giant Smokey in the brutal bear market of '98. He announced to his sales force that his Dow target, which had been 7,000, was now going to be 6,735. Those, like me, who thought that we would now bounce from Acampora's floor, saw the floor pulled out from underneath us. And this from someone with high-stakes credibility forged during years of bullishness ahead of this sell-off. The futures would have sagged visibly after such a call, if they hadn't fallen as far as they could legally go before he made his call. Who knew where the real market was.

Goldman Sachs's Abby Joseph Cohen spoke too. As if I hadn't learned my lesson yet, when Rich, my Goldman broker, buzzed me to say that Abby was coming on the squawk box (the P.A.) at Goldman, my heart paced rapidly and a grin broke through my indelible frown. Ah-hah, I said to Jeff, whom I had barely acknowledged that morning because he too had believed my thesis that we could be in for some lift, "Abby's going to put a stop to this decline right now, stop it in its tracks."

What a clown you can look like in this business, within seconds! My smile turned to anger and I mashed my phone into the side of my personal computer when Rich said, "It's not good, Jim."

Cohen had stayed bullish throughout the painful summer, not wavering for an instant from her Supertanker America thesis that our nation would pull the rest of the world through this financial crisis. Every time she spoke, she turned around the futures, or broke the nasty selling waves, as she explained why panicking was wrong and we were in a rip-roaring bull market. She was my bullish soul-mate, someone who made me feel comfortable holding onto the horns while others fled for the Kodiak dens. Unlike Acampora, Cohen is no technician. Her work is based on the future earnings power of the market as a whole. As long as she stuck by her theory that corporate profits would be bountiful, she would stay bullish.

On this particular morning, when I was in need of Abby's most bullish of Supertanker America calls, she made an adjustment to her corporate earnings view. An adjustment *down*. She took her S&P projections for the following year down a tad, just enough to cause another landslide. In a market that had come to see this frumpy curly-haired nerd as a double-hulled supertanker herself, this change jolted those whom Cohen had steered through choppy waters before. It seemed like a warning that the biggest ship of all, the U.S. market, was just as vulnerable to the financial storm as any leaky rowboat. No supertanker, just a Cunard liner headed for an iceberg.

Cries of "Cohen's getting off" echoed through trading desks worldwide. No matter that she didn't predict a decline in equities, just a decline in earnings, the move seemed like a prelude to the most important bull-to-bear switch this market had seen since once perma-bull Elaine Garzarelli yelled crash from her Lehman perch on the eve of 1987's one-day decline of 508 points. You had to get in ahead of a guru switch, not after it. While the futures couldn't trade lower, I heard brokers tell me that they had merchandise for sale off Cohen's call that was 5 and 6 points below where stocks traded before last night's bell. In another frame of mind I would have noticed that you get that kind of capitulation only at important moments in stock history. This time I just cursed myself that I would soon have to join the sellers because we had to wire out $106 million to my departing partners. I was formulating a way to capitulate with dignity, something that is akin to trying to arrange the egg on your face so it looks less scrambled and more sunny-side-up.

If anyone didn't yet recognize the sinking fortunes of financial companies, Citigroup picked this day to announce a staggering loss, even worse than had been anticipated during a previous intraquarter profit warning. The newly created institution fessed up that it had a Long-Term Capital–like global arbitrage unit that had racked up $300 million in losses previously known to the top brass. The Street buzzed that the isolated collapse of Long-Term Capital must not have been as isolated as we thought. Who else had to take a charge? If Sandy Weill took a charge, someone else had to be hurting, hurting far more than Sandy. He's good! Who else had to fess up about this leveraged lunacy? We had been battling with the financials for months on end. Fortunately my wife had us short Citigroup just the day before, as a hedge to all the other banks and savings and loans we owned. Unfortunately, it was only 50,000 shares short. Not much protection there when you are long about 15 million shares of less-well-run financial concerns.

Those looking for hope from the tech sector, which, until this day, had been holding up somewhat better than the rest of the market—save Cisco, which was still reeling from that Cowen downgrade two days before—had their hopes crushed right up front too. The *Washington Post* reported that morning that the Justice Department had more ambitious goals than just to rein in Microsoft's Internet plans. The stock of Mr. Softee, which had stayed strong throughout this period of turmoil, was indicated down 2 or 3 points at the get-go. We had owned 100,000 Microsoft going into that morning as well as 750 Microsoft calls. Supertanker Microsoft. It was our largest nonfinancial position. We looked to be in the hole for 500 Gs for that one position alone. It was offered down 6 points on the article. You could buy millions of shares there. And there were no takers.

Those who had been playing the Net couldn't even count on a rally, as Yahoo!, which at that time was known only as a search engine company, had just beaten the earnings estimates by a whopping 6 cents the night before. This was the first pure Net company to turn a real profit. It was amazing to this Netizen, a blow-away achievement. I figured a profitable Yahoo! could withstand any selling onslaught. Nah, it was looking down a dozen points! It hovered at close to $100 a share. It had been at $125 at one point the day before. The judgment of the Street spoke loudly: upside surprises don't matter when you are faced with thermonuclear meltdown.

Need more negative input? Merrill chose this day to downgrade the airlines, despite a 40 percent decline from the top already this year, based on worries of an economic slowdown. This group, under pressure for weeks, looked set to roll over again. The cell phone stocks, another set of darlings for this entire bull market since 1990, got axed from Merrill's recommendation list that morning as well. It downgraded both Ericsson and Nokia, and the latter was already down 8 in Finland. Merrill said Nokia, the bellwether for the industry, had slowing sales. Huh? I made the Merrill broker put the phone to the speaker. I couldn't believe what I was hearing. I loved these stocks. These companies were doing fantastically right now. Where did this analyst get this info?

We dodged the airline bullet, but the Nokia downgrade caught us like a dumdum right in the temple. We owned 59,000 Nokia. "Why do we own Nokia?" Jeff asked before he even said hello when he staggered in at 5:45 A.M.

"We owned Nokia," I said, "because as of yesterday sales are smoking. We just got that update."

Jeff glowered. "Merrill says they aren't."

I said, "That's news to me."

Jeff, increasingly frustrated by any attempts we made to make money on the long side, said, "So what, Merrill says they're not." I wanted to buy. Jeff reminded me that at 1:00 P.M. that afternoon we would have to send out a huge chunk of our fund and it wasn't the right time to buy. No buying allowed.

As each broker came in the news got worse and worse. J. P. Morgan, out of nowhere, suddenly came out with a call that because of the credit crunch we were going to go into a mild recession in 1999. Until that morning people had been expecting a robust economy next year. Now we're talking about a recession. "They have to talk about a recession today?" I asked Jeff.

"No time like the present," he deadpanned.

For years, ever since Bill Clinton had brought my old boss Bob Rubin to Washington, we looked to the nation's capital for good news for the economy. On October 8, though, for only the third time in history, the House of Representatives was set to vote on impeachment hearings and the Democrats, sensing that things had gone badly awry, seemed resigned to go along with Republicans' call for a full-blown proceeding. Throughout the morning there would be speeches from politicians from both parties pointing out that no man was beyond the law, not even the president. All morning, any time the market looked like it wanted to rally, a Republican would come on the tube and talk about grave times for the republic.

It was into this cauldron of gloom that my wife bounded in, about 8:30, brandishing some Martha by Mail catalogues, a couple of pieces of fresh fruit, and a completely unnecessary, I thought, in my paranoid fashion, mocking smile. "Hey, chum, looking glum," she said to me. I told her that the world looked like it had caved in overnight and we were already losing millions.

She shrugged. "So what? We'll figure it out." I thought, given the futures, the downgrades, the lack of help from Washington, that seemed pretty glib. She didn't care. She settled in at my seat while I grabbed a Diet Coke. I would be standing around today, I thought to myself. On the day when I can't take it anymore, they take away my chair too. The gods really had it in for me.

Karen asked how Yahoo! was quoted. I told her it was down 12. "Yippee, we have puts!" she said.

But, I said, "The puts are struck at 50, the stock's still up at 100." My wife hated to be corrected, especially in front of the four people who had been brought in to replace her when she retired.

"Who would have been stupid enough to bet that the stock would go down to 50?" I wanted to tell her that we put the position on when Yahoo! was at 60 and it had just run away from us. I didn't want to start the day with discord, though, and just acknowledged that I had been an idiot when I did it. She rolled her eyes, shorthand for "You are a knucklehead and I can't believe I married someone this stupid."

We met as soon as she was ready and mapped a game plan in Jeff's office, with Karen reading down the portfolio just like the old days. I knew we had to do some selling, but Karen, much more cavalier about the Fed margin rules, said that we had to wait until we saw the real whites of this market's—and our—eyes and we shouldn't sell anything until the last second that we had to.

"The market is set to open down huge and we have to buy," she said.

"But how about all of this bad news?" I said, as we went over the morning brokerage calls.

"They can't be right," she said. "You suddenly trust Ralph I-Can-Make-You-Poorer? How about yourself? What's the oscillator?"

When she was a trader my wife had been addicted to the Standard & Poor's oscillator, a measurement of selling versus buying. Whenever there was too much selling, she always liked to take the other side. When I told her that the oscillator was as negative as it had been since the crash of '87, she said, "We blew that one, not committing enough money. This time we can't make that mistake. That's my view."

I reminded her that we were fairly fully invested and would be overinvested at 1:00 P.M. when the money came out. She seemed completely untroubled. "How about this America Online," she said, as she took over my turret. "Max says it's looking down 8. I want to buy it for a trade."

I told her to be my guest and she bolted from the confab to get levels for trades, leaving Jeff and me dumbfounded with her sunny reading of the dire situation. We were astonished at her optimism. We couldn't bring her down despite every attempt we made to tell her how bad things were for us. She wouldn't hear it.

By the time all the Dow stocks were open, at roughly 9:50, the market was already down 100 points, including the new combined lower price for Citi and Travelers. This time, however, the coloration of the decline was distinctly different from that of the other horrible days for the bulls. Each day the selling had been concentrated in the financials, industrials, and techs. This time, though, they were whacking the drug stocks, previously an oasis. We owned a ton of Pfizer and Schering-Plough but were short 210,000 Lilly against it. Karen wanted to cover every share of Lilly at the opening and buy more Fizzy and Plug, as they were called. I reminded her that if the market kept breaking down, we would be wildly exposed to the decline. I made it clear that we didn't share her robust view of the action.

Techs, drugs, you name it, they were being hammered throughout the morning. Sometimes, when the market opens this horribly, there is a pause, related to the trading curbs put in after the 1987 crash, designed to let traders catch their breath and hunt for bargains in the newly created ruins. Not this day. The market not only continued to plummet after opening down 100, but it seemed to lose 25 points every fifteen minutes. "Uguly," my wife pronounced, even though Jeff and I had learned many weeks before how hideous this market could be. She seemed to enjoy the pronouncement and the angst that it spawned in her husband and his partner.

Decliners outpaced advancers by an overwhelming nine-to-one margin, virtually an unheard of ratio. Five points came right out of General Electric despite its reporting a beautiful quarter. On word of an antitrust investigation by the Justice Department, the credit card companies were all opening staggered, some down 12 to 15 points. Our few stabs at buying stocks were instantly met with reports, meaning we had bought the stocks for about a half point *lower* than we were even trying to buy them. People were getting out so fast that they were willing to sell stocks below where buyers would pay for them! Every half hour brought progressively lower prices, more and more put buying, and fewer and fewer buyers. The eerie decline embraced all sectors. Right before noon the Dow had declined 200 points, true bear market territory, and it showed no break in the decline despite the trading curbs. Sliced through them like putty. Any stock that lifted its head got it hacked off. Everything was attracting sellers. Karen seemed even more oblivious to the conflagration as the flames leaped from screen to screen. She bought 30,000 America Online at $85, down $5. When she got the report, the stock was at $82, down $8! She just bought another 25,000. She didn't bother to ask; she said she had no time, stocks were falling too quickly.

She wanted to buy Gap and Lilly and Seagate and Ford. "They are all coming in, it is terrific, we have to buy them when we can, not when we have to. You know that's what we were taught. We can't ignore it now."

I was dying. Here we were supposed to be selling, and she was committing even more capital. "These are once-in-a-lifetime buys," she kept saying.

Did she know something I didn't? I thought. Well, at least we are going down in some serious flaming, and not with a whimper. For months I had been arguing that this market had to bottom somewhere, but these declines, this news, these pressures, the dollar crash, the Japan reversal, Germany, no rally in Britain, the drug stocks rolling over, Abby Jo going negative, Acampora giving up, the impeachment, the goddamned redemptions, no help from the Fed, it was all unraveling right before my eyes. And here's my wife wanting to buy, acting as if nothing's going wrong, acting as if it is just another day and there are bargains everywhere.

I took Jeff aside and apologized that we didn't sell sooner, apologized for being too bullish, too long, and too hopeful. The contrast between my wife, buying them on the way down, committing even more of the precious capital we didn't have, and my own belief that our franchise, the whole thing we worked for, was about to go up in smoke, was getting to be too much for me. I could barely hear myself talk over the pounding of my heart and the pain in my throat and head. Pounding, pounding, pounding that this market is finished, that we are buying into a market that is about to crash, instead of selling and selling furiously like everyone else. We are about to be obliterated, vaporized by a market that is not stopping down 260 points and isn't going to stop until it is down a thousand points. Maybe today. There were no buyers anywhere. Except in our shop! And we had no money and some crazy woman doing unauthorized trades who also happened to be my wife.

And still she bought. And still she sat there and placed orders to buy stocks down 7, 9 points. Schwab, 50,000. Mellon, 50,000. Hewlett-Packard, 85,000. Again with glee in her voice as she announced that they are just giving them away. What is she seeing? I wondered to myself. It is a holocaust out there, everyone giving up, everyone throwing in the towel, and she is buying 35,000 Household down 4 and 10,000 General Electric down every half point. "At this pace you will own more General Electric than Jack Welch," I joked to her after she put in her scale of 10,000 every half down to 60, with the stock trading at 70.5, down 4.5.

"I hope so," she said. "These are going to be great buys, especially these ones below 70. We will look back and marvel at how cheap this stock got." All I could think about was, What were we going to pay the brokers with? How were we going to buy all that General Electric and not go belly-up? How could I ever explain this one?

I wish I could say her optimism was infectious. It was more like an infectious disease invading my sanctum of fear that grew stronger by the hour, as the averages took out the year lows and the Nazz threatened to be down more than 100 points. Only the curbs were keeping stocks from falling through the floor, and we kept buying and buying and buying as if Macy's were having a one-day sale.

At noon, after another episode of furious buying when the Dow had dropped more than 270 points, I had had enough. "Let's get off the desk," I said. "We have to talk."

Karen rolled her eyes again. She had been placing orders with Land's End for a couple of kids PJs as she waited to see if we would drop 300 points, her next level where she wanted to buy. She was taking a little break. "Talk about what?" she wanted to know. "This market's on the verge of doing something big, we have to get ready."

"Ah, now that's a true statement," I said under my breath. As I gathered us into Jeff's office, she couldn't resist pointing out some bargain she saw on the CNBC ticker in Jeff's office. "Look at that. Time Warner down 6." She wondered how she missed that. "Dell, down 7, now down 8, 9!" She wanted to get right back out and buy some Dell as soon as the meeting was finished. "Jeff, what's the matter with Dell? Ooh, baby, it is really coming in. Shouldn't we be buying some of that sick puppy?"

Undaunted by her enthusiasm, I asked Jeff to give us his outlook. Jeff's all fundamentals, and he said that business had clearly slowed because of the declines in the stock market. The spillover from the financial markets, he said, was causing a decline in spending, and earnings estimates for everything from airlines to computers might be too high. Credit card sales were coming down. Information technology spending was dropping.

I listened to Jeff while I kept an eye on the ticker and an ear on what midday anchor Bill Griffeth was saying. "Two staunch bulls growing bearish." "Horrifying losses." "Panic selling." Then a story on staggering losses in mutual funds, and then a story on Clinton's impeachment, and back to a story on bloodshed on the floor of the Exchange, and credit card losses. Recession in 1999, and yet no Greenspan to bail us out.

At that very moment with the Dow down 211, and the Nazzdog composite index off 91, CNBC did a break-in: Greg Smith, the Prudential strategist, was lowering his stock allocation from 60 percent to 55 percent.

"That's it," I said, throwing my hands over my head. "Smith runs big money. All those Pru brokers will now call their clients and tell them to sell stocks. I just don't know if I can take it anymore. We are way too bullish. We have to get out."

My wife looked at me as though I were from another planet.

"Is there any chance Greenspan bails us out, because this market is so oversold it could turn around?" She emphasized that while she had been away, this was the most extreme selling she had ever seen.

I said it reminded me of the selling before the 1987 crash, when she told me we had to get out. Remember: the sell call Karen gave me that had put me in cash for that crash and saved my firm.

She said she couldn't disagree more. This action, right now, was like the crash, she said. "The crash is happening out there, right here, open your eyes. The tick's at 1,700," she said, pointing out a measure that showed an extreme level of selling historically. "Only 300 stocks are up and 2,700 are down. That's an extreme. That's the definition of what you want to see at the bottom. This *is* the crash," she yelled, no longer trying to buck me up, just trying to stop the brewing catastrophe. "You have to buy the crash. You didn't buy it in 1987; you have to buy it now." I thought back to how right she had been then. But she had been away now for so long, taking care of two kids, taking them to school, class mom, for heaven's sake. Hasn't read the *Journal* in months. Doesn't know what's going on. Her instincts, though, her impeccable instincts. I don't know. I don't know. I am so confused, so scared. The redemptions. The selling. The pressure, the pressure. I wish someone would take away the pressure. How do I get my head to stop pounding. How does she know what she's doing. How will I explain how I listened to her when we are down 1,000 points at the end of the day?

She repeated that Greenspan had to be watching this action and had to be considering another interest rate cut. In the background, on the tube, a then CNBC reporter Alan Chernoff was saying from the floor of the Exchange, "Every single component in negative territory, the transports off 158 points . . . serious damage . . . a billion-share day . . . an accelerating sell-off, we are having panic selling once again." The Dow had dropped another 22 points in the few minutes that we had gotten off the desk. It was fifteen minutes past noon.

"Kar, every second counts, this decline is killing us. And all of the new stuff we put on, I mean."

"Give me this," she interrupted. "If Greenspan were to move, or if you thought he was going to move aggressively, would you be buying?"

I said, "Of course. The only weakness is in the financial markets, not in the real economy. But he said on Tuesday there was no crisis." We only had an hour before we had to sell stocks to meet our redemptions. We had waited weeks now, not selling, and now we owned way too much stock, way too much, and all we had done was buy!

"Everything tells me we should be buying, everything," she repeated, exasperated. Now the Dow dropped another 20 points before my eyes, no doubt from the Pru-related selling. I saw GE at 70 on the ticker. We had probably just bought more with my wife's silly scale.

"No, no no," I said, throwing down my legal pad and pounding the marble coffee table in Jeff's office. "We have to get out, we have to get out now," my voice shaking, sick, sick that we had to give up after being bullish all the way down, all the way down for 1,000 points. "That's it," I said, "I can't take it anymore. We are selling, I am undoing your buys and getting us out of this. This market is going to %&#! and it's going there #%$&."

The Dow was down 262 points, the Nasdaq had opened down 103.

I stormed out of the meeting, took my place back at my desk, shoved the catalogues away, and began to sell the stock that my wife had put on. I canceled the GE scale, dumped 5,000 shares of ten stocks, and told my brokers to wait two more minutes and repeat it again and again and again until we had sold everything we had bought and then some. I asked my traders to see where I could sell a million shares of BayView, and 500,000 shares of a couple of other savings and loans. I had been beaten.

And I beat out a piece, a little piece, but the most important piece I had yet to write for *TheStreet.com,* saying that it was time to get out, that the crash was at hand. Big losses awaited us. The piece reiterated my arguments that I had just delivered in Jeff's office, without any of my wife's caveats. As I sent it I looked up and saw some commercial with Peter Lynch and Lily Tomlin talking about how "buying what is hot without research is not investing, it is gambling." Now they tell me, I thought to myself. It was 12:29 P.M.

After the commercial ended, Bill Griffeth came back on and said that Ron Insana, the CNBC evening anchor, had a story about Lyle Gramley, a former Fed official, telling a Schwab client group about a possible rare between-meetings conference call by Greenspan. I saw the market lift 20 points, a visible lift. Maybe a Fed bailout? I thought to myself. Impossible. Not after what Greenspan said earlier in the week. Not after what I just said. Not after the story I had just sent to *TheStreet.com.*

At 12:34 P.M. a rarely smiling Ron Insana—there had been nothing good to smile about for months—came on and said that there was a possibility that the Fed was going to act "relatively swiftly" because the "wealth destruction was so noticeable." He then repeated it, that the Fed would not be waiting until its November 19 meeting, that the Fed knew the markets were being hammered and it would provide the liquidity necessary to stop any decline. He said this would be extraordinary but he had been working the phones all morning and he believed it. As everyone in the office regarded Ron as a bear, his credentials punctuated the report with veracity.

Suddenly the Dow rocketed from its low, clawing back first 30 and then 40 and then 50 points as Ron talked about the teleconference easing, "maybe by as much as a half point." A half point! That would be huge. That would be unprecedented. That would change everything. Now the Dow was down less than 200. Twelve-thirty-eight P.M. And the Nazz was ramping up, down only 100, and then under 90. It was at that moment that my story appeared telling readers to get out. My wife was listening to the TV as intently as I was. She looked at my computer screen and expressed horror when the "get out" story popped up on *TheStreet.com* at the same time that Ron Insana was breaking the news that would cause the bottom not to get lower. "Where are the caveats?" she asked. "Where is the stuff about how the market will rally if the Fed eases?" I shrugged. I had left them out. I hadn't wanted to seem wishy-washy. When I wrote the piece I thought the world had ended. Had I gone for a soft pretzel or for an Italian ice, or if I had just gone out for air, or a trip to the men's room, I wouldn't even have written the story. And why does it have me say "get out"? Karen asked. I didn't say get out. I wanted to get in, she said. What if Insana is right? "You will never live this piece down," Karen was screaming at me. "I hate this stupid *Street.com*. It ruins your ability to be flexible. Ruins it."

What have I done? I thought. Forever I have that image of Alec Guinness falling on the detonator to blow up the bridge over the River Kwai. My bullish bridge blown up right when it was about to take me where I had to go. What had I done?

"I blew it," I said quietly to her as she stood over my shoulders. Then enraged, I shouted, "I blew it." I said it ten times. Giants win the pennant, like. "I *blew it!*"

"No, you didn't," my wife said calmly. "You didn't. You didn't blow anything. Cancel the sell orders. The market is done going down."

But the readers, I said, will forever think that I am an idiot. I can't change my view like that.

"You aren't a guru," she said. "You are a guy, a big fallible guy and you blew it, but you know it. We missed 50 points on the Dow that's all. Sure you blew it. Everybody blows it. Just admit you made a mistake and change. You aren't a guru," she repeated.

It was too late, I said, a correction to the piece won't appear for another half hour.

"Forget the piece. Save the fund. Pull all the sell orders," she said. "Just listen to me. We are done going down. Maybe for good."

"But how about the margin, the money? We only have a few minutes left to make the wires. If we don't sell anything we will be borrowing too much money overnight," I said. "We'll get in real trouble with Goldman." Did Karen not know the margin rules?

She looked at me for a second the way a mother might a child that feared getting yelled at by the principal for doing something that everyone gets away with. "Didn't you always want to be fully margined, 200 percent long at the bottom? Didn't you always want to have a Fed margin call at the bottom? That's what you will have and you will be proud of it. It'll be a badge of honor. This is your chance to do what you should have done after the '87 crash. Just let it ride. Let it ride." She added, noting that with the day's huge volume and confusion, it would probably take Goldman weeks to figure out how much we really had to margin. You could borrow against those savings and loans if they were going up, she said. And they will go up with this Fed news. By that time we'd be well on our way to making it back to the black and it wouldn't matter. "Anyway," she said, "we used to run it up all the time at Steinhardt, borrow way more than we should have. They'll let you go if you do the commish and say you won't do it again."

I wanted to know about the banks and savings and loans. Shouldn't we be selling them now that there were bids developing because of the emergency easing coming? Shouldn't we be taking a chance and selling into this momentary lift?

"You want to be just where you are, with all of these crummy little savings and loans," she said, ticking off the names from her position sheets. "They'll rally with every Fed ease that you didn't expect. You will sell the BayView at $20 instead of the eight bucks you might have gotten a few minutes ago." She then gave me her targets on where the rest of the banks and savings and loans would go to. "Don't you sell a thing. You already didn't listen to me once today, don't do it again."

I could see that she was getting ready to bolt to go home, probably trying to make it home before our eldest got back from first grade. It was only a little after 1:00 P.M. A half day's trading was ahead and who was to say that this rally that began minutes after I gave up could last?

"How can you be sure it is the bottom?" I said, trying to divine what she saw as I stood watching the markets rise on the eight screens in front of us at the top of the trading desk. "What makes you so certain? How do you know this bottom will hold? How can you go now? How do you know you will be right?"

"Simple." She bent down and whispered to me so that others in the room could not hear: "Because at the bottom even the coolest, most hardbitten pros blink. At the bottom the last bulls throw in the towel. At the bottom, there is the final capitulation." She waited until it dawned on me who she was talking about. "At the bottom, Jimmy, you capitulated. At the bottom you gave up. That's how I know it's the bottom. It's okay. Michael Steinhardt"—her old boss—"capitulated at the bottom in '87. It happens to the best."

In the last thirty minutes since Insana spoke one stock after another had indeed bottomed, Microsoft, down 6, Cisco down 3, IBM down 4, Seagate down 4, Dell down 9, Intel down 4, all were headed to the black. The brokers were screaming. The financials were all up fractions, on their way to multipoint gains. The world had changed from red to green on that Fed intervention call. Owners of puts, who had been coining money on the downside, now wanted bids. They wanted to cover the shorts that had made them gazillions in the last six weeks. There were no offerings to be had. None at all. The selling was done, my trader yelled out. "There's nothing but buyers." The tape left not even a small hole of doubt; it was off to the races. Almost straight up for the rest of the hour. Short sellers at last were panicking. Even for the stocks that we needed to sell there were suddenly no offerings. The shorts had disappeared, like vampires waking to broad daylight.

"Should we be buying?" I said, now totally bewildered. She reminded me we bought all the way down, when the prices were much better. Would there be a pullback?

"There won't be one of any significance," she said. "We can't do anything anyway." True, we were borrowed to the max. More than to the max.

"Do you think it will ever pull back? Maybe in a couple of days? Weeks?" She didn't bother to answer, just kept packing up, tossing out a Lands' End catalogue she had ordered from during the height of the downturn and retrieving the Martha by Mails that I had shoved aside when I had panicked and started selling into the maelstrom.

She was leaving some written instructions of when to take off the positions she had bought all morning, positions that would be worth millions of dollars more than she had paid for them in a matter of an hour or two. America Online, Gap, Seagate, and the questioned General Electric. Now all much better to buy. Now not even looking back. "A pullback?" she asked rhetorically. "No. Not likely. Not after this selling crescendo." She jammed some catalogues into her Coach bag, stood up, tidied up my desk space one more time, scrawled on a little Post-it that she covered with her hand, and headed for the exit.

And with that she said goodbye to everybody, just a simple wave. Not even a see-you-later. Hasn't been back since. Never will be. No encores for Karen.

The market rallied from then on for the rest of the year in one of the greatest comebacks in history, one that never faltered. We made back $120 million almost in a straight line, getting off margin about a month later and breaking into the black a month after that. We sold the BayView at $20 and dumped the rest of the savings and loans at much higher prices after the Fed eased and eased some more, causing a mad bull market in the very financials we were hung up on. The market rose until Nasdaq hit 5,000 and Dow 12,000 from their bottom at 12:18 when I pushed aside those catalogues and got to work trying to undo my wife's bullishness with my own bull-turned-bear imitation.

We finished up for the year, still disappointing relative to the averages, which we never caught, but much better than the intraday down 38 percent level that we hit on October 8, the day we should have gone bust. We waived a couple of million dollars in management fees because we didn't make more than a couple of percent and weren't proud of what we did, even though we were proud that we turned the ship around. The crisis occurred early enough in the month that no one other than the minute-to-minute folks even knew it had occurred. If you stayed in the fund you increased your worth by more than 200 percent from that bottom in the next two years. Sweet. Many of the departing partners tried to come back in after we finished up 60 percent the next year, but we didn't let them. Even sweeter. But the pain of those dark days was not exorcised by the pleasure of seeing the fund back in the black and healthy again. Goldman never did figure out that we borrowed some $30 million more than we should have, given the flimsy nature of the collateral, and we were more than fully margined at the bottom, just as you want to be, just as every great hedge fund manager wishes he were. The readers of *TheStreet.com,* however, never forgave me for panicking out, even as I switched direction in my writings a day later. According to Karen, it was a sign of strength, not weakness, that I could capitulate and then embrace the long side again so fast. The worst thing to do is to cling to a losing position even for a minute when you know the facts have changed and you are wrong. Flexibility is what distinguishes a good trader from a bad one. But the readers just remembered me as the man who capitulated at the bottom, who defined the bottom.

Oh yeah, and that Post-it my wife slammed to the side of my machine as she left to go greet our daughter after her day at school? "It's good to be good, but it's better to be lucky."

If only it really were luck, then I would at least have a chance of duplicating the last trading performance of the woman they still call the Trading Goddess.

CHAPTER 17

Inside the IPO:
Part One

The irony of the situation hit me in the face like a four-day-old bluefish every time I thought about it: how could a business so immensely profitable as my hedge fund, one that had never had a loss, one that had generated more than $300 million in profit, be on the verge of insolvency, while *TheStreet.com* sustained hideous eight-figure losses, with very little revenue to speak of, and was suddenly the toast of every investment bank and venture capital firm in the country? Could the capital markets be this wrong? Could my partners at my hedge fund be this unforgiving? Yes, and yes.

In the final months of 1998 as Cramer Berkowitz moved back into the black, on the strength of an equity market buoyed by a panicked Federal Reserve, *TheStreet.com,* as a venture stage company, traded in sync in the private market with the initial public offering market, and that market could not have been hotter if it were located on the sun itself. Usually investment banks were ready with offerings to meet all of that cash the Fed was creating by keeping rates so low and allowing banks to borrow money overnight with reckless abandon, as they were doing. But all summer of 1998, as people in the business stood paralyzed as obscure departments like arbitrage and global fixed income trading wiped out whatever profits and capital the big brokers had, nobody bothered to create enough new paper to sate the public's demand.

The public, with high job growth, and lots of 401(k) money to put to work, needed stock to invest in. The Fed lowered rates to save the brokerage system from Long-Term Capital's wake, and that left the public, which didn't need a bailout, flush with capital to invest and the only game in town was the stock market. Put simply, there wasn't enough public equity to go around, particularly dotcom paper, to equal all of the cash looking for a home. Demand suddenly overwhelmed supply just as the Federal Reserve wanted to relieve the nation's credit crunch. There was so much cash around by November of 1998, so furiously was the Fed printing money and lowering rates, that it began to seep into the private equity market, buoying even early-stage companies like *TheStreet .com,* which was now in its third year, but with no track record to speak of and an organizational structure that lacked a formal board of directors, a chief financial officer, and, of course, a chief executive officer. (Ironically, Kevin English was named CEO on October 8, the day I almost went bust.)

After three years, the company's officers were still reporting to me, Marty, and the Flatiron VC'ers, Fred Wilson and Jerry Colonna, with no one really in charge. Before this era, private companies would gradually move toward the initial public offering market over time, working toward profitability over a multiyear time frame, with formal structures and clear paths to profitability. Now, in the fall of 1998, newborn companies were being sought by investment bankers to come public just months after they had started operation. *TheStreet.com* seemed downright mature in that environment. Rounds of private financing that should have taken years to occur now started the moment the previous one closed, and at a monster premium in value to the previous rounds. For *TheStreet.com* that meant the April first round, which valued our company at $30 million, suddenly looked like a steal versus the next round, once we were finally able to start raising it.

The brokerage houses had never been caught so flatfooted before. The bear market ended in lightning speed—the Nasdaq, where most of these new companies resided, was now beginning its historic climb from 1,500 to 5,000 and the firms that create paper simply didn't have enough equity in the pipeline. The only deal on the books that fall was for some miserable outfit that I knew, from my dotcom hat, had no business to speak of, whatsoever: *theglobe.com.* I had gone to *theglobe.com* before, by mistake of course, thinking that it was *The Boston Globe* and looking for information on the Red Sox. It turned out to be some conversational site, some community where people got together and chatted. When Bear-Stearns, the underwriter, had asked if we wanted any shares, we passed. I knew better. There was no way to monetize chat. Advertisers didn't like the eyeballs behind chat. Amazingly, in the third week of October, *theglobe.com* had shrunk the size of its offering and the price—usually steps that move merchandise—and it still failed to come public. The company pulled its offering a week later. I figured this stuff was just damaged goods forced on the marketplace because of pure desperation.

I was way too smart for my own good. The stock opened up 90 points from where it was supposed to, the biggest single one-day "pop" anybody had ever seen. At first I thought it had been rigged. I knew Wayne Huizenga had an investment in the darned thing, and I figured maybe he bought the opening in order to create some hoopla. Everybody would talk about such a pop, and therefore people would hear about *theglobe.com* and a giant branding event would have been created. "There's genius be-hind this, genuine evil promotional genius," I said to Jeff, who wanted to know why I didn't fire the person in charge of underwritings for not insist-ing that we put in for some of *theglobe.com.*

Every hedge fund that trades a lot has a designated person who goes to meetings for initial public offerings. That person tends to be a low-totem-pole employee. My wife used to dole out this task to attractive young women. They would then sign in that they attended the meeting, would be sure to be seen paying rapt attention to the speakers, and then come back and tell us if there were a lot of people at the meeting and whether people at her table were jazzed about it. If there were, then we could call up our brokers and say that our representative just loved, loved, loved the story and we would try to get as much of the underwriting as possible hoping it would be hot. We would then, of course, flip it—taking delivery of the stock for about thirty seconds, at the price that it came public, and then dumping it at the much, much higher price that it opened—because we would never get enough of it to have it be a core position and because by the time it opened it was usually hopelessly overvalued or a real stinker that nobody wanted anyway. Flipping was a good business when underwritings were hot. Some hedge fund firms lived off it entirely. It was just a line of profit for us.

But this *theglobe.com* was different. Nobody was interested in the road show. Nobody wanted to hear from two college kids who had never made a dime and could have easily been selling shares in a lawn mowing or window washing company that they might have set up if they hadn't been early Web adopters. Institutions could not care less.

We figured it was the Huizenga factor and we dismissed it.

Our judgment was wrong, though, as *theglobe.com* was a transforming deal that led to an amazing confluence: a Fed that wanted stocks higher; a public flush with cash; a brand-new pipeline, the Internet, to sell deals; and a belief that the Internet would usher in a whole new economy. While several dotcom deals had come public in the last two years, including Yahoo!, Excite, Amazon, and of course America Online, this *globe.com* deal signaled the beginning of the hyperventilation, hyperthermia stage of Internet investing. Jeff Berkowitz and I realized it a few weeks later—in early January—when *CBS MarketWatch,* another deal that nobody on Wall Street seemed to care about, went to the exact same premium as *theglobe.com.* One red-hot deal might have meant manipulation; two meant a trend worth mining. *MarketWatch,* our number one competitor, offered 2.75 million shares for $17. The stock rose to $130 on its first day! That's an unbelievable 100-point pop. Now here was some lunacy I understood—I was in that business—and we took down a huge slug of the stock on the deal, enriching our fund even as we benefited the competition by giving them money—albeit momentarily, as in about forty-seven minutes. That's how long we held the stock.

We at *TheStreet.com* had flirted as recently as that summer with merging with *MarketWatch,* talking with my friend Larry Kramer, the editor in chief and chief executive officer of the company. I knew that, although he had no subscription revenue, Larry had put together a tremendous advertising vehicle and had terrific placement with America Online and Yahoo!, the two biggest page-view generators on the Web.

But still I was stunned—as was Larry, he would later confide in me—at the reception *CBS MarketWatch* (MKTW) had in this market. Neither of us had figured that this stock would open north of 100. Nobody, not even the most outrageous of bulls, thought there was that kind of demand out there because, again, institutions had expressed little interest in the company as it made its rounds in what is known as the institutional road show.

At the hedge fund office, the day of *CBS MarketWatch*'s deal, it was just another glum session as we tried to claw our way back into respectability—if there were such a thing. But my ears and brain perked up when I heard the early indications for MKTW. With IPOs, the sales trader, the representative from the broker who covers you, gives you preliminary indications before the market opens about where deals might open. The initial indication for *CBS MarketWatch,* formally priced at 19, was somewhere in the 20s, no big deal, given that there were so few shares offered and the company had gotten its name around via the Net, the best way to attract new buyers who loved taking a few shares in IPOs with their new electronic brokers. But by 10:00 A.M. the price talk for the opening got ratcheted up to the 40s. The underwriters figured when they got to the 40s, supply would flow back and knock the stock down.

Every institution that got stock on this deal would be thrilled with a double, and I thought the next thing we would hear would be that the stock would be reindicated back down to the 30s.

When it wasn't, and instead the indication went 50–60, Jeff cocked his head toward his office, indicating he wanted to speak to me. "Are you thinking what I am thinking?" he said, smiling about as large a smile as Jeff would ever allow given our ailing performance at Cramer Berkowitz.

"I'm trying not to," I said, "because who knows what *TheStreet.com* would be worth if this *MarketWatch* thing opens here?" We suppressed our giddiness until the indication went above 100. Then we simply multiplied our shares (Jeff had gotten a boatload of stock from me personally for helping us make that payroll in the spring as we waited for the Flatiron financing deal to close) and laughed, the kind of laugh that Walter Huston would have laughed if he had kept the gold rather than lost it at the end of *Treasure of the Sierra Madre.* We couldn't contain ourselves. How in heck could *MarketWatch,* which was losing chunks of capital like *TheStreet .com,* be worth a billion? How could the markets be that stupid? And would they stay stupid long enough for *TheStreet.com* to come public?

From that day on, when *CBS MarketWatch* opened at 117 and went up ever so slightly before coming back to the low 100s, everybody from the investment banking or analyst side of Wall Street to the conventional media was suddenly our best friend at *TheStreet.com*. Until the *Market-Watch* deal we were one of hundreds of dotcoms that hoped one day to be considered worthy of the public's attention. After the *MarketWatch* deal we were a front-burner piece of merchandise, ready for the public frying pan even as we were still trying to get the project to look like a real company. The *New York Times*, for example, which hadn't even acknowledged our existence even though its digital head, Martin Nisenholtz, had grown up with me in Wyndmoor, Pennsylvania, and had been my treasurer when I was elected Student Council president at Springfield High in Montgomery County, now knocked on our door and started talking with us about making an equity investment. They wanted a board seat too! We didn't even have a board yet. At the same time Rupert Murdoch's Fox unit came knocking, eager to work with us on a potential show, *TheStreet .com*, for the Fox News Network, if it helped them get some shares in our company.

But every effort to climb on board the company's surging freight train paled in comparison to the fervor of venture capitalists and investment banks trying to get in ahead of what would now be a preordained hot initial public offering. As soon as we had picked Kevin English, he began the fund-raising for our second round of money, a prelude to our ultimate initial public offering. Now venture capitalists who hadn't even let me in the door in 1996 and 1997 clamored to get on board in a round of financing that would end up valuing *TheStreet.com* at almost four times what it had been worth in April of 1998. It was difficult to imagine being treated more shoddily than I had been with my idea of *TheStreet.com* by the same kind of people who now begged for shares because they smelled a hot offering down the road.

The bankers and their analyst minions from virtually every firm on Wall Street were all over us to write the final ticket, the IPO, even before we had finished the crucial second round of financing that English had started. Most of them didn't even know what we were, what we did, or whether we had any revenues let alone profits, but they wanted to be our best friends. Some were beyond shameless. One analyst from one of the Street's largest firms called on us to give me his assessment of the Net so he could make Cramer Berkowitz some money. He knew next to nothing about what was really going on at the time. We politely nodded at his lack of insight and were anxious to show him the door when he asked if he could speak about something personal. My eyebrows always fly up instinctively when I hear "something personal" because, believe me, there is nothing personal at all in the hedge fund world; everything's business.

Sure, I beckoned. "What's on your mind?"

Well, he said, he had a proposition to make. "Give me some *Street.com* stock and I can really help you," he said. I told him that although I was a writer and a large shareholder, I had nothing to say about the underwriting process. "I know, I know," he said. "Just get me some stock personally, and I can see that good things can happen."

Holy cow, I thought to myself. This is first-class corruption to a degree that is beyond even the usual rats in the business. "No dice," I said. This was so blatant a pitch that I mused to Jeff afterward that maybe he was sent by one of my enemies and was wearing a wire, hoping to entrap me. Jeff was always willing to indulge my most paranoid of fantasies, but this one was too much.

"Nah, he's just a corrupt asshole," Jeff said.

The rules for underwritings are so screwed up that as soon as you are officially contemplating an offering, which we did the moment we hired English, you can't talk about the company anymore. You have to "go quiet," in accordance with some obscure provisions of the 1933 Securities Act that were written before there was pervasive interest in the stock market and instant access to information. The government has an interest to protect: it doesn't want you to hype your company to the moon during the process lest you get unsophisticated people too crazy about your stock. So you are simply gagged and can't respond to any questions, reasonable or unreasonable, about the company.

In theory, the prophylactic approach makes some sense. You can't predict who is going to hype and who is just going to stick to a script and tell the facts, so you ban any public conversation about it at all, with the threat that if someone goofs and makes public comments, the government can delay the deal, which could ultimately kill it if the delay is extreme.

In practice, the gag rule is a nightmare. At the very moment when everyone is trying to learn about a stock to decide if they want to make a purchase of it, you have to dodge every inquiry and go out of your way not to answer the most basic of questions. Which of course then makes the press believe you are hiding something because no one in the press is familiar with the obscure "quiet provisions" of some act passed seven decades ago.

Every day some reporter would call me and ask when *TheStreet.com* was going to go public. As I always had a pretty freewheeling relationship with reporters, suddenly I was dodging their questions, too scared even to go on background, lest someone ignore the ground rules and quote me outright.

Meanwhile, of course, all you are talking about is how and when you are going to go public and with whom. And if you are not, you are crazy, because when you are besieged by bankers who want to give you money, you don't say, "Hold it, we aren't ready, we are losing lots of money, let's wait and see." You can't say, "Nope, sorry, we would rather run out of cash trying to make a profit." And you can't tell the venture capitalists to whom you have just sold a huge chunk of the company and have put on the board, "Guys, it wouldn't be prudent right now to come public." Everyone inside and outside wants you to come public. There is no one around to say no. You would not be performing your fiduciary obligation to your investors if you didn't go public.

All winter of 1998–99 as we finalized our second round of equity at roughly $100 million valuation—it went up by $10 million a week for three straight weeks; we were being pursued by the *New York Times* to finalize an even higher valuation investment for a portion of our company. The *Times* wanted to do a deal typical at the time for dotcoms. It wanted to find out about how the dotcom world worked—ostensibly being taught by us—and at the same time participate in a joint newsroom that would contribute copy to the *NewYorkTimes.com* (as it was then called) and *TheStreet.com.* It would give us $15 million, $3 million in cash and the rest in an advertising credit that would have to be paid back, a sweetheart deal for them (they were giving us money to give back to them) but one that bought us their imprimatur. We completed that deal in February 1999, in a transaction that valued us at $11 a share, or almost $250 million. Even as we were still losing a fortune, had no real plan to be profitable, and hadn't even created an official board of directors yet. Such were the heady days of February 1999 that you could be worth millions upon millions of dollars more each day without any reason for you to be worth more. All because of a shortage of equity for a Net-crazed public.

That February, in a few short weeks, as the media seized on *The Street.com*'s pending public launch, I went from being the Pied Piper of capitalism, an individual people respected as a market maven, even after my tough year, to being the biggest hack and charlatan to have come down Wall Street in a generation. For the first time, I, a true fighter who never let someone strike me with conventional weapons without lashing back with a tactical nuclear arsenal, could not strike back. I could say nothing because we were "in quiet" as the government required. The *New York Times* Business Section, in some delicious irony, a day after the *Times* signed its deal with us that virtually assured that my 3.5-million-share stake in *TheStreet.com* would be worth $50 million at a minimum, decided to write a story about Cramer Berkowitz's struggling performance in 1998. Someone had given the *Times* my end-of-year performance letter where I admitted how embarrassed I was to have earned only 2 percent when the S&P was up 29 percent. The article quoted everything in the letter except the fact that I had chosen to waive my fees of $1.2 million because I said I didn't deserve to get paid for such a poor performance. The article made me look like a total fool, one that you shouldn't bother to read, even as the corporate side of the *Times* was investing with an opposite thesis in mind.

At the same time *Vanity Fair* picked this moment to do one of those full-blown hatchet jobs on me, a mortifying piece that basically described me as an underperforming money manager—again citing 1998—a second-rate writer, and, of course, a first-class lunatic madman. I still can't believe that they didn't stamp "HACK" all over my forehead in the opening photo.

I understood the *Times*'s motivation. You can't get a better story than some pissed-off partner leaking my letters to embarrass me at the same time that the business side of the paper is making me a millionnaire with its investments. I would have written the same piece, knowing that the target was totally defenseless for once and couldn't strike back, given the SEC gag order.

The *Vanity Fair* profile, though, stemmed directly from what was now just an out-and-out war with Marty Peretz. We had pretty much decided to stop speaking with each other after he pulled out of my fund and we had failed to land Jonathan Fram as *TheStreet.com*'s CEO. It had gotten so bad that Marty and I, once inseparable, now made sure that we came to that year's *Street.com* Christmas party at different times. I had written many hatchet jobs in my career—and was a natural call by many editors when they wanted one produced during my full-time journalist days—but I was astounded at how efficient and how sharp the axe can be wielded in 8,000 words in a high-gloss magazine like *Vanity Fair.* Virtually every aspect of my life, save my wife, came under enfilading fire. I knew the blade was headed for my jugular before the piece appeared because when the *Vanity Fair* photo editor called to set up an appointment to take my picture in advance of the piece, I asked her if she would sit for the pictures if the piece were about her. She expressed astonishment and told me "of course not," as it was anything but flattering. I let them scramble for pictures of me from my friends; I wasn't cooperating and sitting for anything, even one of those fancy Annie Liebovitz numbers. I couldn't tell what was worse about it, the dredged-up faux history of my family's poverty, courtesy of Nick Lemann (my dad had a job, we didn't grow up in a trailer park, we were respectably middle-class if not higher), or the endless blind quotes from people "on the Street" about what a hack writer I was and the horrid investor I had become.

The combination of the *Times* and the *Vanity Fair* should have sated the media beast's appetite for my scalp, I thought, until Alan Abelson from *Barron's* called me that same week in February "the new Triple Threat," a threat to the well-being of my investors, my readers, and potential investors in *TheStreet.com.*

The *New York Times, Vanity Fair,* and *Barron's* all taking aim at me at once. I was wilting. Of all of the articles, the Abelson piece hurt the most because it was so darned personal about what a bad investor I was, even though I had made so much money for my partners in the last twelve years. It was as mean-spirited an ad hominem attack as when Lalli had trashed me in *Money* after the *SmartMoney* debacle. When Karen caught me moping about on a cold February Saturday morning, while attempting to play with the girls at our country house in Bucks County, she let me have it: "If you hadn't made fun of him for being bearish since 1,100 on the Dow, or mocked his writing in that 'Roundtable' send-up [I had done a parody of Abelson's writings a year before], then you would have a right to be mad. But get over it. You had it coming and he delivered." She said it would have only surprised her if he hadn't hit me.

In March of 1999, *Fortune* and the *Boston Globe* picked up on the Marty-Jim spat after the *Vanity Fair* article made things public, and devoted more ink to our dispute. It got so sticky that when we finally filed our prospectus to go public in April, the Securities and Exchange Commission held up the deal pending an investigation of how much Marty and I hated each other and whether that would affect operations at *The Street.com.*

As much as we might have been angry with each other, when it got to the point where it could kill the very project that the whole war stemmed from, we had the good sense to agree not to speak about the fight ever again. At a tense meeting, the first real board meeting of the company, Kevin English announced that if Marty and I didn't patch things up, our deal could be scuttled. We may have been furious at each other, but we had come too far not to see this project through. We agreed on the spot that we would work things out.

This was a prelude to the entente that we have since reached, and it felt great. I was more than happy by that point to admit I had been a bad partner and a bad friend, and I did so publicly at a dinner at the Côte Basque after the board meeting where Marty and I hugged, in public. Ironically, Marty took me aside that night and asked whether I was as appalled as he was about how profligate, stupid, and totally out of touch English was with what was going on at *TheStreet.com.* He said that given that we had never made a dime and were losing a fortune, what the heck were we doing at Côte Basque. I agreed that we should have been calling in Chinese at the office. We laughed as we hadn't in a year. And we both vowed that we would stop English's excessive spending soon after we came public.

Once we agreed to stop fighting, a pledge we kept that ultimately blossomed into friendship again, there was nothing to prevent *TheStreet* .*com* from going public in the first week of May 1999 except a sudden glut of so many other deals in the pipeline. By mid-spring deal after deal with a dotcom suffix came public with an ever present triple from the underwriting price, regardless of how bright or, more likely, dim the prospects were.

For those of us in the stock-buying business, the inner workings of the underwriting process had remained a total mystery. For all the years I had traded stock, underwritings had been controlled, in secret, entirely by the syndicate desk, in close cooperation with the largest and more important accounts on the Street. The syndicate desk is a remarkable institution in every important brokerage. It coordinates the actual distribution of stock among the firm's best clients, if the deal is liked, and among all of the clients if the deal is disliked and has to be sold. The syndicate desk is the ultimate carrot-and-stick operation. You want some ultra-red-hot deal that you know will go to a huge premium? You have to take down some nasty stinker that the firm writes a big ticket (makes a lot of money) on because some dog of a company really needs the money to maintain its business. Think of it like this: a syndicate desk controls the tickets to Broadway plays. You want a hard-to-get ticket? You have to sit through some real losers first. The syndicate desk is also the funnel that corporate finance goes through to get to the brokers who ultimately sell the deal. It tells corporate finance how much demand there is at different price levels, if any, and how well the deal will do in the aftermarket—how high it will ultimately go—where all stocks trade.

A company's management only comes public once, so most people running these dotcoms knew nothing about how the process or the pricings worked. We relied on the professionals to fix a starting price, based on various metrics, such as price to profits—if there were any—or price to sales if there weren't. These pros would value the company as a "comp" or figure out which companies it most resembled and then determine what the price should be relative to these comparable public companies. If a newspaper company were coming public that had a limited operating history and a short period of profits, it would be priced at a discount, perhaps a substantial discount, to, say, Gannett or the Tribune Company.

A retailer that had 10 percent growth in same-store sales, or sales in the identical stores, year over year, for, say, five years, would be priced alongside those stocks of companies that had similar growth.

With dotcoms, however, there were no honest comparisons, other than to other dotcoms. So, if *TheStreet.com,* with $15 million in revenues that were drenched in red ink and producing nothing near a profit, was to be compared with Gannett or Tribune, that would be just plain stupid. We would be worth less than zero.

Yet, with *CBS MarketWatch,* a company similar in nature to *TheStreet .com,* with prospects relying similarly on advertising (although *TheStreet .com* has a subscription stream of revenue too), trading at a billion dollars, who cared what Gannett traded at? *TheStreet.com* compared with *MarketWatch* and the market had judged *MarketWatch* to be worth more than a billion and a half dollars. That was the underlying economics of the rush to underwrite *TheStreet.com*'s public offering.

The underwriters knew this math when they competed for our business. They all offered us similar comparisons and said they could tell the story best in return for their selling 5.5 million of our shares and earning $1.33 per share sold as a selling concession. It became just a battle of which firm had the best imprimatur and led to the first public friction that I had experienced with our new chief executive officer, Kevin English. The CEO told me that because his brother was a managing partner at Morgan Stanley we had to go with Morgan Stanley, and that because of Mary Meeker, at that time dubbed something silly like the Queen of the Internet by a press that finally realized there were tons of ads to go around Net copy, we also had to go with Morgan. English said that Meeker had assured him of a positive review and that he didn't want to run afoul of her. She was too powerful.

I told him that while I appreciated the input he had just joined the company a few months before and that I felt we owed the business to Goldman Sachs where I had gotten my start. I told him that Goldman had let me keynote a bunch of their giant technology forums and that its research department had supported *TheStreet.com* long before it was perceived as anything other than a thousand-to-one shot. I told English that I didn't want this to go to the board, but if it did, I would make my case for Goldman. It did; I made the case, and Goldman got the business. This was the first in what would become dozens of conflicts with the new CEO, on all of which Marty now sided with me, not against me. Given that Marty and I together had 25 percent of the prospective public shares, we were not to be trifled with.

Once we picked Goldman, Goldman would decide when we could go public. Goldman had excelled in bringing dotcoms public and had so many to bring that we had to jockey for position, coming public almost simultaneously with eToys and *Barnes&Noble.com.*

For about six months dotcoms had been exploding out of the chute while other deals languished. Nobody expected this to last. No one realized that we would have another full year of this hot market. Everyone figured that there would come a deal that would sap all the public's money and fall flat on its face, killing every other deal that was in the pipeline.

I would sit and fret with Jeff Berkowitz that this giddy rocket ride simply couldn't last until our chance to enter the capsule and get blasted off.

As we counted down the days to when the initial merchandise—before the road show—was going to be priced, Marty and I demanded that English let me in to the meetings so I could understand how it worked. I wanted to know how every deal that was coming to market right then could be priced so wrong, so out of sync with what the public was really willing to pay. I needed to know how there could be such a disparity between what the bankers agreed the company was worth—what the company was ultimately going to receive—and what the stock would open at on its first day of trading. Was it because the number of shares offered was too small? Was it done on purpose to help brand the enterprise? I knew that the pop generated headlines and lots of TV coverage, but it was meaningless in even the intermediate term to the prospects of a business. If anything, an unsustainably high opening price would anger a lot of shareholders down the road, if not immediately, if the price didn't hold. Already, in May 1999, we began to see older deals wilt as the capital came out of them, must likely, I figured, to participate in the newer, sexier deals. I didn't want that happening to us. I knew that the underwriters would be making more than $7.3 million (with the potential to make $8.3 million) from our underwriting; I wanted to know what they brought to the table.

It turns out that pricing a dotcom required the rigor of Barnum and the showmanship of Bialystock. I couldn't believe how plainly silly and irrational the whole thing was.

In our first meeting, a telephone interchange, we listened to the head of syndicate talk about how the deal had to be justified within the parameters of other media deals. So the bankers cranked up some figures that extrapolated online trading to its seemingly logical end growth, given the bullish market we were in, and matched these figures with the expected growth in online advertising that firms were projecting. We arrived at a logical guesstimate of revenues in the out years so we could put a multiple to them. We had to do something to come up with "analysis" or else the process was a total joke, and when you are talking about millions of dollars to the company and to the underwriter, there's no joking around. We actually did our best to figure out what could go wrong too, and included that in the projections. On a Sunday morning teleconference, we rehashed all of this data about online growth (we figured on a sextupling of online accounts by 2002) and we tried to decide how to value the 25 million shares we would soon have outstanding. Sure, we didn't have any operating history, but we did have an owner of 8 percent of our company that did, the *New York Times,* which had paid $15 million for 1.3 million shares.

That was a convenient benchmark. For the bankers it was a much better, firmer benchmark than the obvious one, the billion-dollar value of *MarketWatch* (now down from a billion and a half, but still pretty substantial). When the call, which was led by Goldman with limited input from us, the client, was over, we had settled on an initial filing of $9 to $11, with the higher end of the range conveniently being almost the price paid by the *New York Times.* No value added there.

There was only one problem with this sane, reasoned analysis: it took no account of what the public was actually willing to pay for the merchandise. It would be as if you were auctioning off a Van Gogh and you said that bidding started at $2 million. You knew that was a lot, but you also knew that it bore no relevance to what the buyers would pay.

It was, in retrospect, a charade to cover the underwriter if we were ever sued for not doing due diligence. Having come from that world, I probably would have done the same thing. But this process contributed to the amazing absurdity in underwriting in 1999.

And to think that Goldman would get paid more than $7 million to have that discussion over a piece of business that was sold before it even started made my stomach churn.

Yet what had happened with our pricing so far was the sane part! It would get crazier and more irrational by the day now that we had settled on $9 to $11.

CHAPTER 18

Inside the IPO:
Part Two

Nobody would admit that the $9 to $11 pricing Goldman had arrived at in April just before they began the road show to market the company was both unrealistic and a total rip-off for our company. If the *New York Times* had just paid $11, what the heck were we doing offering it to the public for the same price? It should be much higher than what an insider would get; that's the way all pricings were supposed to work. The private value of a news entity previous to its endorsement by the *New York Times,* and the public value of that same entity after, can't possibly be the same. The value of the *Times*'s imprimatur can't be zero, unless you believe that the *Times* isn't worth affiliating with. Instead, it put us on the journalism map. But if you were a newly minted young kid out of business school in charge of our deal for Goldman, you seized on any benchmark that made sense. And if you were a top partner at Goldman, worried about one day getting sued because you priced a deal too high, why not cover your bets with the price the *Times* had paid.

As seasoned as I was about trading, I had no idea how this IPO process worked once the first pricing had been arrived at. It had never been written or talked about publicly before. Still hasn't. The people who do it never peep about it and the execs involved are strictly one-off on the subject and have no ability to compare their deal with others. The IPO process is probably pretty close to the loss of virginity; it happens only once. You have to figure it was good, but it's strictly overrated fun-wise. People just don't have enough to judge the bankers on. Everything they say is taken as gospel, regardless of whether they are forceful or cavalier.

But I did know that our deal was not going to price at $11 no matter what. We could have sold the 20 percent of the company we were offering for $11 the next day if we wanted to. The exercise so far was totally chimerical at best.

We could have just priced the deal after meeting with a couple of people in New York for a few days, maybe do a Web cast for Europe and California and Denver or something, that's how hot the market was. But that's not how this process worked. We were going to do anything but that. As part of the process of marketing the deal, Goldman Sachs put the senior management team of *TheStreet.com* on an airplane and set that plane down in a dozen cities across the globe, including Paris and London. Even though everyone was confident that we could get dramatically more for the company than $11, it was vital that we start the creep up with the big, expensive, time-consuming totally unhelpful road trip just when senior management was most needed to run the business.

Word leaked back after the European road show, where management basically called itself the digital *Wall Street Journal*—much to my chagrin, because there already was a digital *Wall Street Journal*—that TSCM, the unclever symbol we crafted, would now be priced at $11 to $13.

That was another painful fiction. When management was in Europe, the bankers had informally told me that we would ultimately price the deal at $19 because it had a great ring to it. Clients loved deals priced in the high teens, they said. That was the best psychological pricing point (think $19.99 instead of $20, a time-honored discount, and you understand the feeble brains behind this kind of thinking) but you had to make a pit stop at $11–$13 to get there.

As the management team slogged its way across the country, stopping at major mutual funds for the fabled one-on-ones where information is supposed to leak out that is different from the prospectus, but never does because everyone is so darned rehearsed, the price tag crept to $13–$15. It was all informal, nothing written, but it was headed in the right direction.

Midwest meetings, one-on-ones in Chicago and Denver, the latter a hotbed of growth funds that loved this stuff, took the range to $15–$17.

And, as was the case with virtually every deal that was going through the chute at that time, the well-attended, beloved New York road show created so much demand that the underwriters were "forced" to take the range to $17–$19. I skipped the New York road show despite the offer from English, who wasn't telling me much these days about how the company was doing, not that he would have known because the IPO process took him totally out of touch with the operations. Instead I sent our designated road show person as usual, careful to distance myself from a process that everyone in the media thought I was controlling anyway. No matter what I did, nor what English did, the media refused to believe that *TheStreet.com* was anything other than an operation I controlled out of my hip pocket. Nothing could have been less true. I was struggling, and losing, in my effort to try to retain some control over what went on at *TheStreet.com.*

What really happened during this worldwide tour to sell the deal, a tour that distracted management to where for three crucial weeks nothing happened at the company? What was the impact of the big show? Three things: one, no institutional demand was drummed up whatsoever. Everyone was simply playing the game as Cramer Berkowitz played it, sending people to the luncheons, asking for one-on-ones because they knew that *MarketWatch* was a hot deal and they knew that *TheStreet.com* would be similarly hot. They were all going to play the flip game, and Goldman, which monitors that stuff better than anyone, knew it.

Two, a very expensive group of actors traveled around the world for no reason whatsoever, saying the same thing in city after city. The input from the "investors" was worthless; all they wanted us to do was to get rid of our subscription model and go free, something that management now favored after the trip, but had we done, we would have been bankrupt and closed a year ago. A simple Web presentation could have done the trick, saved everybody a lot of time and money and kept us from having to rehash the stupid logic of going free and forgoing whatever revenue we actually had.

And three, management took its eye completely off the ball in a critical stage of the company's development, when it should have been negotiating deals and building an infrastructure that could handle the reader deluge. No one at the company knew anything about what was happening at

2 Rector Street because everyone important was flying all over the world to drum up interest in something that needed no drumming. The whole exercise made me think that maybe those Marxism classes I took at Harvard—all government majors logged time in courses that spent hundreds of hours on that defunct economic system—may have been right; maybe capitalism could destroy itself through its own greed and stupidity.

No matter, believe it or not, the absurd part of the process lay in front of us, not behind us: the launching of the actual stock offering.

There's always a hesitation after the road show, a possible delay by the SEC, the "holdup," as it is called. Not that anyone knows what the gnomes at the SEC are thinking. But whatever is happening in Washington after the road show but before the actual deal gets priced plays totally into the hands of the investment bankers.

Just when you were beginning to think, What the heck do these guys get paid for, they hold your hand as the SEC holds you up and you think, Well, maybe they deserve something anyway. They've been through this process. They know when something is awry. At the moment, believe me, this was a concern. The IPO was a big deal for us, but I never even thought it registers on the consciousness of anyone who had worked at Goldman for more than two years. There was so much business being done at the time that we had the junior assistant team across the board. I kept thinking at the beginning of the process that Goldman had jammed us with junior associates and that as we got closer they would bring out bigger guns for our $7 million in fees. Where did they get these neophytes? I kept wondering. But the neophytes were the most senior people we would deal with. And they never even bothered to learn anything about our business.

At last, the second week in May, when Goldman placed us officially on the calendar, arrived. On May 11, the morning of the deal, there was the requisite article in the *Wall Street Journal* that I knew they had been cooking up.

I figured it would include new revelations of my fight with Marty—not that there were any—something that would kill the deal at the last minute.

Amazingly, after what was supposed to be so much bad blood between us, the article was remarkably upbeat. "Worth 10 points in this market,"

Jeff noted offhandedly about the "Heard on the Street" column on us. Then came the endless morning joking on CNBC about how rich I would be by some reporter who at the time was covering the dotcom bubble and has since gone back to Harvard Law School. I wanted to kill the guy.

And then came the official word that our deal was "effective"—however that comes down from on high by the SEC, I still don't know—and then there was the "final" pricing at $19 a share. Alas, $19. Just as we all knew and thought, and right on time, more cynical, contrived, and foretold than a Kim Il Sung election in North Korea.

Goldman's management assured us that the stock was "heavily oversubscribed," which, at another time in another market would have meant that the big institutions had all committed to taking down huge chunks of stock. But in this market it meant little, because while the stock may have been heavily oversubscribed at $19, what would it be like when it would eventually open, if the stock were to open much higher than $19, as short-term history indicated would inevitably happen.

For the big day I invited my sister and my dad to watch the festivities from my trading turret. I invited Karen too, but she said that I should invite her when I could sell stock; she didn't care much for a process where I was locked up and couldn't ring the register for more than a year. Dad had brought up a corrugated box of Federal Baking's best soft pretzels from 9th and Federal in the heart of South Philadelphia, not far from where he lived in Society Hill Towers. He would have brought cheesesteaks from Geno's, but they don't travel well past 9th and Passyunk.

He and my sister, as well as everyone on television, expected to hear immediately that *TheStreet.com* had started trading. We had a full box of confetti and some iced Veuve Clicquot ready at 9:30. But I had to explain to them that ever since *theglobe.com*, demand for stocks had become so great that stocks couldn't open on time. It had become a badge of honor to see how late and how high the stock would open.

At that point, my father, used to conventional old economy businesses, said, "If they have too much demand, why don't you just print more stock to gain from it?" I said that the government doesn't let you do that. You have a set amount of shares and you can't call for more, even though that would make sense. Then he asked, Does the company benefit if the stock opens incredibly high? I said, No, not at all. Well, then, he said, What's the point? Who benefits?

Dad, I said, nobody, nobody except those who have friends and family stock and the people who got good "indications" of stock can now flip that stock in the open market. Friends and family, at the moment, meant this scam where you gave favored people a bunch of unrestricted stock that could be sold. We had to work hard at *TheStreet.com* board level to try to keep management from giving it to payoffs, to people who could help our business down the road. It was truly meant to go to friends and family of people at the company.

But that didn't keep English from giving 1,000 shares to Barbra Streisand, at that point an inveterate day trader, in return for a promise of dinner for him and his wife. That ought to help the company, I joked to Marty, who was furious about it.

Friends and family stock at that point came to almost 5 percent of all of the stock to be sold, which was a windfall for everybody's buddies but made no sense when it came to anything logical for the business, or capitalism in general.

Dad wanted to know how much I could sell or flip. None, I said, explaining that Karen didn't even bother to come because I could not make any money from the deal that day. I was bound not to sell for a very long time, I said. I had given most of my 25,000 shares of friends and family stock—an allocation English set without my input—to my dad and he didn't want to flip it, he wanted to hang on. (My sister couldn't take stock because her husband is a director of a major arbitrage firm, and anyone in the business can't take hot stock on deals for his personal account. Another quirk of the system.)

Again, Dad seemed puzzled by the counterintuitive nature of it all. He wanted to know if I knew these people who were going to get rich buying the stock at $19 and flipping it wherever it opens. No, I said, they are all anonymous, just a bunch of good clients at Goldman Sachs. The process, I said, allows Goldman to make a lot of important clients a significant chunk of money, and makes Goldman look great even as we look stupid. If these shareholders did nothing for the company, he asked, why do they get the benefit? They took no risk. That's the underwriting process, I said. It encourages flipping, and, indeed, Cramer Berkowitz was often a beneficiary. I told him that even if *TheStreet.com* came out poorly, my other line of business had done well through the years with the underwriting process. It wasn't a total lose-lose. And why, Dad wanted to know, didn't I, who had worked incredibly hard for the company, get to ring the register, instead of the CEO, Kevin English? Only at the last minute did I learn from Fred Wilson, the venture capitalist driving the deal from our side, that English was given 83,333 shares of freely traded stock to sell at the underwriting price, $19. He had bought this stock for next to nothing as part of his wrangling with us when he took the job, and now he stood to make about $1.5 million on it. Wilson kept saying that English had us over a barrel. The venture capitalists told me to shut up about his windfall and keep writing.

On the morning of the absurd underwriting process a true great businessman, my dad, who had built his wholesaling business from scratch and never got anything for free, was the exemplar of common sense. Nothing like a little bit of old capitalism brushing up against the newer, shoddier, corrupt version.

Exasperated as the morning of May 11 wore on and the stock still didn't open, I told my dad, "I don't make the rules. This is how the game is played."

I was really getting upset, between the television's steady blare of how rich I was and the plain fact that it was all on paper. I could now see it coming. I would soon become the ultimate dotcom poster boy after today, I said to my sister, Nan. The ultimate joker, just the opposite of my real job, where I book the gain before I go home every night.

At 10:15, with the stock still not opened, I heard from our trading desk, which was in constant contact with Goldman, that the stock was "looking $25 to $27." That, I said to my dad, meant that our stock could open up 8 or 9 points higher than it was priced. I knew that would bring a new barrage of questions about why our company didn't get any of that, but my dad didn't pester me. Instead, I volunteered that we sure did leave a lot of money on the table. Better I said it than my dad or my sister.

At 10:30 the stock was looking $30–$32. That was enough. I got on the phone to the trading desk and I said, "What's the deal, man? Don't open the damned stock too high or we will lose all of our holders. We'll piss off everyone."

The pop of 12 points was enough already. No sense in making it so that everybody who learned the story on the road show took the quick buck and we were left with a bunch of weak holders.

The trading desk said it was getting ready to open any minute. Fifteen minutes went by; $35–$40 was the new price tag. Now in two hours we had doubled what it had taken three extravagant weeks to do, and we all had known it was going to go there anyway. I picked up the phone again and told someone on the line to tell someone else that this was getting too crazy and we had to open the stock. I said that we were setting ourselves up for a huge fall because the company would now be worth close to a billion dollars, a price that would exceed that of *MarketWatch*. It would leave us no room to grow, no room for error. The voice on the other end didn't seem to care and I hung up. My point was too subtle for the guys on the other end of the line.

At a little after 11:00 the folks on the tube were yucking it up that every half hour I seemed to be worth another $30 million. At this rate, by 4:00 P.M., I would be a billionaire! I began to break out in a sweat. Oh God, I yelled, we have to get this stock open before it gets even more absurd. I called Karen. She said, "If you can't book it, it ain't worth jack."

At 11:15 the price talk for TSCM moved to $45–$50. I kept waiting to hear the TV people talk about how we were worth more than the *Wall Street Journal* or the *New York Times*. Somehow they forgot to mention it, but they did harp on the billion-plus valuation for a company with nothing but losses and $5 million in revenues.

Heading surely for dotcom poster boy status now. Ugly. I picked up the phone and demanded to speak to the head of the trading desk at Goldman. When I got through, I went ballistic, swearing at the man, whom I had known for fifteen years, that $50 was just plain ridiculous and what did we pay him all of this money for if he was going to open the stock so much higher than what we all knew it was worth. Why, I said, didn't he just sell a boatload short? Why didn't he take the other side of the trade and get the damned thing open, as he had every right to do? Why wasn't he committing capital to get this stock open at some price having something to do with reality?

He didn't have a handle on the opening, he said. Nonsense, I told him. You're Goldman. Goldman's in charge of the deal. You're running the books. You're being paid $7 million to get this process working right, to take some risks, for crissakes. You can measure where the demand is. You know better than anyone how much stock there is to go at various levels. I told him that his buyers were nuts to pay these prices.

He was quiet for a second, and then he explained to me the key to the whole dotcom craziness, the missing piece of information that I would never hear from anyone else, even to this day: "I don't control the buyer."

Huh? I said. Goldman's running the show and it doesn't control the buyer? That's right, he said. Knight/Trimark controls the buyer. Knight/Trimark? How can this be? How can Knight/Trimark, which I barely knew as some sort of small retail house of tiny orders, never a factor in any stock I ever traded, be in command here? How could those schmoes be in charge? Who put them in charge?

"They are in charge of all of the dotcom deals," the voice told me.

"Bet against Knight/Trimark then," I said.

"Can't," the trader said. "They're too powerful."

The trader didn't know how much Knight had to buy and at what level. Some outfit that didn't even exist a couple of years back was trumping fabled IPO king Goldman Sachs at its own job. What an embarrassment.

"Come on, you are Goldman, get control!" I yelled, but I don't think he was listening.

He rang off and I heard from my salesman that the stock was going to open $55–$60, probably top end of the range, in a few minutes.

"Congratulations," he said to me. "For what?" I said. "You're rich," he said. "Damn it, I was already rich, I wanted this to be good for the company, I can't sell anything. This is the worst thing that could happen. Everybody will hate us till kingdom come. Everyone will lose money today!"

With those words, all of the confetti that our clerk Joe Mastellone had cut up for the big moment looked mighty soggy, not to mention the soft pretzels. Everyone in the room was bewildered. Wasn't this supposed to be a joyous occasion?

Nan, who knows me all too well, wanted to know if this was just my finding the dark lining to the silver cloud. "Nah," I said. "We're fucked. This will be the highest we ever trade. We're fucked."

I then told Pop, "Listen, you've got 5,000 shares of friends and family stock, and I want you to dump every share."

To my dad that was sacrilegious. "Never," he said.

I told him, "Nope, do this for me. Sell every share. This will be the highest we ever trade. We will never be worth more than today. Ever."

I then proceeded to call everyone I had ever given friends and family shares to (I gave my assistant, Jeannie, the stock of those whom I couldn't reach), urging them to dump the stock when it opened.

At 11:30, I rang the trader again. "Knight's come in with 400,000 to buy at the open market," he said.

"Fucking lunatics," I said. "They are screwing everybody. They just batched those orders together." I urged him, once again, to take the other side of it.

No, he said, he couldn't. If Knight found out that he was short, they would simply batch some more market buy orders and squeeze him up. Too big a loss to risk, he explained.

"So Knight/Trimark runs this show?" I screamed, still in disbelief about that fact. But there was no one on the other end.

At 11:43 the stock opened at $63, with almost the entire buy side coming from a bunch of e-tail market orders all batched together by Knight, which had totally hijacked our deal. Within minutes the stock was at $70.

"Dad, listen to me, I want you to sell every single share. Dump it, dump it. We are too high. This is nuts! Sell it."

Dad didn't protest but he sold only half. He still has the rest, which he paid $19 for. I sat there dumbfounded. Knight/Trimark had just collected a giant bunch of retail sell orders and taken the other side of the trade— shorted the stock—leaving them totally in charge of the game.

At the moment of truth, Knight, not Goldman Sachs, controlled both sides of the operation. What a miserable misallocation of our fees. What a strange process that allowed Knight to turn market orders from an oblivious public to their own personal advantage. They knew where all of the demand was and they totally abused the IPO. They could have opened the stock much lower. But controlling both sides, they wanted it to open as high as possible, and then with their own capital, take the other side of the trade, short the opening, and then watch it go down and profit from each point of decline. The higher the opening, the more TSCM would fall, the better for Knight. What a killing they must have made—they don't break out how much money they make per deal but I bet this was one of their biggest moneymakers of the year, if not for their whole corporate existence. They were the only winners on the 11th of May. Goldman, *TheStreet.com*'s shareholders, and TSCM were the losers.

We had succeeded in making all the buyers lose money and all the sellers win. TSCM got one third of what people paid for the company, a colossal pricing screw-up. The rest got left on the table. It is a fiasco that haunts me to this day. I was so thoroughly convinced at noon of that day that the IPO was a total and unequivocal disaster that I had no choice but to do what I did whenever I was most upset. I went for a walk around the block. I told everybody I had to get some air. The moment I got out the revolving doors at 100 Wall, I knew it was a mistake.

"Hey, how about a loan?" said one of the half-dozen smokers outside the building.

"Slap me five, rich guy," said another from across the street.

"Mr. Dotcom," shouted another as I walked toward the Exchange.

Yep, "Mr. Dotcom." Somehow I had the vision to know that this moment would do more to tarnish my reputation as a businessman than anything else I would ever do. No way this stock would stay at this price level. No way it would last. As I went up the hill on Wall Street I could have sworn I heard voices saying, "We're all going to laugh at you," like Carrie on prom night. I was just going to have to sit back and take it. I had become a quarter-of-a-billion-dollar joker, a paper multimillionaire with no more hope to cash out in real dollars than if I had just won a huge game of Monopoly.

My premonition of what would happen to TSCM stock became a reality immediately. Our stock never lifted again after that morning. It was straight down with a couple of rest stops and an occasional total breakdown.

Yet everyone at *TheStreet.com* that I talked to seemed immensely proud of that first day. The stench lingered for months, right up to the celebratory dinner for the IPO that Goldman threw on July 21. Why July 21?

There were so many deals that late spring and early summer that Goldman's junior team that shepherded our deal couldn't put it on the calendar any earlier.

At the dinner in a private room at Picholine, Goldman Sachs took our senior team and me out for a party in honor of our deal, complete with commemorative menus made out to *TheStreet.com*. I kept wondering how much of the roughly $7 million we paid them went to that celebration. The young junior associates at Goldman who played the key role in our deal gave out funny little awards—at least they thought they were funny—like a case of Altoids to a financial fellow from our team that I guess either had halitosis or a thing for Altoids. It was a real insiders' bash. And I was no insider. However, I was seated next to Larry Calcano, the ultra-cool lead investment banker who was always so, so busy during our road show that he didn't get to focus that much on us—but at least he returned our calls! Calcano never flinched even when I pointed out the irony that by the time we had our "celebration night" our stock had already lost two thirds of its value. Calcano never flinched at anything.

A few minutes into the dinner he knocked over his glass of cabernet mid-sentence, and even as it drenched the white tablecloth and seeped up the white cuffs of his blue-and-white-striped shirt, he just kept right on talking about how proud he was of our team and what we had done. He wanted to toast our long-term relationship and emphasize that this IPO was just the beginning of a really solid partnership between Goldman and *TheStreet.com*.

I stopped him near the end of the paean and said, "Larry, look, I think you have to get some club soda on that sleeve."

He looked at the sleeve, dripping cabernet as if he had slit an artery, then looked at me and just continued to talk about how the best stuff between us was yet to come, not even bothering to staunch the flow. Talk about unflappable!

Toward the end of the dinner, there were more toasts about how Goldman and *TheStreet.com* would work closely together in the coming years. The Goldman people gave out little chunks of Lucite with a four-inch plastic street signpost jutting from it that said "Wall Street" and "The Street.com."

Mine came broken.

Within a few months Goldman's investment banking team would rarely return our calls. The research department, after writing desultorily about us a couple of times, dropped coverage a year later. We never saw any of those folks again, nor worked with any of them again. Excellent cabernet and pasta at that Picholine dinner, though, the only thing that Goldman ever really gave us.

CHAPTER 19

Media Madness

TheStreet.com CEO Kevin English seemed to feel his most important mission was keeping me out of the loop.

Our relationship didn't start out adversarial. English seemed like he knew what he was doing. He dressed well, always in a nice blue suit with a white shirt and a rep tie. He was well coiffed. He definitely looked the part of the chief executive. I even called him the "graybeard every dotcom needs" in a puff piece that *Business Week* wrote about English when he came on board. He sounded the part too. He always gave the appearance of being serious and getting his hands dirty with the details.

But it didn't take long for me to realize that English was a hands-off CEO, which would have been all right if there had been a great team of top lieutenants. Instead, though, he seemed to delegate all authority to editor in chief Dave Kansas, who began to regard me as if I were the major obstacle to the success of *TheStreet.com*.

I had crossed swords with Kansas earlier in 1998 when I dashed off an e-mail to a reporter on the West Coast, Marcy Burstiner, about an error she had made. Even though I was right about the error, Kansas sent an e-mail to me and to his whole staff banning any direct contact between me and *any* reporter. He said he would not bow to my intimidation. For heaven's sake, it was an error, I said, a simple correction was what was called for, not an all-out ban on contact. That was never a part of the SEC agreement regulating my involvement at *TheStreet.com*. But Kansas was good as his word. So from then on, whenever I had a good story or insight, I had to give it not to the organization I co-founded, but to CNBC or *SmartMoney* or Dow Jones. I complained to English that I was a better source for other journalists than for our own Web site. English said he would look into it, but later said that the newsroom was off-limits.

At a November 20, 1998, "off-site," one of those expensive confabs meant to be away from the action for God knows what reason other than it is expensive—we never held one at the hedge fund—I saw that if I wanted to play a role in the new *TheStreet.com* under English, mine would strictly be as a figurehead. At the meeting, which I regard to this day as the beginning of the downward spiral that *TheStreet.com* only recently broke out of with the removal of Kansas, I broached the idea of some sort of site director who would keep the site lively, like the director of a television program. Kansas disagreed vehemently, saying that he would never cede that kind of control. English agreed with him on the spot. I then suggested that perhaps there should be more cooperation between business and editorial, because the business side told me that editorial wouldn't even give them the time of day. Again Kansas said no to any cooperation with the business side, and again English agreed with him.

Instead they spent the whole day trying to figure out what the "mission" of *TheStreet.com* was. Huh? We knew the mission: to try to make the readers as much money as possible. That's why I set the damn thing up in the first place. I was embarrassed and ashamed of what I had created after watching the monkeyshines of Kansas and English. I left the off-site early. Everyone outside the organization thought I was an important cog in the company, but it was clear that internally I was a meddlesome, doddering uncle, even though I was the only one in the room with any Wall Street or serious financial journalism background. English was out of LexisNexis, the information outfit that was completely outflanked by the Web. Kansas had been a markets reporter, somewhere midlevel in the writing ranks at Dow Jones, with little editorial experience. But together these two had made a decision that my input had to be disregarded either because, in Kansas's case, I was considered somehow corrupt, or in English's case, because he wanted to run the show without any interference or input from me. From my perspective, my company had been hijacked. I should have been able to stop it, but the venture capitalists, who were now going to dominate the board of directors, used the bad blood between me and Marty to seize authority and to define the vision for those toiling every day at the company, not for those who created the concern.

I had no idea, however, how adversarial things were going to become among me, English, and Kansas. A week after the off-site, I was back on *Squawk Box* with Joe Kernen subbing for Mark Haines as co-host. The market was hot as a pistol and many stocks were doubling or tripling if they appeared on television and told a good story. I decided that it was time to point out to people how dangerous the heat could be if they got in late. I knew that one of the companies on the show, Wavephore, had just tripled in a couple of weeks. I asked the *Squawk* staff before the show began whether they wanted me to find out if Wavephore, which was at $15, was up on a short squeeze or not. Sure, they said, that's exactly why they have real money managers on *Squawk*.

So I called my trading desk and asked if Goldman, our custody broker, could loan out any Wavephore to be shorted. Remember, you can't just bet against a stock by selling it short. You have to be able to borrow the stock physically first, so the buyer actually gets something. Word came back immediately that Wavephore could not be shorted, "tight as a drum." There were no shares out there to be borrowed. That meant it would be an illegal short; you can never sell stock short without locating the stock first.

I also could see that Wavephore needed to raise cash from looking at its balance sheet and its burn rate, something that I had become quite good at figuring from our experience at *TheStreet.com.* I could see a situation developing where Wavephore could hype its stock, traders could make a few bucks, but anyone who was watching the show could get killed if they bought Wavephore after this move. And I said the same when the show began, mentioning that Wavephore shares could not be borrowed at Goldman. When I mentioned to management later in the interview that the stock might have been up because of a short squeeze, management was furious. The stock's momentum had been broken and it started plummeting. It went from $15 to $8 almost immediately after the interview.

I didn't think a thing about it. I had always been tough on execs, and always tried to warn the public when I thought they could lose money. But my e-mail in-box was filled with people who wanted to kill me for ruining Wavephore. Almost at once management threatened to sue me for knocking the stock down and "benefiting" from the decline. Management accused me of shorting the stock, even though I had never even traded it.

At the request of Wavephore the SEC called me immediately to see if I was short the stock, and, just as quickly, I was able to show the government that I had no position. CNBC kept me out of my rotation for a week pending its own investigation that I wasn't short it. That "suspension" as the papers called it, caused a firestorm of ethics charges. Once again, some people said, I had used the media to benefit my portfolio. Almost every story that I read about this incident mentioned that I was short the stock and that I had made good money on the short. Every time I tried to explain to reporters and columnists that I wasn't short the stock, they would ask me why I knocked it if I wasn't short it. I told them I did what I did because it was up on a short squeeze and I didn't want people to lose money. I couldn't believe how few people believed that I would say something negative about a stock if I weren't short it. I wish I were that cynical; I would have been making a heck of a lot more money in 1998 than I did!

No matter, CNBC had me back in a tough session a few weeks later, where Mark Haines grilled me on the incident. I was cleared and then back in the co-host rotation. I paid the $40,000 in legal fees this fracas generated, and tried to move on.

But even after CNBC cleared me, English demanded that I sign an affidavit saying I wasn't lying about the incident, something no one at CNBC had demanded. He insisted that I swear that I wasn't short the stock, even though my records clearly demonstrated that I wasn't. This piece of paper was necessary, he said, in order for investors to have confidence in *TheStreet.com*. I signed it.

Then, in a series of meetings that I knew nothing about, English somehow pledged my services to Rupert Murdoch's Fox network in return for an investment in *TheStreet.com*. I told English informally that maybe close to 50 percent of our readers had heard of us through my appearances on CNBC. He said I would still be on CNBC, but I would also be on Fox at the same time. I told him I didn't think television worked like that and that I didn't need any more trouble with CNBC after they had just defended me in the Wavephore incident. He told me not to worry.

But the next time they saw me, the CNBC people pressed me about whether I was going to be a regular on Fox, something that they said would not fly if I wanted to stay on *Squawk Box*. I swore that I would not be a regular, just an occasional guest, and that my allegiance was to *Squawk*. I said that I would never leave *Squawk* for any other show, that it was my favorite program, and that I was simply at odds with management at *TheStreet.com*. Like everyone else, CNBC couldn't imagine how this was possible, how I could not be in control of *TheStreet.com*, given my number of shares and the fact that I was by far the most important marquee columnist on the site.

I knew my goose was cooked with CNBC, though, when as *The Street.com* was filing to go public, my face appeared in a full-page ad in the back of the *New York Times* as a regular on the new Fox show *The Street.com*. I was horrified. This happened on the morning of a regular appearance on *Squawk* in the spring of 1999. I had just pledged my allegiance to CNBC, and now an ad appeared clearly showing otherwise. When I reached English, telling him that I was going to be finished on CNBC because of this, he said it wasn't his fault, it was the fault of Fox. He never would have placed the advertisement, he said.

I did *Squawk* that morning, but right afterward, management called me in and said that I could no longer appear on CNBC because of the show at Fox.

English had killed the golden goose, the single greatest branding event we had going. He had yanked me from my favorite show because of plans for some sort of half-hour show on the Fox News Channel. *Squawk* had been the thing that I liked most about my workday. I could not have imagined what I would get myself into when I agreed to cede any control over *TheStreet.com*. I had funded my own personal nemesis, and everyone thought I was in control of the company. Even as paranoid and as miserably masochistic as I could be, this CNBC axing caused by my own people took me right into the realm of total looniness.

I began to resent *TheStreet.com* as a rogue operation, run by people who wished I would go away. But I owned 3.5 million shares, was by far its most popular columnist, and I had founded the damned thing. I couldn't—and wouldn't—just wash my hands of it.

And besides, English had other ideas for me.

"You gotta keep me away from Roger Ailes," I told Berko. "I'm gonna love him but I don't want to work for Fox, I want to work for CNBC." Berko knew what I meant. Ailes was a businessman, someone with a background in politics that would make him irresistible to me but would hurt our company because we needed to be where people focused on stocks, not politics.

I had given my anti-Fox rap to Kevin English a dozen times, but he wouldn't hear it. He wanted the pop, the first-day homerun that an initial public offering with pizzazz would generate, and to him that meant getting Murdoch to buy on the IPO, which he ultimately did. So what if it meant that I, who had made *TheStreet.com* known through my appearances on CNBC, had to move to Fox. English pleaded with me at a series of dinners to at least meet with Ailes. Each time I explained that I didn't think that the branding we would get from Fox could equal the branding we could get from CNBC. Then that ad appeared for Fox's *TheStreet.com*'s TV show, and the deed was done. I was finished at CNBC so I had to go meet Ailes.

I liked him immediately. His whole being, his whole essence was to make Fox News successful, and I was to be part of that success, he said. He could make me into a star, he said. Oh man, I said, I thought I *was* one, but, whatever. Our first lunch went smoothly, although it was complicated by the *Vanity Fair* article's appearance. Ailes wanted to know if I was a trustworthy lunatic or just a lunatic. I assured him I was the former, and he made it clear there would be ample punishment if I were the latter. Everything with Ailes was "playing ball" or "staying on the reservation." To me these were simply versions of "my way or the highway," which I used at Cramer Berk, and I understood the consequences of casting my lot with Ailes. I signed a hasty contract with him that he said would allow me to be on CNBC whenever if I wanted, as long as I was identified as a Fox News person, which meant, of course, that I would never be on CNBC. That's okay, I knew that English had burned that bridge whether I liked it or not.

Associates told me that Ailes liked me, but that if I were ever to betray him, you could bet our television show, our half hour, would be put on at 2:30 A.M. on Saturday or against NFL football. And I wouldn't even want to contemplate what would happen to me personally if I crossed him.

At first all worked well, as I began to appear on Fox show after Fox show, promoting our own weekend half-hour episode, always with the intent, endorsed by Ailes, of helping *TheStreet.com.* Our show, hosted by Brenda Buttner, now on Fox, was a simple bull session about stocks. *TheStreet.com* writers, including me, would shoot the breeze with one another and argue about stocks. We would then make predictions; it was a snappy format that worked, but it didn't get much traction for the Web site at all. Still, I was having a terrific time showing up and talking stocks on all the shows, and then popping up to see Roger after a show was over, to see how to make things better and to learn, because one thing Ailes knew how to do was teach—teach media, teach popular culture, teach message.

At all times he was totally charming. We would often deviate from straight programming and talk politics. Despite what I had read about Ailes and about his deeply Republican ties, I always thought that he was gratified to have a liberal around. He welcomed the repartee and was more willing to hear and support outside views than any executive at any network I had worked at or been exposed to. I had an opportunity, at least a dozen times, to be told that Ailes didn't want my politics on air, but it was always just the opposite. He just wanted conviction. He wanted debate. He wanted to know whether people believed what they said or whether they were just mouthing it because they wanted money or some endorsement, even if they knew it was bad for the republic. I kept thinking at some point Ailes was going to tell me I was totally full of it in my support for Democrats in general and Clinton in particular, but instead he was amused and encouraged me.

That's the side of Ailes people don't talk about.

Unfortunately, initially through no fault of my own, and then ultimately, through my own sheer stupidity, I met the Ailes that people do talk about, the Ailes who had to dispense punishment because I had strayed from the reservation.

The initial tension came, once again, from English. Ailes, like just about everyone else I worked with from outside *TheStreet.com,* thought that I ran the place and was in charge of everything that happened. He couldn't believe that I had actually ceded any power, regardless of what I had told him about the rules that I had to adhere to. He was sure they were a ruse.

Ailes has sources everywhere at every organization and is certainly among the most powerful and knowledgeable people in the media, if not *the* most powerful and knowledgeable.

Which is why, when English said he wanted to talk to *CBS Market-Watch* about merging, right after I had signed a contract with Ailes, on August 25, 1999, I knew that I was a dead man. I told English that we simply couldn't go talking with CBS after I had signed a three-year contract with Ailes, that Ailes would go ballistic when he found out.

English knew nothing about Ailes or about the media, or from what I saw, nothing about business for that matter. He said that we would have the meeting in secret, uptown, in the apartment of Allan Tessler, a *Market-Watch* director who owned a big chunk of *MarketWatch* stock. I asked, would anyone from *CBS MarketWatch* be there? He said that Fred Reynolds, the CBS CFO, would show. I told him I wouldn't know what to say when Ailes learned of the meeting. He told me that I was being ridiculous; Ailes would never know.

We had the meeting, which indeed, seemed top secret, because Larry Kramer, the CEO of *MarketWatch,* who would have been immediately sold out if we merged, didn't even know about it.

But the very next day Ailes called on my direct line, said he needed to see me, that it was about "playing ball." I told English about the call and English told me I was just being paranoid. Once I got to 47th and Sixth, though, and entered into Ailes's chilly corner office, in one of those meetings where he would stare at you with those tungsten eyes of his, the same eyes that stared down everyone from Nixon to Manson, I knew he knew.

"Why are you talking to CBS?" he said straight out. I fessed up, no need to compound it by lying, saying that English was old friends with the people at *MarketWatch*—true. Ailes said that he didn't want to have to remind me that I had a contract with him.

I said I understood. When English brought up the merger at a board meeting shortly thereafter, I mentioned that we had burned CNBC and now we were going to burn Fox and that each time it looked like I was doing the burning.

That put a spike in the talks. But I always felt that Ailes never trusted me again. I couldn't blame him, given that he figured that I ran *TheStreet.com.*

Dutifully, I threw myself into working for Fox after that close call.

Every Friday morning at seven, I would go to Fox's Midtown studios and tape *Fox and Friends,* where I became a kind of in-house clown cum stock market guru, doing jazzercize, funny outside gimmicks, whatever was called for. I would then at 4:00 P.M. go back uptown and tape three more Fox shows, including the half hour for *TheStreet.com.* I did it reluctantly, though, because I was dog-tired from running the hedge fund and couldn't quite get fired up for all of that Fox action after tough weeks. No matter, I played ball.

Until November 19, 1999, fresh off the red-eye from California, I committed the cardinal sin: I spoke critically backstage into an open microphone of the power of Roger Ailes to do something to help us. I had been out in California at E*TRADE, trying to pitch a half-hour prime-time television show about what to buy in the next millennium. As an aside I mentioned that we at *TheStreet.com* were getting close to Fox. E*TRADE head Chris Cotsakos, a friend of Peter Chernin, the president of Fox's parent News Corp.—Chernin is on E*TRADE's board—said that was unlikely. According to Cotsakos, Fox wasn't committed to the Web and not committed to us.

Bleary-eyed and depressed by Cotsakos's "news" that Fox wasn't that interested in *us,* but was interested in *me,* I came into the *Fox and Friends* studio angry that I had spent so much time working at Fox and yet nothing would ever happen between our two companies. I was wired for sound and when someone off camera asked me why I seemed annoyed, I said that "Ailes didn't have the juice" to make something happen between our companies.

Of all of the harebrained things that I have done in my lifetime, this ranked right up there. Ailes had done everything I had asked to help us.

Stupid, stupid, stupid. And although I later apologized when I learned that my intemperate comments had reached Roger, I was finished. You never overcome that kind of well poisoning. I just didn't have my heart in the Fox setup, though, never did, and the more I stayed away from CNBC the more I missed it. I got tired of people saying "Weren't you that guy who used to come on *Squawk*?" Wherever I went I heard that refrain, family reunions, plane trips, even in London and the Caribbean. Drove me crazy. Worst of all was how much my dad missed me on the show. When he later had a difficult procedure at Jefferson Hospital and I asked him what I could do for him, he said, "Get back on *Squawk.*" I can't believe how much I missed that show. I can't stand to let my dad down.

I went through the motions for the next several months, but I had ruined our prospects with Fox, whatever they might have been, with my big mouth. I compounded the pain, a week later, when I missed a *TheStreet .com* television show filming that I was supposed to attend, and then, finally, in a moment of total disgust, I mentioned our own stock as a buy on our own show. It happened right at the end of the show, when we had to give predictions. I thought that our stock, well below its cash position, represented a good buy. Even though the stock subsequently did double—and I sold none—Ailes was furious that I used his show to promote our stock and told the press that the next week. I had strayed so far from the reservation that I was about to be taught a lesson in why no one crosses Roger Ailes. Anxious to promote my return to *New York* magazine with a cover story entitled "Dot's All Folks," I appeared on Chris Matthews's show on CNBC and then the *Today* show on NBC. What was I supposed to do, pass those up?

But when I got to my office soon after these appearances, a process server hit me with a suit by Fox seeking damages and forcing me to appear only on Fox for the next two years, the duration of my Fox contract. Nasty.

For three miserable months we duked it out in print and in court, until a settlement was reached that freed me to appear elsewhere. It was bittersweet; I had gotten free to go back to CNBC, but I had let my emotions screw me up again and had betrayed someone who had meant no ill will for me, simply because I wanted to be on some television show that I liked a lot. The suit and the intrigue had sapped my spirit to do both the television and the hedge fund, though, and throughout the fall of 1999, even as we were coining money, I was more miserable than ever.

CHAPTER 20

Taking Back *TheStreet.com*

If you had to come up with a terrible scenario for a start-up company like *TheStreet.com,* it would be to give an unseasoned chief executive officer a pot of money and a bunch of kids to spend it on. With almost $150 million in the bank, Kevin English proceeded to try to buy every investment Web site in the universe, while giving editor in chief Kansas a blank check to build a worldwide newsroom. Marty and I, now united again and suspicious of English, managed to nix all the major acquisitions, any one of which would have put us out of business. But we couldn't stop the spending, because it was endorsed by the venture capitalists on the board, who believed we had to get big fast or get out, whatever getting out meant.

Even as we had very little knowledge about our own market, who signed up for us, what people read, what people liked, and even though we were obviously linked in our growth to the initial public offering and Nasdaq markets, English became fixated on taking the money and establishing a base in Europe. For the life of me, I couldn't think of anything more stupid. We knew nothing about Europe, nothing about the London market, hadn't established ourselves well enough in America, and yet the U.K. became our focus. Kansas and English both believed that's where the growth was. As the venture capitalists agreed with this moronic course, as did the *Times* guy, Michael Golden, and since Marty and I were just still trying to get back together, the European juggernaut couldn't be stopped and we proceeded to spend millions of dollars opening a European branch that, within a year, almost threatened to bankrupt the U.S. operation before we closed it.

Prior to *TheStreet.com* coming public, Marty and I had a modicum of cost control, knowing that we had a finite amount of money with which to play. Now TSCM could only spend, spend, spend, without, it seemed, denting our cash. We were on a mad dash to get to 300 employees, to hire 100 reporters, to build offices around the globe. Right after the IPO, in June 1999, English went to the board to urge us to drop the subscription revenue stream that amounted to an $8 million annuity, our only consistent revenue stream. He said it was constraining our growth, which should be 100 percent advertising-related. He said that he heard this information from "valued accounts" who had participated in the road show for the IPO. He said that the emphasis on paying for content, a bedrock issue that the company was founded upon, was wrecking his ability to do his job.

I argued that advertising was not a sure thing and that who in his right mind would ever give up a real revenue stream for a chimerical one. I said that advertising's cyclicality could lead us to become dependent on something that could dry up in a bear market. Plus, I said, we had 25,000 people willing to pay $100 a year—why not see if we could keep that and get advertising too? He said we needed to do it to please the analysts and Wall Street, to keep the stock high. I said it didn't matter what the stock did, what mattered was what the business did, and we needed the money for when advertising eventually cooled. Anyway, I said, pleasing Wall Street was an exercise in losing your integrity and your mission. I knew from the hedge fund what Wall Street wants is faddish; what Wall Street likes changes from day to day. Wall Street was about fashion. Right now advertising was in fashion, subscriptions were out. (Later it would be reversed, when advertising soured.) What you should care about is what's best for your business, I argued, in one of my first forceful challenges of English at the board level. Giving up a certain revenue stream for an uncertain one was just plain idiotic.

When Marty launched into a strong defense of my views and my position, English retreated. His reaction, I would find out later, was to put the company up for sale to anybody who wanted it. But as our stock was in free fall two months after we came public, cascading to the 20s from that

$63 opening, any negotiations to acquire us seemed downright ludicrous. We had just come public and he wanted us sold whether we wanted to be sold or not. I remember telling Karen about how English wanted to give up, and that it sure would have been nice to let me know who I would have to end up working for, as I was the largest shareholder and contributor. She urged me to get rid of English as soon as possible, especially because I had signed an ironclad contract to work for *TheStreet.com* until 2003 and I was beginning to resent the operation I had founded. The fact that I wanted to build the company into a business before we contemplated dumping it didn't factor into English's thinking, though, and he busily set up meetings with E*TRADE and *CBS MarketWatch* to merge our companies. This was the *CBS MarketWatch* meeting that soured my relationship with Roger Ailes.

English, I always felt, figured he could get away with just about anything, spending recklessly, putting the company up for sale, because Marty and I had been warring. But the peace treaty English brokered right before the IPO came public stuck, courtesy of English's mistreatment of both me and Marty. I don't think there could ever have been as easy a reconciliation if we weren't so appalled by the reckless spending and the lack of oversight management that English brought to *TheStreet.com*. At the end of May 1999, shortly after we had come public, I had placed my fourteen-year-old nephew, Cliff Mason, son of my sister, Nan, and her husband, Todd, on *TheStreet.com* payroll, as a summer intern and told him that he could earn a couple hundred bucks a week if he would simply count the hours that English was there and find out what the heck he was spending his time doing.

Every Friday Cliff would walk the four blocks over to the hedge fund, get some Chinese food, and spill the beans on what was going on over at *TheStreet.com*. It was all bad. English wasn't around much at all, Cliff explained. He came in late many days. He played a ton of golf. He took an occasional meeting. The whole place was being run by Dave Kansas, the editor in chief, who Cliff said knew nothing about business whatsoever. If English was really working on improving *TheStreet.com*, it was news to just about everyone there, Cliff said. Oh yeah, and by the way, he was hated. Enough people didn't know Cliff was related to me that he found out that senior staff were supposed to do everything they could to keep me out of the loop. It was remarkable to have my worst fears corroborated by a freshman in high school. (Others confirmed what Cliff told me.)

The absurdity of the spending spurred me to ask Marty if we could do more together than just make up. I said I needed to apologize fully and get us back on track to retake the company from the hijackers. He graciously agreed to do so and at a crowded downtown restaurant named City Hall a month after we came public, we agreed to patch things up as best as we could, as fast as we could, to save the company. Marty was more than eager to start a war with me on his side. We decided on the spot that we had to get rid of English or minimize his involvement before he either bought something that bankrupted us or went through all the cash we had raised.

In August I took a week off at the beach, and asked that, if possible, we have a quiet week at *TheStreet.com*. That was precisely when English went into overdrive to sell the company, forcing me to come back to work to ask him what the heck he was doing. We had several tense sessions in August and September where I demanded that he hire a chief operating officer, someone who could mind the business day to day as he was off doing his big thinking. He agreed, and I decided to head up the search for the person. We quickly hired Tom Clarke, from the respected financial firm of Technometrics, which had just been bought by Thomson Financial. Tom was a seasoned hand, someone who had actually been in financial services and understood that we had to get our costs down before it was too late and we had run out of money. He was a specialist in restructurings, and even though we had just come public, we were in dire need of a restructuring after the layers of management and staff English and Kansas had piled on.

At the next board meeting at the 2 Rector Street conference room in October, English began by passing out a proposal saying that the meddlesome nature of two board members made it impossible for him to do his job and that it was time either to sell the company, or to boot off the two intransigent board members. He said he had no intention of going anywhere. I looked around in the room at the faceless venture capitalists who now dominated the board and at Dave Kansas, whom I had agreed to have on the board because of the need to preserve editorial integrity in the eyes of the SEC. Nobody seemed to be disturbed by English's attack.

I had flipped through the presentation, which listed all the initiatives that I had fought, and had skipped to the ultimatum in the back. I was fuming, beyond anger, shocked that a company that had relied upon me for its cash, its branding, and its readership was willing to get rid of me just like that. When the room got to English's ultimatum, I got up, and said, "Hey, if you guys think you can do this without me, be my guest, I have a lot of work to do at the hedge fund." And I walked out. I didn't speak to anyone. I just headed to the elevator bank, went down, and returned to the hedge fund. I had had enough of this lunacy. I didn't care that my stake was worth $50 million at the time. This company had become an embarrassment, and I had no desire to work for it anymore.

English seemed so thrilled at the turn of events, Marty later told me, that you could tell he thought the game was over. He suspected that my rapprochement with Marty was bogus to satisfy the regulators. That's why he was shocked when, after I had left, Marty spoke up and said that he wanted English to leave the room so he could discuss the situation. Once English was gone, Marty told the board that while I was no picnic to work with, I was the franchise and we couldn't dump the franchise for English. He called for a board vote on the spot to fire English and replace him with Clarke, who had been with the company less than two weeks. The board agreed with Marty and English was fired immediately.

The venture capitalists, mortified by the turn of events, insisted on rewarding English with a massive package of stock that he was free to trade—the second time they caved to him—and the only man to work for *TheStreet.com* and make millions of dollars from it was shown the door one year after his appointment. The venture capitalists said that paying him off like that was the price of dismissing him without a legal fight. I didn't even care. I would have paid him personally to go. He was a disaster. We were through with him at last. He would subsequently drift on to a succession of dotcom jobs. We never spoke again after that showdown.

In his place, Clarke came in and immediately put in spending freezes and dismantled the European operation. Clarke understood that the dotcoms would never be able to get financing again. He slashed expenses, fired hundreds of people, and set the company on a course that ultimately would keep us alive long after most dotcoms died. He fired every single executive save one who was with the company under English—whom he agreed had indeed hijacked the company from its two founders—got rid of all the venture capitalists who had demanded that we grow with no dis-cipline (they sold all their stock) and at last set the company on a course toward profitability. And he agreed that I could visit all I wanted and talk to anyone at the company I wanted unfettered. He said he wanted me *in* the door, not out. It was Clarke's open-door policy and shrewd manage-ment that would, in the end, allow me to work side by side with him to save the company from financial oblivion.

English's departure and Clarke's arrival made it possible for me to re-build my relationship with Marty.

CHAPTER 21

Repositioning Cramer Berkowitz

We needed another brain at Cramer Berkowitz, someone who could handle all of the new tech companies that were being created like dandelions overnight. That's where the action was, in the new stuff, the stuff that came public like *TheStreet.com,* the companies that were "new economy" companies. That stuff moved, and, for a hedge fund, movement is all that matters, not direction or velocity. Going into 1999 we could no longer just make money trading traditional blue chips or growth stocks and owning small capitalization stocks. We had to change our style. We had to adapt to the new companies that the economy was creating like mad, or risk being irrelevant and underperforming.

Oh, now, don't for a minute believe that we were into the new economy at Cramer Berkowitz. I think we might have believed that hype, if it weren't for *TheStreet.com.* But I knew that the new economy was simply a combination of overheated stocks, a desire to start an Amazon, a desire to kill an Amazon, and a desire by investment banks to take advantage of a good thing until they killed it, as they always did with something new and different and momentarily profitable. We saw through the pure dotcom nonsense. Again given the huge costs of running a dotcom, I knew that the new economy was more expensive and, in many ways, less efficient than the old one. I understood the momentary love affair with the picks-and-pan sellers—how many times did we hear those silly Gold Rush analogies—and we were willing to buy those stocks because we knew that Exodus, the now bankrupt Web-hosting company that traded with a $40 billion market cap two years ago, was shaking down TSC. Hosting was just a place to store a bunch of Sun microservers. We knew that Akamai had fooled off-liners wanting to go online into thinking that many more people would come to their sites if they were a nanosecond faster, which gave Akamai a $30 billion valuation. (Believe me, I toyed with a "Powered by Akama" sign on the site, dropping the i, as I knew from our internal studies that Akamai had no real discernible effect for our readers.) Sure, why not buy Vignette, the $25 billion Web commerce company that had us over a barrel at *TheStreet.com,* charging us a fortune for a commerce system that really didn't work well with our publishing system and didn't allow us any flexibility? The upgrades from Vignette buried us. And who wouldn't buy the e-brokers like E*TRADE and Ameritrade given the business they were doing and the advertising they were placing? We plowed into the Scients and the Viants, multibillion-dollar-capitalization companies that were simply consulting firms that did nothing but design Web sites, mostly for offliners. We played them to the hilt during their ascendancy into their $25 billion market caps, as seemingly every company in America sought to build a Web site, take the division public, and then reap the sums that the public would throw at them.

These trends, however ephemeral, had to be played if we were going to make our nut, which, by 1999, meant making $300,000 a day just to meet our historic averages. And we did play them, both on the way up, as long as the IPO market funded companies that could spend the money on these tools, and then on the way down, on the short side, once the IPO window closed in mid-April of 2000 and left these companies without new customers.

But what we needed was a metric, something to grade these stocks by. Earnings didn't matter, revenues didn't matter, valuations didn't matter. We needed to measure heat, what was hot and what was not. We needed to measure fashion, to try to figure out what would be popular with the buyers, not what we liked ourselves. And we needed someone to look at these stocks in a manner as analytically cynical as that in which they were created, someone who would buy into the notion that these were ambush stocks, where you ambush the shorts, take the stocks up, and dump them to the mutual funds who couldn't get enough and were constantly pumping the stocks on television as long as their performance held out. We needed to run with these stocks and dump them just when they got cool, or better yet, short them as they returned to the dust that they emanated from.

How do you find a brilliant cynic who can at once buy into the new trends and then dismiss them as if they had no bearing or importance? How do you locate just the person who understood the faux nature of the companies but was willing to get them while they were hot, so to speak, and scorn them a day before they turned cold? Someone who recognized that the game was musical chairs, or hot potato, and the winner coined money for the partnership while the loser lost a pile of money *and* his job?

I had pretty much given up hiring, for fear that I would kill the next person who lost me money. I had grown increasingly bitter toward all but our most inner circle and wasn't going to reach out to find another numbskull who told me how smart he was and how much money he had made, only to discover that, like everyone else, he would fold under that first one-and-three-quarter-point decline. I had been through dozens of people and still couldn't find one moneymaker, one person who didn't need the market to go his way to make some bucks. There just weren't enough good people out there who recognized that they would have to "Wear the Post-it" if they screwed up—and wear it miserably until I said they could take it off. When you own the firm and you have the most capital on the line, you need to find a way to make the hired folk feel the pain when they botch the job and go long a bum stock or go short the next Microsoft. To me there was no stronger way to drive home the point than writing out the symbol of the piece-of-garbage loser of a stock on a Post-it and making the poor slob who picked it stick the Post-it on his forehead and wear it all day until I felt the shame had registered. It was unusual but not cruel, because I never made them wear it outside the office.

Who would come in and be willing to handle the pressure when I told Jeff, "Let's see how fast we can make him cry," after the knucklehead had taken his first $50,000 loss? Who could handle the pressure that comes from reviewing a stock every half hour and paying the $2,500 fine I instituted for every half point that the stock declined after I said I didn't like it but the person hadn't sold. No better way to find out a person's conviction than making them write you a check for the losses. Who could handle my selling your stock out from underneath you when you went to the gent's (or ladies')? Who could take my incessant badgering about how little they knew about the stocks they wanted us to own and how I would never forgive them or their children for losing my partners' money. Who would take that pressure?

Only someone who knew that Berko had made 400 Gs that first summer he worked for me. Only someone who knew that I paid $10,000 bonuses on the spot for good ideas, as I did to one employee who noticed that Dr. Pepper was featured prominently in *Forrest Gump* and that might spur Dr. Pepper sales, which it did, causing my firm to make a quick 200 Gs.

Only someone who knew that my assistant got paid a half-million bucks to take the abuse I dealt out every day when we were losing money. Only someone who accepted the bargain of Cramer-induced misery on bad days for big money on the good ones. Someone who wanted to be right and be paid more than he would anywhere else on earth to be right.

That's why when Matt Jacobs, an analyst at the Carson Group, a PR firm, sent me an e-mail saying he would regard a turndown as the beginning of a beautiful relationship, I was intrigued. Of course, I rejected him out of hand—why not save him the angst and me the losses. But as he said he would, the twenty-four-year-old, whose job it had been to advise CEOs about how to handle the media, came right back with another e-mail saying that he was the best that I would ever find and that he would know more stocks and make us money faster than anyone since Berko. Hmmm, at least he knew the cast of characters. I can't tell you how many times people would try to get a job at my place and spell my name wrong, and not even know that Berko played a role. They figured it was all me, all of the time, judging from my incessant appearances on TV.

I asked him to give me three moneymaking ideas by e-mail. If all three panned out within a week *and* we made multiple six figures in profits from them, regardless of how the market did, then I might give him an interview. His picks worked, so I said he could come in the following Thursday, in the third week of November, on these conditions: one, he had to be there at 4:15 A.M.; two, he had to have five more great ideas; and three, he had to bring the food that I had once written in a 1997 column in *TheStreet.com* that people had to bring me before I would take them seriously.

That Thursday morning came and I stepped out of the Mercedes-Benz 500 at 4:12 A.M. to see an incredibly thin guy with wire-rim glasses and close-cropped hair smiling at me. "You must be Jacobs," I said, perturbed that he really took me up on this early morning gambit. I didn't want to have to go through the hassle or I would have made him come in during regular hours.

"And I have a dozen Krispy Kremes here, just made." At least he got the password food right.

I said to him, Look, before we go up that elevator you have to understand that I have tried to murder research associates and that I always regarded it as justifiable given the losses they generated. He nodded and said that "capital punishment" made sense for those who generated losses for Cramer. I told him that I would make fun of him mercilessly and that he would cry to his mother and dad and break up with his girlfriend and want to kill himself if he lost my firm money.

He said in that extremely unlikely event he would deserve whatever befell him. I told him I had thrown probably 300 water bottles at Jeff for mistakes he had made, or mistakes that I made that I blamed him for, and I always wished they had poked out Jeff's eyes when I threw them. "Probably deserved it," he said. I told him that I was mercurial and arbitrary and capricious by nature and a total monster to work for. It was my way or the deathway, etc.

He said he wouldn't be here if I weren't all those awful things and more. My kind of guy.

Three hours later, when the rest had arrived, I insisted that Matt spend time with everyone.

Jeff was livid. "No more hiring. No more hiring," he said. "They kill us."

I said this guy was different.

He said, "They are all different."

I told him, "Spend time with Jacobs, just grill him, treat him as I treated you," I said.

"Send him to look through waste cans? Send him to hang out outside offices and ambush CFOs?"

Okay, I said, just give him a chance.

By the end of the day, Jeff said Jacobs deserved a chance to come by again. He said we couldn't hire him no matter what, until he came by several times, because we were so terrible at hiring.

I agreed. Each time Jacobs came in with Krispy Kremes. Each time he had more good ideas. Each time the ideas made money.

So on December 10, 1999, after the third time, we hired him. We paid him $2 million in his first full year working with us. He deserved every penny, because within a year he had a Rolodex as big as Jeff's for the new economy, the best young talent I had ever seen. Within a year Jeff stepped up to be my equal and we made Jacobs research director.

At first, I insisted he work just with me. We developed rotisserie leagues to learn new stocks, where we would risk phony money to draft our favorites and only after we had traded them for a while would we invest in them. Just like those rotisserie leagues where you pretend to coach a football or baseball team. The pressure of wanting to win—and not wanting to look stupid, in my case—drove us to learn dozens of companies that otherwise we would have spent no time on. We had to break up the game and play with real money when we started making more money on paper than we were with the real fund.

Jacobs understood the chimerical nature of what was hot. He understood which companies would raise the bar, and which mutual funds would then come in and walk stocks up to levels that were unsustainable.

Best of all, he understood that the most important part of investing in the late 1990s was knowing when the sizzle was gone and the steak was burnt—or putrid or maggoty. It was an awesome talent and Matt made our firm the most intense fundamental place on earth in 1999, a place where knowledge of news and valuations combined with catalysts and market mind-reading on a daily basis to make big money.

Still, coming into 2000, we lacked one critical element toward making our firm the ultimate destination for wealthy people's capital. We needed a trader, someone who could step in and do what I was doing so I could think more, someone who could swing, who could make profits from the desk, who could "see" the market and "read" it and make use of all the great information that we saw and heard every day from all of the institutional desks. Someone who, in a hurry, could "get something done," who could put a position on, a giant position, without hurting any broker or moving the market, setting us up for what we knew would be an inevitable end to the bull market, as the Nasdaq kept climbing, absurdly, toward 5,000.

At the beginning of 2000, we made Todd "Cookie" Harrison head trader at Cramer Berkowitz. On Wall Street nicknames abound and we rarely even know the reasons for them. I'd been calling Todd "Cookie" on the other end of the line for ten years and had no idea why. Still don't. I didn't even know what he looked like before we hired him. That's pretty typical of Wall Street. But we had done billions of dollars' worth of trades together—by phone—and I trusted him implicitly. Ever since my wife left the firm, I had preferred to have a head trader who did not play an active role in the choosing of stocks, just in the execution of orders given by me.

In other words, an order taker. "Buy 25,000 General Electric, don't pay more than $40." Or, "Sell the Lilly down to $77." Now that my wife was out of the picture I didn't want anyone who was more than just an extension of my brain. Todd changed all of that. Like Karen, Todd brought his own perspective and his own moneymaking ideas. He was an aggressive capital committer and he liked to swing for the fences. He is also volatile, like me, wildly emotional *except* when the big money could be made. Then he was cold as Saturn. Todd made my stock life easier even as his personalities and my personalities together, plural intended, would cause fire marshals to groan with fear of overcrowding the trading room.

We came into 2000 with a full head of steam and a belief that the Nasdaq wasn't done yet. Ever since our switch in strategies after the debacle of the fall of 1998, we had chosen to go with the flow. We recognized that the stock world had changed, even though we knew, mostly because of the chaos at *TheStreet.com,* where being a dotcom ultimately put you at a disadvantage against your television and radio colleagues, that the business world hadn't. Unless you had seen how Net companies frittered away their advantages and faced an increasingly hostile consumer, who felt that everything on the Net should be free, if not subsidized by the offline parent, you really would believe that a new economy was being created. We had seen the Nasdaq vault to 4,000 at year-end, seemingly leaping every day, and I was convinced that this market would see 5,000 before it again saw 3,000, even if it deserved to be at 1,500. Where it deserved to be never mattered. Justice is an irrelevance in the stock market. Where it was going is all I have ever cared about.

Part of our great strength at the company was the recognition that investing is almost all psychology and very little substance, despite what the multimillion-dollar research staffs of every Wall Street firm would tell you. We know that Wall Street is more a fashion show, short-term, than an exercise in rational pricing and capital allocation. We knew coming into 2000 that the prices of stocks could not be justified by the prospects of business. They could only be justified by those who were paid to justify them, the analysts and brokers seeking to get you to buy them. If stocks had to be sold, tales would be crafted to sell them. I knew that from my sell-side days. We knew that you could spin any story, fundamental, or otherwise to justify any investment. We had seen, since the market bottom in 1994, that, increasingly, it didn't matter what a stock was valued at. It seemed that each year we were paying more and more for the same level of earnings. Prices that we would have puked over in 1995, we paid without blinking in 1996. Prices that we couldn't stomach in 1996, we lapped up in 1997. And whatever discipline the market might have had in 1997 disappeared entirely in the fall of 1998 when the Net bubble expanded. You had to believe in nothing when it came to buying stocks, because if you believed anything rigorous—price-to-earnings, price-to-book, price-to-sales, dividends, cash flow—you looked like an idiot. An old fogey. Someone who would be drummed out of the business, as many of the old growth and branded folk were. I know it: on television and in print I did a lot of the drumming.

After the redemption fiasco of 1998, I knew the truth. If you stuck with a style, stuck with what you were comfortable with, then eventually you stuck with nothing. They would take the money away from you if it underperformed, as I certainly learned with the $100 million in redemptions in my first bad year versus the averages. And if you lost money? They shut you down. That was the lesson of 1998. I knew this well ahead of all of the mutual funds that eventually went belly-up in the great massacre of 2001. I knew it because of the dry run I had in October of 1998, when people no longer liked my style of stock picking because it didn't keep up with the Nazz, even as I had been conditioned that the only benchmarks that mattered were the Dow Jones and the S&P 500. How could I not feel this way? I had made money for eighteen years, and in my first stumble almost half my assets came out in five business days, even though I regarded myself as a shrewd observer and evaluator of what stocks were really worth. I was never going to be foolish enough to let that happen again. If people wanted to own tech, well, let's make the tech bet. If people wanted to own new tech, let's hire Matt and learn new tech. And if people wanted to trade the new issues, the most exciting ones, the ones with the least seasoning and the most downside? Let's get a new trader who can handle it. Let's get Todd Harrison. If people wanted dancing bulls that could pirouette on the head of an Internet pin, all the while knowing that the stuff could turn out to be built on gossamer pillars, so be it. I can handle that. I can play that game.

Todd, like me, is a solid citizen of paranoia and psychosis. I knew I had a kindred spirit when, after his first good day of trading he wore the exact same outfit to work the next day. And then wore it again and again and again. He knew, even though he had worked at Morgan Stanley for ten years, and not Goldman. He knew, even though he had done millions of trades based on fundamentals. Those clothes determined the outcome of the trades. Isn't it irrational and mortifying that the best traders actually think like this?

Todd's all karma. I live in a world where if you lose money, I hate you, hate everything about you and want to pillage your home, until 4:00 P.M. when the closing bell rings and I love you again. Todd, on the other hand, knew that if you lost money you deserved to rot in hell and have your liver picked out each day by strange birds of prey. You didn't, however, need Cramer to pick at it too.

We were a fiery combination, and one that was so combustible that we had to have daily hug sessions and "I love you, man" instant messages to keep from slitting each other's throat and then second-guessing whether we should use dull or sharp knives to do so. We were, in Todd's words, our own minyan, a Jewish term for a quorum of ten; we were more than that, we were dozens of personalities in two bodies seated across from each other. Almost immediately we clashed on what was happening in the market. A month into 2000, with the Nasdaq going up virtually every day, Todd "hated them," meaning he thought that stocks were wildly overvalued and going lower. Oh man, did he hate them. He had watched as Matt and I jammed the sheets with new economy stuff, stocks that would go up 10, 15, 20 points an hour, and were pure short squeezes. He knew we knew that these were all overvalued, that they would one day be colossally slaughtered. But he didn't want to catch those last points.

To me, a student of manias, I knew that the best point to be maximum long would be the blow-off stage, the stage where stocks would explode upward with trajectories that defied imagination, as short sellers would be pushed under by the wave of bullishness. You had to get off right at the peak. Until then maximum price appreciation beckoned and if you didn't get in on that, you shouldn't be a fund manager. Plus I never loved or hated stocks. I saved those emotions for the real world, or the sports world. Not the financial world that I played in by day. Hate stocks that are going up? No, hate terrorists and murderers, not a runaway Qualcomm or an over-priced Amazon.

I relied on Matt Jacobs to fuel me with the ideas, the new world ideas that would capture the market's fancy. By the beginning of 2000 they were printing them so fast I couldn't keep up with them. We piled hundreds of millions of dollars into these names in November and December of 1999, when their trajectory resembled a rocket escaping earth's gravity. The path continued in 2000 without skipping a beat. I had long since accepted that what was really happening in the Net world was coming to an end. That had been a process where you came public, got bid up by the day traders and electronic traders who now lived on the Net, and then took the proceeds and gave them to Yahoo! and AOL for slotting and placement fees. This was some racket; we all played it. The idea was simple. If you had a lot of eyeballs coming to your site, you could, theoretically, sell ads against those eyeballs. To get as many eyeballs as you could, you needed placement at AOL and Yahoo!, anchor tenancy so to speak, so people could click on your icon, or a mention of your story, and be sent to you. If you had lots of people clicking to get to your site you could sell more ads. Yahoo! and America Online demanded fees to place your stories above other stories—whether they were better or not. At *TheStreet.com* we thought this was wrong because we were doing proprietary analysis and we were being put behind commodity stories that were unhelpful to the consumer but gave a bigger payday to the portals than we could provide. Once advertising started drying up, though, you were stuck with a parade of eyeballs that came to your site that you could no longer monetize. You were then paying for nothing! I could see that happening from our numbers at *TheStreet.com* and I knew that the dotcom-comes-public, dotcom-pays-AOL-and-Yahoo!-for-traffic days were running out. There simply weren't that many left that hadn't come public that could play this game anyway. The pipeline was exhausted. Every single e-area had been IPO'd three times over. When we had gotten to the e-parties of the world we were simply running out of merchandise to be sold. We were waiting for some real confirmation by people in the real world of business to tell us we had vastly outrun the fundamentals.

I knew that the game should have been up a year ago, after so many companies, including *TheStreet.com,* had come public at lofty levels and then been crushed into smithereens. But there were so many believers out there. And it didn't matter if I was an apostate; no one was listening. I had twice tried to write an obituary speech for the Web, once in London for Goldman Sachs as keynote of the firm's international tech conference in September of 1999, and then in New York a month later at a *Crain's New York Business* presentation. Both times absurd events had made me look like an idiot. I annoyed everyone at the Goldman tech conference by saying that the Internet was overhyped and repellent and expensive to use. Who needed someone telling the truth in the midst of the great underwriting boom? Anyway, within a few days after the speech *TheStreet.com*'s DOT (Internet) index rallied to new highs, making me look like a total moron! Then I tried it again a few weeks later in front of 2,000 people at the *Crain's* breakfast, talking about how there would only be a few dotcom companies that would survive and those would be the ones whose sites people paid to use. Sites that generated revenues would win, sites that generated just eyeballs would lose. That very morning, I had to rip up my speech because, an hour before the speech was given, Excite@Home announced it had paid $730 million for Blue Mountain Arts, a company with no revenues that just relayed Internet greeting cards. I was wrong before the ink was dry as the speech rolled out of the printer. (American Greetings would later purchase Blue Mountain Arts for $35 million from Excite@Home, which went bust.)

All around me deals were occurring at astronomical valuations that were being greeted as positive for the buyer *and* the seller. How could the

Net be near death if Yahoo! was paying $5 billion for GeoCities and another $5 billion for Broadcast.com, or if start-up companies with no revenue were getting rounds of financing with no products and a $3 billion valuation? Maybe it was just me. Maybe it was just the management at *TheStreet.com* that was telling me, increasingly, how awful the Web was to do business on. Maybe it was how crowded everything was on the Net and I saw it from the inside. Eyeballs were still king even as I joked that only ophthamologists get paid by the eyeball.

Until one day it all changed, the day that Time Warner merged with AOL. No one understood the Net as well as Steve Case, except maybe Bob Pittman, his co-officer. Their decision, in retrospect, to merge with Time Warner was recognition that growth had peaked, but we just didn't know it yet. When the rest of the Nazz sputtered but failed to decline after the AOL news, I thought maybe there was still more money to make. At the time I was buying a list of stocks I called the winners of the New World, companies that stood to benefit from the so-called revolution that I knew wasn't happening, but was tired of fighting. On February 29, 2000, in a Gartner Group Internet and Electronic Commerce conference in front of a packed house at the Marriott Marquis, I revealed that list and said that these stocks were the hottest stocks I have ever seen. I told people that these were scalders. I derided the fuddy-duddy managers who refused to buy them. I can't even find most of those companies now. They have almost all gone Chapter 11 or been wiped out. They are history. But at the time they were worth billions upon billions of dollars and we didn't want to leave them yet. In the two weeks after the speech many of them went up radically in price. They were making more money for us in a day than we could make in a lifetime of ownership of Heinz or General Mills or Procter & Gamble.

Todd, a trader, knew the truth—these stocks were all in weak hands. Some were held by quickdraw guys like us, able to pound them out on a second's notice. Others were in the hands of the momentum-oriented mutual funds, and we knew these funds had no tolerance for stocks if they started failing. The rest, the vast bulk, was all being held by insiders anxious to depart or venture capitalists with 4 cent cost bases, even though they, for the most part, were bound by federal rules barring them from registering their stock until a certain amount of time had passed after the underwritings had occured. These were people who would sell their grand-mothers if they had a big gain on them. I have always refused to underper-form even for a day, no matter how great the opportunity to make money eventually. I wasn't willing to short the stocks that we all agreed were overvalued because shorting on overvaluation is a chowderhead's game. There is always some fund manager out there who can claim a stock is un-dervalued on 2010 earnings and will buy it up seemingly forever or until his fund runs out of money. As long as the mutual funds kept the balls in the air, even if they were trillion-dollar overinflated balls, I wasn't saying goodbye to them. I would continue to trade them to the long side. Todd, not willing to go head to head with me, instead shorted the indices against our individual longs. We pretty much nullified each other every day.

Until the second event occurred after the AOL Time Warner deal that dealt the death blow to the seemingly never-ending tech rally: the day that MicroStrategy blew up. When the tawdry era's history is chronicled in the textbooks, March 10, 2000, will be recorded as the high for the Nasdaq. On that day the Nazz peaked at 5,010. But that's right only statistically. The heart and soul of the Nasdaq died ten days later, when a company that had products so integral to the notion of the new economy, MicroStrategy, MISTER to everyone on Wall Street because of its symbol, MSTR, re-vealed that it had committed fraud in reporting its results. We always talk about darlings. Cisco, the network darling. Intel, the semiconductor dar-ling.

MicroStrategy was the Internet and Internet infrastructure and business-to-business darling. It was a company with real revenues, real earnings, real management, and real prospects. It was the next IBM, Microsoft, and Oracle put together. You couldn't get prospects brighter than this one. Until March 20.

That's when we found out that all of those prospects were strictly vir-tual in nature and nothing was real at MISTER—least of all the numbers. It had made up its revenues and its earnings and had fooled everyone into thinking that it was around the corner from making huge money. Until this revelation, MicroStrategy, like many Internet companies, seemed to be going up a dozen points a day. Institutions, particularly mutual funds, had developed an insidious practice that reached its zenith in March of 2000. They would glom on to certain stocks, sometimes from their inception, and keep them perpetually moving up by buying them, talking about them on television so they would go higher, and then drawing more money in as their performance was boosted by their own hype on the air. As long as they "controlled the float" of the companies, and as long as they all bought the same stocks, everyone was coining money. I had been well aware of this pattern for more than a year. I knew it because many of my friends worked on desks where they had to short stock to these mutual funds and lost fortunes doing so. The funds were running a sophisticated version of a Ponzi scheme that depended on ever more money coming in.

The valuations, of course, could be justified by new economy rules. How did you know that a company was following new economy rules? That was easy too. All it had to do was, first, make up a series of entirely beatable estimates for earnings and revenues. Then give those estimates to the lackeys, the analysts who had helped bring them public. Then the company would beat those estimates handily when they reported. How could they not? Companies have a clear idea in good times what they are going to earn. If you knew you were going to make 3 cents, just say 1 cent, and then report the better-than-expected number. If you knew you were going to have $5 million in revenues, tell everyone you would have $4 million in revenues and then blow the number away. Everyone played this game, including the old management at *TheStreet.com.* No one quarreled with the charade of beaten expectations. It was too much fun and way too profitable. As long as those numbers got beaten, and estimates moved ahead inexorably, the analyst community could conspire with these greedy mutual funds to keep the prices in the air, going ever higher regardless of the valuation. That's how companies with no earnings to speak of and little revenues found themselves with valuations ten times the size of General Motors, Boeing, and Ford together.

Until, that is, the game ended with the fraud uncovered at MicroStrategy, a tiny Washington, D.C., company that made intelligent software for Web-based applications and that had, somehow, amazingly, skyrocketed to being almost equal to what Merck or Bristol-Myers Squibb is worth today. What was the reason to own a $300 stock that had no earnings and no prospects, you could hear mutual funds managers asking themselves—the same managers who had created this behemoth out of nothing. As the market capitalization melted, it dawned on other, lesser darlings that stocks can go down too. Before MicroStrategy's implosion, most of the selling of these stocks had been short-selling by brokerage houses trying to appease mutual funds that insisted on walking stocks higher after the MicroStrategy debacle. An institution that wanted to buy two million shares of MicroStrategy couldn't just go into the open market and buy the stock. It would move the stock price too much. So, instead, the institution went to a brokerage house, a Goldman or a Morgan, and asked the firm to "short me some MicroStrategy." In other words, create stock by shorting it and then find the stock by canvassing its account base for sellers. Until the announcement of the fraud, so many mutual funds had gone in and gotten so many brokers short who could not recover their stock because there were no sellers, just believers that the stock had been virtually walked up by the accounts getting the brokers shorter and shorter and shorter, to where some of them had to break ranks and turn buyer themselves, making the rocketship go even faster.

After MicroStrategy revealed its fraud, the world seemed to change overnight. Now insiders were selling and registering shares hand over fist. Venture capitalists who professed to be long-termers now did everything they could to sell stock. Now, short-selling hedge funds, who knew that many of these stocks had been bid up by mutual funds to well beyond where they could be supported, came in and furiously sold these stocks to anybody who would buy them. They would then cover when the mutual funds capitulated and sold. Sure enough, the tsunami of stock hit the market, all in the last week of March. The supply was way too much for this market to bear.

For us at Cramer Berk, the realization that it was at last over came hard. We had been making so much money on the long side we were extremely unwilling to switch direction. We were happy to bolt from the stocks, but the idea of shorting them, something that had put many hedge funds out of business in the last few years, seemed antithetical to all but Todd. As someone who had to sell merchandise short to buyers to please them for years at Morgan Stanley, just as the brokers had now been forced to sell stocks short to willing buyers, Todd was actually more comfortable shorting than being long. We cleared the decks in the last week of March, taking off positions that we had kept on for most of the bull market since 1999. When April came in, and the Nasdaq was still in the 4,500 area,

Todd suggested that we were on the verge of a collapse of titanic proportions, that the whole Nasdaq bubble was about to burst and would shortly
be at 1,500.

Man, that was bearish. Todd, like my wife, couldn't articulate why that
would be. It was, again like my wife, a feel. Did I hate that! I wanted more
than a feel. I wanted why, why it would keep unraveling. In the meantime,
I suggested we take all of tech off the table—something I communicated a
dozen times to my Web site—until we figured out why it would crash. I
had gotten so jaded about the mutual funds' ability to raise cash and bash
the shorts, keeping stocks at absurd prices, and, believe me, it was almost
entirely the go-go mutual funds' fault, that I didn't want to get short until I
knew for certain that there was more than just valuation at work.

Fortunately, I had *TheStreet.com*. By 2000, it was clear to me that even
with fantastic management, the management that broomed English and
was still firing his acolytes, the Web was not a commercial endeavor except
for America Online and E-Bay. And AOL, by its merger with Time Warner,
signaled the end of the Net as a stand-alone investable concept. As we tried
to game what would happen with the market, increasingly I came to look at
all the companies that supplied infrastructure to *TheStreet.com* as overvalued, because they existed only because of the overvalued market. If you
took out the props, the tight supply, and the better-than-expected ruse, and
you loosened supply and disappointed in earnings, I argued that there was
no end to where your stock could fall. Todd pushed me daily to be even
more negative than I was, and given that we had sold almost everything
tech by April and had as our largest positions General Mills, CPC (which
Unilever bought), and Anheuser Busch, I became more and more comfortable with the lifetime top thesis that Todd was espousing.

We sold almost all our technology stocks that had made us so much
money since the bottom in October of 1998. On April 7, I found myself on
TheStreet.com's Fox show outarguing our house bear, Herb Greenberg, in
warning people to get out now. I was manically vocal about it, some would
say scary, shouting that people had to get out, like Kevin McCarthy trying
to scare people into believing their worst fears at the end of *Invasion of the
Body Snatchers*. The Fox show would only have a couple of months left in
it, but I used it to do my best to get people out of the Nazz while there was
still something to sell. Unlike October 8, 1998, when I was panicked and

alone, fighting margin calls and redemptions, my head this time was crystal-clear.

By the second week of April, I finally let Todd win out and we shorted the market because we believed we were going to have a crash. And we did, a week where we had a 20 percent decline that our firm made a ton of money trading. What a contrast with October 8, the bottom of the bear market of 1998, when I was so wrongly worried that a bear market loomed. Then earnings were set to boom; now they looked ready to collapse. Now the Net was imploding. All of that merchandise pumped out in the most excessive IPO era in history was behind us. I found our gains painful. Unlike Todd and my wife, I hated betting against stocks, even overvalued stocks, because I had become so conditioned to the fact that everything worked out well in the end for the bulls. Plus I am an optimist at heart; I dislike betting against U.S. companies. That weird combination of buy and hold merged with tech creating a plethora of "tech blue chips," which I now knew to be an oxymoron, even as I had wanted to believe in the stock market at all times. For me the short-side gains were gut-wrenching.

As we profited from the decline in the market that week, I sensed that there could be one more long-side killing to be made into a bounce. As the market unraveled that Friday, April 14, just as it had every other day that week, I took us into Jeff's office, and said we had to bring in our shorts. Everybody's thinking that this is the Friday before the '87 crash, and I think, as in 1998, we just had a crash and we had to cover. At three, with the market down 200 points and the world looking, once again, like it was coming to an end, we put $100 million to work. With the help of new software that Todd had installed, I was able to see that that $100 million was now worth $94 million roughly nine minutes later. I don't think I had ever lost $6 million that fast.

At 3:07 my wife called. We were supposed to go to Mexico for spring vacation after the close of the market. The kids had the week off. I had put off all vacation since the bottom of October 1998, unwilling to miss out on any opportunities in that amazing bull market period. This one I was in for. This one I was going to get right. I didn't even want to interrupt the meeting when Jeannie Cullen, my assistant, said Karen was on the phone and needed to speak to me. "The vacation, the one to Mexico, after the close,"

I said to Jeff by way of acknowledging that she was breaking up our confab. It was 3:30. Karen said she had seen on the news that the market was down some 400 points. She said she knew I would regard it as irresponsible to go away at this time given that we were the largest partners in the fund. So she had gone ahead and canceled my ticket without even asking. She said she knew what I had to do. I was barely paying attention. I was riveted to that E-Z-Castle software program, the one that showed instantly how much we were losing. In bright flashing red. Mesmerizing. Hard to resist. We had lost another $900,000 while she was talking about the trip. I wanted to vomit, the pain was so bad. Were we going to blow our great year, the one that we had already made because we had taken so much off the table earlier in the year and switched out of tech into drugs and foods? She was chattering on about how duty and honor were really screwing up our lives. Really upsetting the trade. The big bottom bounce trade. Make that $950,000 while we are discussing this stupid vacation.

"What should we do instead? Go to the country?" I asked, oblivious to the fact that she had canceled only *my* ticket. This time they were going without me.

"Enough's enough," she said. "We're going to Mexico without you. The hell with this letting down the kids every single vacation. The hell with your work ethic."

She told me to check the fax machine in a minute. On it would be a piece of paper that I needed to sign: "TO WHOM IT MAY CONCERN: I, James J. Cramer, being of sound mind, do hereby acknowledge and consent to my wife, Karen L. Cramer, leaving the United States with our children." I told her I would do it and retreated back to the crisis meeting without thinking another thing about it. Jeff wanted to know if everything was all right at home. I frowned.

"Man, what's with her?" I said to Jeff.

He looked at me with crinkled brow over one eye, and said, "Hey, she's thinking the same thing about you."

Yeah, I said, "She's going without me."

Jeff looked at me and said call her back, tell her it's fine to go. I told him that as long as I was running other people's money I knew I was doing the right thing.

I would have to resign before it was wrong. Resign and give it all up.

And I wasn't ready for that yet. "No way. Not yet." And I walked out to check the fax, saw the document, signed it and gave it to Jeannie to fax back. Time: 3:45. I noticed we were down $7 million on our bets with fifteen minutes left and I decided to put another $10 to $15 million to work.

We did. And by 4:10 we had done all the buying we could, we had waited, waited perfectly, I thought, and gotten it just right, perfectly positioned for next week. And then I remembered. My wife had asked me to call to say goodbye after the close of the market.

I dialed. Too late, gone already. It dawned on me right then, when I got Karen's voice mail. They really were going without me.

That was me all over: a true king, no, a Stalinist, a colossal fixture at the office, someone who knew he had mastered that sell-off, playing the short side and then switching perfectly to the long side, making partners move up on the Forbes 400 list of the wealthiest solely by his own trading prowess. And a total fraud at home, who knew he really didn't matter anymore to those whom he had routinely and faithfully disappointed because he always made money for his partners. Things had finally reached the point where Karen and the kids would have a better time without me. Not that I knew. I was too busy, thinking about how much money we would make when the market opened on Monday from all those delicious longs we bought at the bottom.

CHAPTER 22

Getting Out

We nailed it that Monday, April 17. We nailed it perfectly. We were dead right, top of our game. Those buys into the weakness after what would be one of the worst weeks in the market's history paid off in spades and we ran the register for $14 million in profits within the first couple of hours of trading. It was sweet revenge for blowing it October 8, 1998.

Unlike then, when we were margined to our eyeballs, we had come in to that horrid second week of April almost entirely in cash, and some food and drug positions that actually went up during the Nazz downturn. Unlike October 8, when we initially sold into the panic, we bought the panic this time. Sometimes we were the only buyer. And unlike 1998 we made a mint over a weekend while other hedge funds, like those of George Soros and Julian Robertson, stumbled and crashed. (We would later learn that they compounded the severity of the sell-off by folding up shop.) We were sitting pretty with a huge double-digit lead on everyone else, with the Nazz down down double digits and the Dow and S&P rolling over too.

It was just as I liked to be going into the middle of the second quarter. Champs in the making.

When Karen called me that Monday from the Four Seasons in Punta Mita, though, it was joyless. She had broken her wrist Rollerblading shortly before taking the trip and while I bragged about how right I had been and how much money we had made, she tortured me with painful stories about how rough it was to carry all of those bags with one hand,

and how much the kids wished I had been there. Sure took the joy out of the $14 million in gains. I was as oblivious as ever, trying desperately to re-create for my wife the courageous stand we took on Cisco and Veritas, not buying them until the last possible moment. I compared it to when Mel Gibson was saying "Hold" in *Braveheart.* She wanted to know if I were out of my mind and taking my medicine. "Who cares about the great Veritas Software stand? The kids want you to board a plane right now and finish the vacation."

I said no way, the volatility was too great, the opportunities too numerous, but that I couldn't wait for her to get back home. I knew she understood why I had to stay, I told Jeff. "She was in the business, for crissakes, she should know," I told him. Jeff mentioned that after the fifth or sixth vacation canceled by market volatility, that doesn't seem as precious a reason to stay at your turret.

After that great hit to the long side we decided we were done with committing a lot of capital to stocks as long as they remained as precarious as they had become. Now that the market had finally seen its spirit broken, we no longer feared the short side. We decided that we would trade with a bias to the short side for as long as prices remained as high as they were.

With the Nasdaq rallying almost back to 4,000, there was a tremendous amount of hope put back into the market. But it was undeserved as the Fed kept hiking rates, and the underwritings kept coming but fell on buyers too full-up with equities already.

With the help of that big Monday rally and a subsequent spike in the morning of April 18 that allowed us to sell even more and clear the decks of all tech, we were up some 25 percent. We didn't need to do anything but day-trade for the rest of the year—be flat at the end of the day with no exposure—so what was the point of trying to be a hero? Running money had nothing to do with heroism.

Throughout the 1990s we had heard from the sages that the returns had been too outsized, too great, and would come to an end. I never wanted to believe it. The money was too great and ignoring the possibility of racking up some big gains seemed totally counterintuitive.

Now, though, things were different. A generation of stocks had been created without any of the rules or rigor that had typically characterized our equity markets. A generation of stocks that were worth billions and should have been worth nothing if capital hadn't been so poorly allocated. That combination of hot IPOs, electronic trading, and the brainwashing of America into buying and holding—whatever it is as long as it is equity—created a mind-set where prudence was disguised as recklessness in the form of selling, and ultra-aggressive went by the name of long-term investing.

From my perch at Cramer Berkowitz I was astounded at the kinds of companies that trooped through my offices in the first and second quarters of 2000, when the market was topping. Major companies, valued in the billions of dollars, visited my office and when closely questioned knew nothing about their own business or the way analysts categorized them. Anything went. Capitalism unbounded and unrestrained.

Wacky stuff happened every day. A few examples suffice. After an article I wrote saying that *Stamps.com* would be worthless one day, John Payne, the chief executive officer of the company, said he wanted to see me and that he would donate $10,000 to the charity of my choice if he couldn't prove that the company was viable and a long-term winner. I took him up on the challenge. He came in and gave a credible story and I even bought some for a trade. A few days later though, he stopped returning my calls. A few days after that he was gone. The stock plummeted. (I couldn't find him to collect that check.)

The management team of Portal Software, a $7 billion company, came in to see me. The company, according to Wall Street analysts, was on the come, expected to crack into the business of billing online for brokerage houses. When I asked about this possible new line of business, the company blanked on me. They wanted to know if there was anyone at Merrill or Goldman they could call to get some of that business. Oh brother.

Or how about 360networks? You may not remember that high-flyer based in Vancouver. It was going to reinvent just about everything telco, fastest lines, worldwide network, fantastic growth. I panned it, predicting it would go to zero. Within a few days the chief executive officer, Greg Maffei, a man I had known from Microsoft, where he had been the chief financial officer with an impeccable reputation, called to lay into me for not understanding the story. They were fully funded, had lots of cash, and I didn't know what I was talking about. I quickly did a pro to my own con for the Web site. Three months later it would file for Chapter 11, the projections all bogus, a clerical error cited.

For us, the recognition that maybe you could never again go long a high-tech growth company without trepidation came when Naveen Jain visited our offices. His stock, InfoSpace, was at $255, and valued at $18 billion.

Naveen had been at Microsoft before InfoSpace. He had created this Net company to be the Yellow Pages for the Internet, a worthy objective. I caught his act on CNBC, where he promised that his company would surpass Microsoft in size because the Internet was so big.

He came by my office as part of a road show to boost his equity after it had fallen from $300. He had a story to tell and he wanted to tell me. He had a new piece of software that enabled you to find the best deal for a pizza south of 14th Street on the fly and get a coupon too. He said it didn't stop with pizza. He could do books, pasta, movies, anything. Right on your cell.

And the Bell operating companies would pay him fortunes to embed the software. He was going to coin money. Just coin it. And InfoSpace would soon be worth a trillion dollars.

I loved it. Naveen was bullish as all get-out. He was high-fiving me and Matt Jacobs, telling us about how much SBC Communications and Verizon were going to pay him. A gold mine.

When we walked Naveen out, I heard Jeff whispering in the phone. I couldn't tell what he was saying. As I escorted Naveen to the door I told him I remained one of his biggest supporters.

I circled back to Jeff. He had dumped all 50,000 shares of InfoSpace right into our meeting. "I saw you do those high-fives. And I said to Todd, 'This meeting is going to cost us millions of dollars,' so I sold everything."

I didn't question it. The high-fiving era was over.

InfoSpace never looked back. It trades right above a buck now. We would have lost millions upon millions of dollars.

There were hundreds of InfoSpaces out there, hundreds of companies that turned out to be all hype and worth not much more than a warm bucket of spit.

As they paraded through our offices we grew more and more bearish despite the lower stock prices. Not long after my canceled trip I said that I would read Miranda warnings to anyone who actually suggested we buy a stock. We would have long and elaborate meetings before we bought even 5,000 shares of a stock. This from a company that would buy 500,000 shares at a clip without a second thought a few months before.

Every stock, every possible move, got scrutinized by four angry guys in a room who could agree on very little. Todd hated it. Matt was assigned strictly to find companies that could beat the quarter and kept coming back with fewer and fewer names. When he did, Todd would try to shoot them down.

Jeff would go to meetings, meeting after meeting, and hear about the coming slowdown, and we would have to bail out of whatever we had put on. Everything on the long side seemed wrong. Everything.

When I first got started in the business, if we had a down quarter, I would be furious with myself. Five years into it, a down month caused great angst. As we had now put on fourteen years with no losses, I got increasingly more conservative, anxious not to blow that great record. A losing week would be a fiasco.

Going into the end of the fourth quarter of 2000, I became obsessed with not having a losing day. A losing day would send me into paroxysms of anger, intense anger, where I would threaten routinely to fire anyone who lost us money. And I would follow up on it if anyone did more than once. At forty-five years old, the daily struggles during the long workdays often became overwhelming. By Friday I would be so exhausted I would go into the conference room at 1:45 P.M., lie down on the black couch beside the big table, and pass out, literally falling asleep the moment my head hit the pillow I kept for these now frequent occasions. "Wake me up 150 points or down 150 points," I would say, "or wake me at 3:15 no matter what." For that market, it was the perfect set of instructions. I was just that exhausted by the mental stress of trying to get it right.

And then, with the new software that enabled us to see how we were doing in real time, I became irritated and angered if we were down at all, even for a few minutes. With a lead and a great record, who was jeopardizing us? I would scream. Who is putting us at risk? Who is doing this? Half the time it was me, not being able to resist a trade.

We traded in that straitjacket all summer as the averages kept coming down. We made more money and I grew more miserable.

In late summer, a book called *The Fortune Tellers* by the *Washington Post* media critic, Howard Kurtz, came out. It explored the curious intersection between those who talk about stocks and those who trade them. I came off as a man possessed by money and possessed by the need to succeed and gain respect at all costs. Kurtz—who had written about me before—described me as someone who would fight with everyone, all in the name of performance. Anything could be justified by performance. People who read the book and knew me were aghast at how negative I looked, and wanted me to defend myself. But I couldn't. Kurtz had it right.

I clipped a review of the book from the *San Francisco Chronicle* and put it on the top of my Bloomberg machine. I still have the part about me: "In his office by 5 A.M. each day, Cramer gives workaholism a bad name. It's amazing that a man so wealthy and successful can still be so manic and miserable." Got that right.

Just before Thanksgiving I had been asked to give a speech in Vegas at The Money Show, one of those late-twentieth-century rah-rah cheerleading sessions for stock market players, the type of gathering you don't hear much about anymore. I said I would go if they paid for my dad and me to stay at the Bellagio. My father saw that I could not, even for a minute, stay off the cell phone to the office. The moment that the pilot okayed the airphone, I ran a three-hour call to Jeff, trading online over the country. When we landed, I switched back to the cell phone and traded up until the moment I was being checked in. Only then at 4:01 in the East could I take a deep breath and relax. My father was aghast. He couldn't believe that I could live with so much pressure. He was thrown off even more when instead of going to the tables I went off on a jag when I couldn't get my phone jack to work and had to switch rooms so I could file five pieces about trading and answer about 400 e-mails. He worried that he would have to bury me, even though he was almost twice my age.

Once I was back, we had our first bad trading day in months, one where we had lost almost a million dollars, mostly betting with the market. The next day when we were down $500,000, Jeff had wondered whether I would mind if he went to see his kids' play. I said fine but that I was going to sell everything we had because we had lost almost a percent in two days and I couldn't take the pain. He took off and said he would try to check in but because of the play, he might not be able to. Soon after, the market rallied and rallied big, right after I had sold almost all our long exposure.

When he checked in I was going out the door taking the subway uptown. I was furious, furious that we had sold and locked in losses, furious that the market rallied without us, furious that he went to the goddamned school play when we needed him. I let him have it for dereliction of duty. I screamed at him, mercilessly. And then in the middle of my breath I realized he wasn't on the phone at all. The line was dead. The next morning Jeff came in and said he had to talk to me. I said sure. As he ushered me into his office he said he had to apologize, that he had been too harsh, too mean, too angry. "What are you talking about?" I said.

"What I said to you after you screamed at me."

I told him I didn't know anything about it. He laughed. He had spent four minutes ranting about how I should fuck myself and he was quitting if I ever yelled at him again like that.

"Anyway, I am sorry," he said, "but you have to do something about yourself. We are having the best year of our lives, the best year ever, better than anyone. Everything we do is exactly as it should be, we are winning, we are Superbowl-bound and you will not relent. You will not stop. You are killing yourself for nothing."

I nodded. I know, I said, but I worry every day we will give it back.

"We won't," he said. "We won't."

I dismissed his comments as patronizing and went home. I knew better. We could give it back in a flash. You could always give it back. History teaches that if you screwed it up, even in November, where we were, you could give it back.

Jeff walked to the elevator with me. I reminded him that in the third week of November in 1988 I caught the flu and made a wrongheaded bet on the earnings of Service Merchandise and Zayre and gave back 9 percent in a flash, cutting my return from the 40s to the 30s.

Another guy would have noticed that Service Merch and Zayre no longer existed, that the shortfall occurred twelve years before, that I was much better now, that we were much better now.

Jeff just nodded. I had trained him too well.

The next day, November 22, we started fresh out of the box and quickly put on $3 million in wins by 10:00 A.M. and then grabbed another $1 million trading the QQQ (Nasdaq 100) index and Microsoft into the bell. We had made back everything we had lost and then some. It was booked. You can't take booked profits away.

And it was done despite a big decline in the market. That's my kind of outperformance. I love that, the double whammy of making money when everyone else is losing money. Yesss! Huge, huge, huge. A magnificent trading day. It was vintage Cramer Berk. Jeff and Matt had provided us with continual trading gossip out of the Credit Suisse First Boston conference. Jeff was always able to pull something out of the hat at these meetings. (When Nortel was in the 60s, and John Roth had tipped his hand that $12 billion in sales would be hard to do, only Jeff braved the wrath of the Nortel execs and whispered into his cell phone to bolt Nortel *now.* Everyone else waited and the stock never recovered.) Now Matt could do the same. By finding out what everyone else was looking for—every analyst at a major investment house—and then comparing that with what was said, we were good for a couple of hundred Gs a call from these meetings and we got it spot-on that day.

Todd and I manned the office and made terrific bets, mostly on the short side, against stocks. I would have gone home high-fiving just then, after penning my closing column—I was now writing a column an hour and would do twelve a day routinely from my turret—but there was still one more big report to come. After the close that November day, on 4:40 P.M., we huddled around our screens waiting for Brocade to announce its quarter. Long a favorite of mine, Brocade represented the remaining momentum position on our sheets, a hard-won position in an office where we thought the momentum stocks, or the onetime momentum stocks, were poison. Owning Brocade, a computer storage company, had become a great source of internal tension. How could we be long a momentum stock at a time when momentum funds are being taken out and shot on a daily basis? What made Brocade immune? Who was I to demand that Brocade stay even after I had bashed all of the other momentum stocks in our meetings at Cramer Berkowitz and in my columns? To which I always said the same: Brocade is outexecuting everyone—everyone! And until it is done outexecuting everyone, I want to be long it.

Then Brocade reported. It was a perfect number. Picture perfect. There was some smashed fly-on-the-wall site that was looking for a better number, something stronger sequentially, but I knew this number was all upside, a thing of beauty. Mesmerizing in its perfection.

Of course at that very moment, the very moment when I decided to add a few thousand shares to our 20,000-share Brocade position, Altera, a semiconductor company, announced weaker-than-expected earnings. Bigtime.

Although Altera barely correlated with Brocade, the latter started sinking like a stone. I knew it was a buy anyway, so I bid $150 for 1,000 more shares.

Next thing you know it was down 6. In sixty seconds. Like some sort of Mercedes in reverse. I was out of answers. I thought it was plain wrong. We were playing lean, however, and I didn't want to inflict any damage on the pristine year. I listened as someone on the tube yammered that the stock was going lower. I saw the bids disappearing. I saw the loss mounting. I was sweating, and angry, shaking my head. Todd looked at me and asked me what was wrong.

He said that it was no big deal. We blew it, move on, no big deal.

"No big deal?" I screamed. "No big #%*&! deal?" He coolly reminded me that we had made several million dollars trading that day. I could not be soothed.

"Who cares about the millions of dollars we made when we just lost money on Brocade? Don't you understand that?" I said into his face. "Don't you know that's how I think, that's how I am?"

Todd walked out, shaking his head. I threw a water bottle at the door when he left, disgusted that he wouldn't argue with me. Furious at him.

I ran into my office and tried to reach Jeff at home to complain to him about Todd not caring about the loss I was inflicting. I got him on the phone but the line kept cutting off. Disgusted, I threw the cell phone at the pillar next to my desk.

Everyone knew the drill by now, though, as I ran from my office back to my desk. They knew what to do when the boss was upset with a trade, the simple 21,000 shares of Brocade that I was now down 7 points on. First to go was the keyboard. Sometimes I would just smash it with the phone. This time I picked it up, turned it on its side, and gave it four good whacks with enough force to send the QWERTY keys to the left and the ZXCVB keys to the right—that's where Jeannie Cullen sits, my sidekick, deskmate, and confidante. She's been picking flying letters out of her coffee, her sweater, and her hair for six years now. She shuddered and would later tell me that she was praying I wouldn't slam the monitor with the staple gun or overturn the whole desk. The last time I tossed the desk—my systems froze as I thought Intel was going up and I was taking it furiously, and then I found out it was actually going down and I had bought a million shares at terrible prices and had lost a million bucks in a few moments—there had been shards of broken glass scattered everywhere that gave the whole staff splinters during the ensuing cleanup.

Next came the phone. As Brocade continued to fall—it had now plunged into the low 140s—I angrily yanked the phone from the cord and pounded it into the desk until it split into dozens of sharp pieces. I was beating the phone to a cadence of furious curses, yelling "Fuck Brocade" each time the stock broke another point lower. Still no one looked up. They knew that as long as the stock kept sinking, everything on their boss's desk could be turned into a missile launched right toward them.

As it hit $143 the second keyboard went into orbit, the space bar and the backspace key separating in midair, before it collided with the stuffed animal totems that lined the partition between my desk and Todd's, who had known enough to slink out before he became a target.

At last, without much left for me to break, the stock bottomed. Then, mercifully, it bounced, my cue to go back in the office to scream at Jeff some more about how I would be right but how tough it was and how I had screwed it all up and how I could have blown our year but I didn't. I always did that too, partly so that Jeannie could pull out the backup keyboards and phones, tidy up, and have everything ready for the next outburst. She kept a closetful of spares. I was shaking as I got back to my desk, staring at the shattered pieces on the floor, looking at the new keyboard all set up, and hitting up Brocade, which had since stopped trading for the night at $145.

Shaking and numb all the way down from my shoulders to my fingers. Tingling and numb. Jeannie urged me to go home. She said that she had only one more keyboard left so that I better be careful with what I had. I couldn't tell whether or not she was joking. Better not be joking on a greater than $100,000 loss.

But there would be no more tantrums. Because the very next day I quit the job. Jeannie's hoard of backups would be safe. I went in, stood up in front of the desk, told everyone to shut up, and said, "Ladies and gentlemen, I am out of here. I am getting out before they carry me out. The firm now belongs to Jeff Berkowitz."

I had broken enough furniture and monitors and keyboards to last a lifetime. More than a lifetime in fact. As a forty-five-year-old hedge fund manager, I had already overstayed my actuarial table. Time to get out before the game killed me. Time to get out before I killed someone else.

After the close, over a cup of hot chocolate down where Wall Street meets the South Street Seaport, I formally gave the firm to Jeff Berkowitz, my thirty-four-year-old partner. He wanted to pay for it. I wanted to pay him to take it! It was his turn to slam phones and shatter monitors. It was his turn to wonder if his heart would hold out under the pressure of the day-to-day.

Someone who could have a heart attack over a $60,000 loss, after taking $400 million in losses already that year—and, fortunately, $535 million in gains—needed to move on. Not because the angst was wrong, but because the angst could now kill me. It was Jeff's turn to sweat and worry and fret about how well he's doing in the viciously competitive world of hedge funds. I no longer wanted it. I knew I didn't care enough come January, when it would be time to feel the worry of starting at zero again. The only way to lock in what we had accomplished was to retire, and I wanted that locked in more than anything else. I wanted to get out before it was obvious that I had lost my edge. A gain of 36 percent when the averages were down double digits seemed as good a time as any to leave my trading turret.

To those not involved in the high-performance game of hedge fund management my hysterical anger after a loss like Brocade probably seems excessive, childlike, and totally unnecessary. Pure petulance.

You are wrong. The reason we in the hedge fund game have such a high burnout rate—the reason why there are no old hedge fund managers—is that if you don't care after watching a stock fall 10 points the moment after you bought it, then you shouldn't be in the game anymore. The moment you say, "You know, I am so good and secure that I could give a rat's ass about Brocade's decline," that's the moment that the partners should cash you in, and give it to someone younger, hungrier, and better.

You have to want to win so badly that you don't care what others think about your behavior when you don't win. Good money managers constantly compare themselves to others. I followed the performance of hundreds of managers when I was at Cramer Berkowitz, hundreds, and I never liked being beaten by any of them. It drove me nuts if Richie Freeman beat me on a day over at Smith Barney Aggressive Growth or if Paul Wick picked up 3 performance points when I gained only 2. I watched these scores the way a playoff team keeps an eye on the scoreboard to see how its rivals are doing during a crucial game. It was never enough for me to win, they had to lose at the same time to make it worthwhile. I had to choke back tears on the days when the bad guys—everyone else running money—made money and we *lost* money.

The manic misery of nonstop performance, day in and day out, can't be sustained without believing in the fiction that poverty still lurks just around the corner, that I am back in that Ford Fairmont sleeping off of Interstate 5 an instant after a couple of bad Brocade trades. But trying to stay hungry when you are making $10 million a year is difficult stuff.

Taking all that risk—that necessary risk—if you want to see outsized rewards seems logically stupid once you have made all that money. As my old Goldman associate Jack Shepherd used to tell the super-rich clients such as I had become, "You only need to get rich once." But you did have to pretend that you need ever larger sums just to stay hungry enough to make as much money as you can for your partners. So the great ones are either pretending that they're driven by crushing insecurity, feeling that no amount of money is enough, or some of both, I guess.

When you are thirty and you have a tantrum after losing money, you can go work out afterward—run a few laps around the Reservoir in Central Park as I used to or go lift some weights at the health club. When you are thirty-five and you smash some computers you can head to the nearest watering hole. Two Grey Gooses later you are thinking, What the heck, good night's sleep and right back at 'em.

When you are forty and you try to throw your monitor out the window because you bought Intel too soon, you are too old to have a drink after work without ruining your trading acumen the next day, so you just go home and hug the wife and kids.

But when you are forty-five and you smash two keyboards and a phone, you can't breathe. You feel like you are choking. Your head spins, everything goes numb, and your assistant wants to call 911. You can't sleep that night without taking something to sedate you and then you walk in the next morning unrevived by two extra large cups of coffee cart joe. The stress is just too great for a forty-five-year-old to handle without lasting damage. It takes a little more out of you each year until there's nothing left, and that's when you screw up. That's when you are Willie Mays, hanging on too long, not being able to hit second from the outfield. You want to go out on top, and I had been given my chance. And it was a perfect one.

When I got home that night no one came to the door, as usual. They had all stopped doing that years before. Who wanted to deal with my angst over my performance after *their* hard days? Who wanted to hug some grumpy hedge fund manager after he had one more miserable day at work battling the market?

I walked behind the kitchen to the liquor cabinet, opened the bottle of '37 Warre's Port I had been saving for who knows what, poured myself a stiff one, and entered the kitchen, where Karen was readying dinner.

"What's the occasion?" she said, barely looking up at me.

"I quit today," I said.

"That will be the day," she said, completely ignoring me.

"I gave the firm to Jeff," I said.

"Very funny," she said.

"I retired, I mean it," I said.

"You did, didn't you?" she said suddenly, recognizing that for once I was sincere about doing something right after doing everything wrong for so long.

She gave me a huge hug and a kiss and then asked me: "How much are you up?"

I said, "Thirty-six percent."

Instantly she asked, "And how much are the averages up?"

I smiled. "They're down double digits."

She laughed. "You know what I always say, you are only as good as your last trade, and that's damn good."

I told her, I think I really got it right this time.

One last thing, she said, "You aren't going to sit on that couch in the living room and watch the CNBC ticker all day, are you?"

Nope, I said. I am done trading. I am going to be what I always wanted to be: a writer.

"With an office in the city, I hope?" she asked. "Not too close," she said with a smile.

"Of course," I said. "At *TheStreet.com.* I am going back to being a full-time writer."

With that she called the girls downstairs and told them that their daddy was never going to miss a soccer game, a back-to-school night, or a vacation again because he had decided to change jobs.

Cece, my older daughter said, "I'll believe it when I see it."

And she has.

CHAPTER 23

Confessions of an Ex–Street Addict

It's been more than a year since I have smashed a keyboard or slammed a phone in anger. It's been more than a year since I have mortified employees over a $25,000 loss or threatened to fine those who lost me money doing stupid trades. It's been more than a year since I have affixed a Post-it with HWP or IBM scrawled on it to some hapless associate's head to remind him of how losses should not be minimized or forgotten. It's been more than a year since I have done a trade, a quick in and out of a stock for a fast profit.

During that year I haven't missed a kid's play, a back-to-school night, a parent visit, or a soccer game. I can't afford to miss the latter; I'm the coach. We just ended a triumphant fall season, taking the Summit Charge to a 4-3-3 record, and not once did I scream at a ref or tell a child she let me down. I cherished holding practices midweek during hours when I would have just been taking Brocade or ramping Yahoo! Sometimes I scrimmaged with the girls. I know my kids' teachers' names; heck, they know me. All of the teachers know me, as does the principal, not because I am on television talking about stocks but because I make it my business to be in school as often as I can.

It turns out my kids and I have a lot in common. We go to baseball games together although we root for different teams. Cece likes basketball so much she named her cat Iverson, after the 76ers' greatest player of the era. (She would have named him Kobe, but that would have hurt my feelings because I still cheer for Philadelphia.) I took eight vacations in 2001, and called in only on the first one, when I couldn't get used to the lack of responsibility. I sleep until 5:30 every day, and I need an alarm to wake me up. I haven't dreamed about missing a final exam once.

I visit 40 Fulton Street now and then, where Cramer Berkowitz resides—Jeff kept my name on the door—and I have been thrilled with the progress the new owner's making at the firm. He's making some money. I found it difficult at first to walk in and see someone else at my turret. I felt old and used up. But that didn't last. Now I feel like I'm returning to an old college campus that I loved, although my memories of the highs are much greater than the memories of the lows. I see that Jeff's losing his hair, if not his mind, from the pressure, and I know I taught him well. He *should* feel the pressure; it's real and it won't go away until you quit. It's good for the bottom line. I don't dread the end of the year anymore either. I don't have to worry about preserving my gains or worry that the clock will start ticking again soon and my beautiful year will be history. I am no longer as good as my last trade.

I am through with paying people to take my misery away by offloading it on them. I still come to work at *TheStreet.com,* but I have no official responsibilities. I do a daily radio show, which I love, where I talk about business and give away every single secret I learned in twenty years of picking stocks. On the program, *RealMoney,* I give the running commentary on the market that I used to abuse my employees with, but without the caustic comments about how my people missed this or I blew that. I can't trade even if I want to. I have a contract with CNBC that I entered into after severing my relations with Fox that forbids me from selling any stock that I buy for one month. I can't buy stocks I talk about on air for five days. And I am strictly forbidden from betting against stocks and using puts and calls. So I can't respond (and neither can my emotions) to the market's volatility. My friend Mark Haines now introduces me on air as the Reverend JimBob from the Church of What's Happening in One Month. I've recently begun co-hosting an evening program on CNBC called *America Now,* and that, too, is a blast.

I have enjoyed more workdays this year than in twenty years of slogging it out against the market. It's true that *TheStreet.com* is still mired in the low single digits, and it is true that I bear some responsibility, along with others, for the tremendous boom-bust we had. I had liked the market to its top, and a few weeks after, but unless you read *TheStreet.com,* you didn't know I had turned into a bear and you may still blame me for putting you in Yahoo! or Cisco, even as I had blown them out at much higher prices. You can knock me for thinking that stocks had replaced baseball as America's pastime. They can't; they lose you much more money than baseball can and they can break your wallet and your heart even more than the Red Sox can. But I never cut and ran from the dotcom, as so many of my rich Net compadres did, leaving the poorer ones to fend for themselves. I cut and ran from the hedge fund and still own all my shares of TSCM. I vow never to quit until we are triumphant, bankrupt, or taken over. It beats the hell out of me which one will happen.

I call my dad after every appearance on *Squawk,* and we talk endlessly about how much fun it is and how great David Faber, Joe Kernen, and Mark Haines are.

I talk to my wife now without looking at the screen at work and without thinking about stock prices at night. She has not asked me about those averages in more than a year and the only stock conversations we have are about uniform gifts to minors. She's in bonds; stocks rarely come up anymore. I come home smiling from *TheStreet.com* and everybody greets me at the door.

I know I could have done all of this years before. I could have checked out if money were all that counted. But I believe, knowing myself, that I would have been dogged, though, if I had not gotten out at my high, and if I had not permanently put to rest the notion that I always feared, that I am nothing but a hack and a simple bull market player. I have many insecurities, but those are no longer among them.

As someone who worked two blocks from the Twin Towers, who lost many friends in the cataclysm, and who reads the obituaries in the *New York Times* profiles-in-grief every day, I can tell you that had it been me in those towers, up until this year there wouldn't have been anything about me in my thumbnail that anyone could be proud of. Oh sure, I could have gotten lots of accolades, and charities would have praised me for all of that check writing, but I was not a family guy. My wife, in the brutal honesty that I love her so for, would have said, "He worked really hard, and was really proud of his performance. He trounced the averages." My kids would have said, "We wish we knew our daddy better. We saw a lot of him on TV and he was really funny."

Now here's the real clincher, the thing that is the most damning indictment of my previous life, the one that really benchmarks the irony: I am a much better stock picker now than I was at any time in the last decade. I see and hear things and have a feeling that is based on real life, not Wall Street. I have a clear head about it with none of the hold-to-buy, upgrade-downgrade machine guns going off in my head.

No, I am no picnic to deal with. I still get in some scraps, but not the kind that dogged me for years at the hedge fund, the kind that caused me steep legal fees or required me to change the locks at my house because of a stalker. My friend Tom Clarke, now chairman and CEO of *TheStreet.com*, describes the new me as a "statesman," and while I chafe at the mellowness of it, I can see where being a goodwill ambassador has its advantages. I can still inflame and I still feel a deep sense of passion for stocks. But it's not as deep as the sense of passion I feel for my family.

Do I miss the action on the Street? During Thanksgiving week 2001, I noticed that the market had rallied nearly 20 percent from its low on September 21 after it reopened following the September 11 tragedy. I mentioned this to Karen, and for a moment—just a moment—I thought, Wouldn't it be great to be back at the hedge fund, pulling the trigger on hundreds of millions of dollars to make a killing when everyone else is so bearish?

But only if the Trading Goddess came back. When I mentioned this to her, she didn't even let me finish what I was saying.

"Don't even think about it," she said. "Not for all the money in the world."

Can I really stay away? Why don't I just return, stand behind that HIGH VOLTAGE sign I brought with me from my old job, and start whamma-jamming them again? Swinging them around, making all that money?

To which I say, Sorry, no can do. I am no longer an addict. I am free of the demons that drove me to go to work at 3:15 A.M. in that last year because I thought I was losing it to younger, better guys. Nope, I am never going back.

Now I know the truth: I am lucky, and it is better to be lucky than good.